Wilder's V

STAND-ALONE NOVEL

A Western Historical Adventure Book

by

Zachary McCrae

Disclaimer & Copyright

Table of Contents

Letter from Zachary McCrae

I'm a man who loves plain things; a cup of strong coffee in the morning, a good book at noon and his wife's embrace at night. I want to write stories that take you from the hand and show you what it meant to be someone who tried to make ends meet and find their own way in the 19th-century United States. I've been this someone for a long time in my life, always looking for my next gig after my parents' sudden death, always finding new friends but somehow not being able to stick with 'em. It's easy to find quantity in your life but what about quality?

At the age of 50, and after my baby boy, Jeb, and my sweet daughter, Janette, went away to study East, with my sweet wife, Mrs. Maryanne McCrae, we moved back to my hometown and my dad's ranch close to the Rockies. After a series of health issues that have brought me even closer to our Lord, I've officially started writing those stories I always loved to read. I'm tending my land and animals now with the help of Maryanne, and I'm grateful for each day I get to walk in this world we call Earth. As the saying goes, "Nature gave us all something to fall back on, and sooner or later we all land flat on it," so I want to take care of it just the way it has taken care of my dad and mom, and my cousins.

My adventure stories are my legacy to my children and to all of the readers who will honor me by following my work. God bless you and your families and our land! Thank you.

Stay safe but adventurous,

Zachary McCrae

Prologue

Pecos River, Texas

1878

"Sheriff Wilder! Sheriff Wilder!"

The loud, commanding knock came at the cabin door just as John settled his long, lanky body into the creaky rocking chair beside the fireplace.

I'm not the sheriff.

"Drat it all!" he muttered, annoyed at the interruption. Fingers stiff, he gripped the worn arms of the chair to push himself up. All day long, he'd been cleaning brush from along the corral fence. A short time earlier, he'd figured to rest a spell before starting evening chores.

Whoever it was, they'd shot down his peaceful evening.

"Who is it?" he hollered, as he shoved his stockinged feet back into mud-caked boots and headed for the door.

A young voice called out, a voice he recognized. "It's Ethan, Sheriff."

"And Lily," a sweet, feminine voice spoke up.

Sam's kids!

"Why didn't you say so?"

He strode across the room, limping a little with his game leg, and pulled open the stout wooden door. "Come in, come in. Where's your old pa? He come along too?"

Ethan shook his head, a wary glance at Lily, his brown eyes hiding something. "No, that's what we need to talk to you about."

John held the door and motioned the kids inside, although, come to think of it, they were no longer young. Ethan must be at least nineteen now. Lily, that cute little pigtailed girl just a few minutes ago, had to be sixteen; almost a woman.

"This is a surprise. Thought you all would be busy on your ranch with the spring chores and all. I keep meanin' to get over there and visit but…"

A slight hiccup from Lily gave John the first indication that all wasn't right. When he looked at her closely, John saw the girl had been crying for a long time. Her brown eyes were red rimmed, her nose pink from wiping, and a limp handkerchief was crumpled in her tight fist.

"Sit down and I'll get some coffee, if you want a cup. Or there's fresh milk. Bossie's still giving plenty these days." He gave Lily a wink, "might even round up a few cookies. You always were partial to my oatmeal raisin cookies, Lily. Baked a batch a couple of nights ago."

Lily gave him a slight smile that didn't quite reach her eyes. Shook her head no.

"No, thank you, Sheriff," Ethan said, "we came to talk to you about…"

John lifted the coffee pot from the pot-bellied stove and poured himself a tin cup. "Been a long time since I was sheriff, Ethan. Me and your pa, finest deputy I ever had, did right proud for the town. Now, that's all in the past."

For years he'd tried to get Sam's kids to stop calling him sheriff, but maybe some names got to be a habit.

7

"Maybe it's time you went back to being a lawman," Ethan said, still standing beside the table, his hands clenched at his sides. "Maybe you could…" his voice broke, and the young man came as close to tears as John had ever seen him.

A shudder passed through his body. A feeling Ethan was going to tell him something he didn't want to hear. "Why don't you tell me what's in your craw, boy."

"Pa's dead."

Dead? Sam?

It wasn't possible. The words felt like a punch in the gut. John couldn't form words. He swallowed hard, moistened his lips and managed to ask. "How? He was younger than me. Was it an accident?"

Lily didn't try to hide her grief. Tears cascaded down her soft pink, baby cheeks, and sobs shook her slender body, her green-flowered shoulders shaking. "Oh, Sheriff, it's worse than that! He was murdered."

Murdered?

The tin cup trembled in his hand. John sat down heavily in a kitchen chair. An ache shot pain from his thigh down his gimpy leg. "Are you sure it wasn't an accident?"

Ethan scowled, his intense eyes so like Sam's. "Someone hit him over the head with a board in the barn. Left him for dead. When we found him, he was still breathing, but he couldn't tell us anything. He just…" Ethan gulped, swallowed hard and blinked back his own tears, "he just grabbed my hand, then he was gone."

Sam had been murdered? It didn't make sense.

"Are you sure it wasn't an accident?" John didn't want to believe in any other possibility.

"It was no accident." Ethan shook his head, ran distracted fingers through his dark curls until they stood on end and made him look like a wild man. His brown eyes glared at John with a tinge of madness too. He was too intent, too angry.

"Pa's been worried about someone following him for a long time now. I tried to get him to talk to you, but he was too stubborn. Said he'd work it out himself. One night, he was sure someone was hiding in the barn when he went to do chores. A couple of times, he thought he'd been followed in town."

"Did he go to Sheriff Crane?"

Lily shook her head, distressed. "I told him he should, but you know Pa." As if realizing what she'd said, she corrected herself in a mournful voice, "...knew Pa. He told Ethan he'd seen a few men in town he might recognize, from the old days. Outlaws. He wasn't quite sure. Said he wanted to make certain."

"He mention who they might be?" John stroked his short beard, deep in thought.

"No." Ethan said. "Just that they were men he thought he recognized. He told us to watch out, be wary. Pa worried about you too. Said he planned to talk to you as soon as we got the fields plowed."

"You have to help us, Sheriff," Lily wailed, gripping John's hand in a tight-fingered clasp. "If those men killed Pa, they might try to kill you, too. Can't you stop them somehow, before anyone else gets hurt?"

The idea of refusing Sam's kids didn't sit well, but he knew he must. John set the tin cup on the table and squeezed Lily's cold, slender fingers with the other hand.

"Been a long time since I rode as a lawman," John looked from Ethan to Lily, knowing they wouldn't realize. No, their grief was too raw yet. They were too young to understand how sometimes a man had to back away from violence. "I'm past all that. Got a gimp leg from the last shootout me an' your pa were involved in. I'm not a sheriff anymore. Don't see how I can help."

"But..." Lily's eyes widened, shocked at his refusal, "but what if they come after you next. Pa feared it."

John shook his head and watched the respect die from Ethan's face, disdain shuttering his brown eyes.

Ethan interrupted, "Let's go, Lily. Guess Pa wasn't as much a friend as he used to say. We wondered why you didn't show up for Pa's funeral, guess it's because you didn't care."

"It ain't that at all," John argued, "I never even knew he died. You should've sent word and I'd have come." John reached out and grabbed the gray linen sleeve of the boy's shirt, "Me an' your pa was the best of friends. I cared about him like he was my brother. But I'm old. I'm tired. Me an' Sam made plenty of enemies through the years. I can't reopen the door to the past and walk in. If somebody comes to kill me—well, I can't do much about that neither. Reckon I'll face that moment when it comes. If it comes..."

"You won't help us find who killed Pa?" Lily's voice trembled; she gripped her handkerchief in a white-knuckled hand.

"I'm sorry. Go talk to Sheriff Crane. Or Sheriff North, he's probably the closest law to your ranch. If someone killed your pa, justice needs to be done. But, I ain't the one to do it."

"Come on, Lily," Ethan grabbed for his sister and almost dragged her to the cabin door. The girl sobbed as Ethan helped her outside, into a waiting buggy.

"You all don't need to go off mad," John followed them out onto his small porch, "stay here tonight an' we can talk about it in the morning."

"We're done talking," Ethan answered, almost shoving Lily into the buggy. He snapped up the reins and urged the horse across the barnyard.

In the west, the sun had begun its downward journey. Pale shoots of pink and orange slashed across the blue of the sky. The hens squawked, pecking at bugs in the dirt around the cabin. John stood, one hand on a porch railing, staring until Sam Garrett's buggy was just a bug-sized speck in the distance.

Sam. He and his deputy had spent years together, tracking outlaws, talking beside campfires, laughing over pranks they'd pulled on one another. Hard to believe Sam was dead.

Gone.

What would Sam want him to do now? John thought about the level-headed man he'd known. If Sam's death was murder, then justice should be done. *But not by me. I'm tired. I'm old; too weary to fight anyone.*

The idea someone might be after him didn't worry John as much as the safety of Sam's kids. *Maybe I should talk to the sheriff myself.*

Bossie bellowed from the barnyard. Time to milk, settle the animals for the night. John headed toward the barn, gritting his teeth at the pain in his leg. After he tended to evening chores, he would rest in the rocking chair, with his leg close to the fire.

Time enough tomorrow to figure out how to help Sam's kids. A tear slid down his weathered face. *Sam's dead.* He simply couldn't believe his best friend was gone. If somebody killed him, they sure oughta pay, and the law should see justice done.

I spent my years as a sheriff. Let someone else take over the job. Won't be me. Sorry, Sam, it can't be me.

Chapter One

Pecos, Texas

Next Day

Money sure goes.

Annabelle Hollis sighed as she glanced down at the wooden box holding the supplies on her grocery list. Behind the counter of the Dawson Mercantile, Clara Dawson chattered on in the sing-song voice most of her customers had learned to ignore. If there was one thing Clara loved more than totting up sales, it was gossip.

"I'm sorry, Clara, what were you saying? You better give me a ten pound sack of flour too. I want to bake some extra bread this week."

"Got company coming?" Clara asked, her blue eyes wide with interest. "Hank didn't mention anything to me."

Clara's husband, Hank, had been helping at Annabelle's ranch since the death of her husband, Thomas.

Shaking her head, Annabelle let her long, auburn braid flip over the shoulder of a blue-and-white-striped blouse. "No, I'm baking extra for that family a few ranches over. They just had a new baby. Figured I've got more time than they do."

"You don't say." Clara plucked a sack of flour off the shelf and set it down on the counter. "Now, what was I saying…"

No telling.

"I know!" Clara snapped her pudgy fingers and rearranged the crate's groceries to add in a small sack of tea. "That hideous fabric, Miz Montgomery bought. So red I'm sure it could start a bullfight."

Despite herself, Annabelle snickered, imagining the thin, squinty-eyed old maid staring down a bull. Maybe waving a cape in her blue-veined hands, hollering in her squeaky voice, "Tora, Tora, Tora."

"I know!" Clara agreed, mistaking Annabelle's humor for agreement. "I told her how awful it looked but she bought it anyway." Tsking, Clara gave a good-natured shrug and added up Annabelle's order. "This all you need? If you forget something, I can have Hank bring it out to the ranch tomorrow. We've got to take care of our best friend."

Distracted by Clara's change of subject, Annabelle blinked. Tears dampened her eyes when she thought of all Clara and Hank had done for her since her Thomas's death. "You and Hank," the words sounded thick to her own ears, but Annabelle felt honor bound to express her gratitude again. "I don't know what I'd have done without the two of you. Ever since Thomas's fall, well, Hank's been the best ranch hand I've ever had, and he's like a doting uncle. And you…"

A tear slid down her cheek. Embarrassed, Annabelle brushed it away impatiently, "what would I have done without you? You've been the best friend I've ever had. Almost like the mama I lost when I was little."

"Now, you shush that kind of talk. We're glad to help, you know that." Clara flushed, the strands from her messy gray chignon drifting around her chubby, apple cheeks. This morning, the small, birdlike woman wore a soft green dress in an expensive cotton with delicate lace at the collar and cuffs. It often amused Annabelle that Clara could dress so fashionably, and be such an impeccable storekeeper, but be so untidy at the same time.

Annabelle felt downright dowdy in her blue-and-white-striped blouse, well-worn brown riding skirt, and runover boots. Until she looked at Clara a bit closer.

Hairpins settled at half-mast in her hair, a splotch of butter smeared her bodice, and Annabelle pretended not to notice the dusting of toast crumbs on her ample chin. While Clara often went through life at full gallop, only her body showed the fact.

The large mercantile store was neat, tidy as a pin, and swept within an inch of its life. Clara saw to it that the wooden floors were freshly mopped each night by her thirteen-year-old son, Herbert. "I honestly don't know how you do it Clara. You make everything look so easy. My life has always felt so...difficult...especially since Thomas died."

Clara reached across the counter and clasped Annabelle's hand in her own. Squeezing tight, she spoke words of comfort. "It just feels hard right now because you're trying to do too much alone. You let Hank help more and I'll send Herbert out to help too. A woman can try to run a ranch alone, but you need a man."

"Oh, I know, and Hank has been a blessing. It's just, maybe I can't help thinking how happy Thomas and I were. It doesn't seem...fair, I guess, that he died in such a stupid way. Falling off a ladder. Who falls off a ladder and dies? Thomas was so careful. It makes no sense."

Clara's blue eyes turned wary. "Hank and I were talking... it never made sense to us either. Hank thought...well," she took a deep breath and plunged on, "he thought things looked kind of funny, that maybe Thomas..." Clara stopped, for once looking at a loss for words.

"Maybe Thomas what?"

Annabelle didn't get to hear what Clara suspected. The little bell over the mercantile door tinkled as someone else entered the store. Right away, Clara shook her head and slid behind the counter, straightening her white apron, dotted with jam specks, across her slender middle. "Good afternoon, Mr. Glover," she said in a voice neither welcoming nor I'd-rather-not-speak-to-you. Not to one of the richest men in town. Clara depended on his business; she'd told Annabelle too many times to count.

"But I wish there was somewhere else he could shop," she'd often whispered. "Mr. Glover makes my skin crawl."

I know how she feels. From force of habit, Annabelle reached to touch the Colt revolver in the holster around her waist.

Isaac Glover stepped up to the counter, smelling of bay rum and the expensive cigar burning between two of his fingers. He wore a dark, broadcloth suit, pressed white, linen shirt with a black string tie, and his leather skin boots gleamed with polish. Annabelle could see her wobbly face in the tips. If a man could give off the scent of wealth, Mr. Glover had that air about him. Like he walked on streets of gold.

"Good morning to you, Mrs. Dawson, and to you, Mrs. Hollis. How are things out at your ranch?"

"Just fine, thank you." Annabelle coughed as the cigar smoke drifted past her nose.

Not that it's any of your concern.

"Hmm, well, that's good, very good, but you know anytime it gets to be too much for you," his piercing blue–black eyes pinned her with an intense glance, "a widowed woman like yourself, I'd be glad to take it off your hands at a reasonable price. You know I'm always scouting land for the railroad. You could settle somewhere in town."

As always at the suggestion, Annabelle stiffened her back, kept a tight smile on her face, and answered as politely as

Mama had taught her. Even if she did want to spit in his face and stomp the shine off his boots. "No, thank you, Mr. Glover. Thomas and I bought the ranch, and I intend to stay there and run it. Now, if you'll excuse me, I have chores to do at home. Clara, have a pleasant day."

"You too, Annabelle."

"Well, well," Mr. Glover chuckled in his slimy snake voice, as Annabelle turned, "Aren't you the feisty one, Mrs. Hollis? One day, you may wish you'd sold the land to me."

Is that a threat?

"Over my dead body!" she snapped, grabbed up the sack of flour and stormed out the door.

Chapter Two

Early the next morning, John finished his chores in record time, saddled up Ranger, and headed into Pecos River. He needed more coffee, and a hunk of Clara Dawson's cheese would go right nice for supper. Not that he couldn't do without both things, but after Ethan and Lily's visit, he'd spent a restless night, unable to sleep. Frustrated about not being able to help them, he decided a ride might do him some good and take his mind off things. While he was in town, he could stop off at the sheriff's office and see if Crane had any ideas about Sam's death. Maybe it was an accident, and the kids didn't want to accept it. Or it might be possible that things were more sinister than they seemed.

Once in town, John rode easily down the hard-packed dirt path they called a street. The town had grown in the few years since he'd settled here, although it had been around for quite a spell. He knew people traveling on wagon trains using the Butternut and Chisholm Trails had passed through, crossing the nearby Pecos River.

Located as it was near the river, the town sat squat on the high prairie at the northern border of the Chihuahuan Desert. It was a good 210 miles to the big city of El Paso. John knew the distance well from his years as sheriff. He ought to, he'd ridden it often enough with Sam by his side.

As he rode along, nodding to friends and neighbors, John looked around at the wooden buildings, tall with false fronts. He noticed a new section of the boardwalk in front of the stores; the ladies must appreciate that refinement. At the far end of town, he saw a corral holding a teeming, bawling herd of cattle, probably getting ready to head across the Pecos River for sale. The dust and stench filled the air with the town's normal perfume of cow manure, sweat and rawhide.

At the corner of Main and Side Alley, John reined in Ranger, slid easily out of the saddle, and tied the stallion to a hitching post. A buggy with a swaybacked old mare stood in front of Dawson's Mercantile. Clara ran the store while her husband, Hank, worked as a ranch hand and managed a small herd of Guernsey cattle.

The store's windows gleamed from elbow grease and vinegar, sparkling in the first rays of the morning sun. John stopped to admire the wares inside as he pulled off his wide-brimmed hat and brushed the trail dust from his long, linen duster.

The front porch on the outside of the store showed shiny tin buckets, a stand of new brooms and shovels, bins of early potatoes, and barrels of staples like beans and cornmeal. A clear-throated canary warbled from a wire cage hanging from the rafters. A pleasant aroma of freshly baked bread drifted through the air from Millie's Café and John's stomach rumbled. It wasn't often he had fresh-baked bread.

John stepped up the two stairs, headed toward the door, and reached out to open it.

The door burst open, and only his quick jump back kept him from being knocked on the head.

A woman barreled out, sidestepped him, and then managed to bump straight into his side. A linen sack in her arm burst open and flour drifted out in an exploding white cloud. It coated them both as the woman stopped, turned, and glowered at him. The angry expression in her eyes was dimmed a tad by the rim of flour coating her eyes like a sideshow clown.

"Why don't you watch where you're going?" John snapped in a sour mood. He brushed down the linen duster, getting flour all over his fingers. Probably all in his beard too.

"Me?" Outraged, the woman glared, green eyes shooting off sparks. "Why were you standing in the way?"

"Standing in the way?" He brushed his beard, the sifted flour falling like snow. A glance at his once clean brown shirt and trousers made him crimp his lips to keep from cursing. He took a deep breath. "You're the one who came barreling out like a bullet out of a pistol and socked me with your flour."

"Well, I'm sorry; maybe I was distracted," she snapped. "But you could have watched where you were going."

A growl erupted low in his throat as he stomped his boots, a drift of flour shifting around his feet. "How'm I supposed to get this stuff off?"

"I said I was sorry," she brushed at the flour on her own face. She crimped her lips, then muttered, "Seems to me you came running up here too fast, without looking where you were going either. It's not all *my* fault."

Darn, fool woman!

"I was minding my own business when you shoved open the door and hit me with your sack," John argued back, shaking his duster, and hitting his trousers with the hat. A cloud of flour wafted out.

"Hit you? Why you…you…" the woman couldn't seem to get the words out. Red splotched her cheeks, and she grabbed the brown riding skirt and stomped past him.

Even though John took an instant dislike to her, he couldn't help giving her a second glance as she hurried toward the buggy, tossed in the limp flour sack, and climbed into the driver's seat.

Too bad she's so disagreeable. She's pretty.

He didn't know why he was staring, but he couldn't help it. John knew he stood there like a half-grown pup, admiring the tall, stately body all stiff-necked and proud. As she settled into the buggy seat, she flung a long, auburn braid over one shoulder. Usually, a woman with hair that color had pale, creamy skin. Sometimes freckles. John could tell by her weathered skin, bronzed by hours in the sun, that this woman was different. While there were some women who always looked as pale as ghosts, protecting their skin with a bonnet, fearful of the sun, John admired a woman who wasn't afraid to let the sun kiss her skin to the color of fine leather.

"I'm sorry about your clothes." She said as she grabbed up the reins and gave him another annoyed look. "Please tell your wife I'm sorry for giving her extra laundry. I'll bake her a pie or something for the inconvenience. Now, if you'll excuse me."

She shook the reins and drove off before John could sputter that he no longer had a wife. Ada had left years ago, not being able to handle being the wife of a sheriff.

Darn fool woman.

John went on into the mercantile.

"Oh, my," Clara said, looking over the counter at the flour dusting his clothes. "Looks like you had an accident, John."

"Accident nothing!" he grumbled. "Some fool woman hit me with a sack of flour."

The storekeeper did her best not to laugh, but John could see her shoulders shaking. She stepped over to a counter, picked up a clothes brush and handed it to him. "Here, go out on the porch and brush off what you can. I'll fill your order if you tell me what you need."

Embarrassed, John took the clothes brush, noticing Isaac Glover standing beside the shelves holding books. He nodded, feeling his face heat again. "Morning, Mr. Glover."

"John."

"I'll just have a hunk of cheese and some coffee beans, Clara."

He took the brush and went out to the porch. The woman was nowhere in sight, and John wondered about her, remembering those green eyes. Annabelle something, wasn't *that* her name? Her husband had died not too long ago. A widow.

Not my concern.

Before long, he had the brown wrapped parcel of cheese, and a small sack of coffee. After telling Clara goodbye, he left Ranger tied to the hitching post and headed to Patrick Malone's saloon. It might be nice to wet his whistle before the long, hot ride back to the ranch.

He also wanted to hear what news Patrick might share. Patrick usually heard all of the doings in town before anyone else. For more years than John cared to count, Patrick Malone had been a bounty hunter and often worked alongside him as a temporary deputy. He and Patrick had spent hours riding on a posse, hunting down outlaws. To many, Patrick seemed gruff, but John considered him a valued friend. If there was one person—other than Sam—he could depend on, it was Patrick.

Guess now Sam's gone, Patrick is one of the few people I can trust.

"Top o' the morning' to ya, John," Patrick greeted him in a thick Irish brogue as he walked into the dim saloon.

This early in the day the place was almost empty except for Old Man Gower, slumped over at the corner table in the back, palsied hand clasped around a glass of whiskey. He'd sit there all day and nurse along one drink. Patrick's had been his home away from home since he'd lost his family to an epidemic four years ago.

The room smelled of stale beer, sweat, and tobacco. A damp sheen on the scratched wooden floorboards showed someone had given the room a lick and a promise with a mop. Most of the tables were still scattered helter skelter from the night before, and a couple of oil lamps did their best to fight back the gloom. Later in the day, the bar would fill, and Mr. Squire, the hired help, would jingle the piano keys. Now, it was too early for most.

"Hi, Patrick. Morning, Mr. Gower."

Standing beside the scarred top of the bar, John leaned his elbows down. "How about a beer, Patrick?"

"Sure 'nuff." The chubby Irishman poured out a glass and pushed it along the bar to John. "What brings ya inta town?"

"Needed a couple of things at Dawsons. And maybe some information." John sipped off the foam of the beer, then took a deep thirst-quenching swallow. "You hear anything about Sam Garrett getting killed? His kids rode out to the house last night."

Patrick brushed a hand through his thinning strands of red hair, dusted with gray. His deep-set brown eyes looked at John as he crossed himself before speaking of the dead.

"Turrible, turrible," he muttered "Sam gettin' killed. A good deputy and a friendlier fellow I never met. Always took time for a kind word, he did." Picking up a rag, Patrick wiped down the bar, shaking his head at the unfathomable mysteries of the world.

"Did you hear how it happened?" John asked. He took another swallow of the beer and kept his eyes on the pudgy bartender. From his days as sheriff, John knew Patrick often overheard stuff. Men might get drunk and spill secrets they'd rather keep. If anyone knew more about Sam's death, it would be the bartender.

Patrick laid down the rag and swiped damp hands down a wrinkled white apron over a red plaid shirt. "Heard it be an accident." Almost like he might be afraid of being overheard, Patrick leaned over toward John and lowered his voice, "but then again, it coulda not."

"What makes you say that?"

"I heard Ransom's out of jail."

Ransom! Just the mention of his name caused John's blood to boil. Ransom Baxter had been the leader of the Red Hand Gang. For years they'd terrorized anyone they came in contact with robbing banks, stagecoaches, and trains around Texas.

John could still remember the day he and Sam had finally managed to capture Ransom and put him behind bars. The outlaw should have hung, but at the last minute, a bleeding-heart judge gave him a prison sentence instead. All because Ransom turned in some of his old gang members to keep his own neck out of a noose. "How did he get out of jail? He got life."

"Escaped, word says," Patrick informed him, a worried crease between his eyes. "No one knows where he went, but...I hear people talking. They say, Ransom managed to gather his old gang together. The ones who didna die or go to jail."

John set down his beer, the clink of the glass loud on the bar. Although he kept his fears to himself, he had to admit, he felt a cold fist close over his heart. If Ransom Baxter were around, if Sam had seen him, and recognized the outlaw...

Maybe Sam's death was murder.

Maybe mine is next...

Chapter Three

Wilder Ranch

Bang!

The gunshot jolted John from a deep sleep. He jerked away, half awake and groggy wondering if he'd only heard the sound in a nightmare. A glance toward the window, the muslin curtains swaying in a gentle breeze, showed him the first pale gray, pink light of dawn. Ichabod, the rooster, crowed. Somewhere, a shutter banged against a wall, stirred by the sagebrush scented breeze.

Must have been a dream or the shutter.

He laid back against the pillow knowing he'd hear Bossie bellowing before too long. Before he could settle down completely, he heard another sound, more like...horses?

This time John jumped out of bed, padded barefoot to the window, parted the curtain and looked outside.

Horses!

A man on a tall, well-muscled Palomino rode past hollering like a drunk after a Saturday night saloon visit. He galloped past the window, close enough for John to notice his masked face. The man had tied a dark red bandana around his mouth and pulled his hat down close to his eyes. Only a slit for the eyes and nose showed his face—not enough for John to get a close look or to recognize the man.

"Hey! You! Get outta here!" he hollered out, then regretted it, realizing he felt vulnerable standing at the open window in just his long underwear, with no weapon in hand.

Another wild whoop—this one from a second man—galloping around the barnyard, scattering the chickens. John's eyes widened in shock as he saw at least four men riding around in front of the house, whooping and knocking over stuff. Already they'd torn down part of a fence near the corral, chased poor old Bossie, udders dragging, into his corn patch, and pulled down the post holding up the clothesline. Two pair of his trousers were being dragged through the mud by the rain barrel. *Durn them anyway!*

One of the men rode a liver-colored mare through the newly planted kitchen garden where John knew he'd seen onions popping up just yesterday. The horse's hooves stomped them flat.

"Get outta there!" He yelled, nostrils flaring and a vein throbbing in his temple.

They must have heard but they kept on, galloping around, hollering, and every so often shooting up in the air.

Who were they? What the devil did they want?

John hurried to the bed and pulled his Winchester rifle from underneath. Ever since his days as a sheriff, he'd slept with a weapon nearby.

Should have taken it when I got up.

He ran back to the window, pulled back the trigger and shot into the ground near one of the horses. All he got was a waft of dust, but it startled the rider. Not enough to drop his handkerchief and reveal his face, but enough for the horse to rear back in fright and rise on its hind legs.

John felt vulnerable, trapped in the house while four men pillaged his ranch. He loaded in another bullet and fired again.

This time, the men took one last round of the barnyard. The rider on the liver-colored horse knocked over a water barrel, spilling the precious liquid, while the rider on the Palomino shot holes in the side of the barn. Bossie mooed in terror and the chickens squawked and darted around in frenzy. The men took off down the farm road toward the main path to the south.

The whole episode left John strangely shaken despite having spent years as a sheriff, living with danger every second of the day and night.

He thought of Sam's kids telling him the gang might come after him next. *Had one of the masked men been Ransom? Were they after him? Was he next?*

Well, he wouldn't just sit there and let them come storming in one night and take him asleep. Nobody would sneak up on him in a barn and conk *him* in the head.

John laid down the Winchester, pulled on a pair of brown trousers, a dark blue shirt and the tan suspenders Sam had given him for his birthday one year. Yanking on his boots, he grabbed up his linen duster, the holster with his Colt, and headed to the barn.

After rescuing Bossie from the cornfield, milking her and feeding the barn cats, he saddled up Ranger. No telling where those men had gone, but sure enough they'd have left some kind of trail. John figured to follow it and see if he could learn more about the men. If it was Ransom and the Red Hand Gang, he wanted to know.

The men had headed away from town, toward the south. John kept his distance, in case they'd stopped along the way, but he rode for about an hour with only hoofprints and horse droppings to show he was headed in the right direction. Or maybe he wasn't.

John had spent years tracking as a sheriff. Sam used to say he must be part Indian, he could do it so stealthily and so well. Well, he didn't know about that, but he had been competent. If the men had headed in a different direction, he should find some sign soon.

He'd ridden for almost two hours when he noticed smoke in the distance. Normal, everyday smoke from a chimney or cook fire. Although he'd lived near Pecos for years, John didn't know all his neighbors. There never seemed to be time to go calling even if he'd had the inclination.

After Ada left, there wasn't any excuse for any of the women nearby to visit. John kept to himself and figured other folks could do the same. So he didn't know who lived in the ranch as he rode down a hardpacked dirt road leading past a field of newly plowed ground. It was too early for whatever crop was planted to show, but whoever owned it had plenty of land, unfenced he noticed.

As he rode past the field, he could see a sturdy barn ahead and a small ranch house. The closer he got, the more he could see someone had been busy fixing up the barn—new boards had replaced old, there were patches on the shingles, and the beginning of a large kitchen garden with a split rail fence.

A woman's scream shattered the morning. "Help! Someone help!"

That was all he needed to hear. John kicked his heels in Ranger's flank and galloped to the barn. Just beside the barn he could see a couple of men, beating an older man. He jumped from the saddle, pulled out the Colt, and fired it into the air. "That's enough! You heard the lady, leave him alone."

One of the men, a tall man with a shock of chestnut brown hair, dropped the older man to the ground, and came at John. He wore a red bandana tied around his lower face, hiding his looks, except for menacing eyes narrowed to slits. Fisting his hands, he stalked toward John, almost into the face of the Colt's barrel.

Is he crazy? I could blow his face off!

The second man gave off a wild laugh, ran at John and kicked him in the stomach. Caught completely off guard by the attack, John doubled over as the Colt dropped from his hand.

I'm dead.

He realized, a second later, that the men had no intention of killing him. The chestnut-haired man kicked John in the leg. A searing, knife-sharp pain took his breath away. It figured that they'd aim for his gimpy leg. Someone fired a rifle but John had no idea who or where. Doubled over in agony, John swallowed past a lump in his throat. While he struggled for breath, the men jumped on their horses and rode off, leaving him and the bloodied man behind.

The older man's moaning forced John to forget his own pain. Half crawling, he managed to drag himself to the man's side and turn him over. Hank Dawson—Clara's husband! "Hank, what happened?"

"I ... I ... they beat me purty bad," he panted, his eyes held a wounded look, "but, I think I'll be all right."

"Let me help you up." Putting his arms beneath Hank's, John managed to half lift, half carry Hank to a nearby bale of hay beside the barn. He'd just helped Hank sit when he heard a gun cock.

"Turn around real slow," a feminine voice spoke, "If you don't want to lose anything vital."

"Annie, it's all right, he came to help," Hank panted in a strained voice.

Still John didn't take any chances. He put up his hands, turned slowly and stared into the green eyes of the woman who'd sifted him with flour.

"You!"

Chapter Four

Hollis Ranch

Earlier

The shouts had woken Annabelle from a sound sleep. Not that she usually slept so deeply. Most nights she was lucky to sleep for a couple of hours, before the longing to have Thomas by her side nudged her awake. On those nights, Annabelle thought of a woman she'd know before she and Thomas had married—Mrs. Carlyle. She'd been a widow for all the years of Annabelle's growing up, having lost her husband in the war between the states. She'd been just nineteen when he died. On the nights she couldn't sleep, Annabelle counted all the years Mrs. Carlyse had been a widow—fifteen. How did she stand being alone for fifteen years?

I'd go mad. Thomas has only been gone a few years, and the ache never leaves. How did a woman last for fifteen years or longer?

The loneliness of the nights was often more than Annabelle could bear. Some nights she reached out beside her dozens of times, expecting his death to have been a nightmare. Surely, she'd wake up and find Thomas asleep beside her—strong, sturdy, his loving arms cradling her as she fell back to sleep.

"Get outta here, you varmints!"

Startled out of the first deep sleep she'd had in months, Annabelle realized she heard Hank's cantankerous voice, the one he used when the pigs got into the garden.

He must have got here early. Darn those pigs! If they trampled my new cabbage shoots, I'll...

Annabelle jumped out of bed, legs twisting in her long, white muslin gown. Rubbing the sleep from her eyes, she went to the window to see what trouble her animals had gotten into now.

Startled, she gawked in disbelief. The sight that met her eyes made her gasp. Her eyes widened in alarm, wishing the trouble *was* just the pigs.

It wasn't pigs, but men, masked men. They had Hank down near the barn and were pummeling him with their fists.

Blood streamed down Hank's battered face, and he doubled over.

Without a thought for her own safety, Annabelle ran into the parlor, grabbed Thomas's rifle from over the mantel, and ran outside. The early morning dew tickled her bare feet and sent a shudder up her back, but she didn't stop.

"Help someone," she screamed, realizing how futile that sounded. Who was around but her and Hank? Although the thought crossed her mind that maybe the masked men would think she was calling other ranch hands to come help. "Someone, help me!"

To her shock, another man rode up, jumped from his saddle, and entered the brawl. At first, she thought he might be one of the men beating Hank, until the two masked men turned on him. One punched him in the stomach and another kicked his leg. Annabelle fired off a warning shot in the air, realizing Thomas's rifle only held one round. Maybe it frightened the masked men or maybe they were done with Hank. They dropped him to the ground, grabbed up their horses and rode out of the barnyard. It all happened so quickly; Annabelle reeled in shock.

The stranger helped Hank half crawl, half walk to sit on a bale of hay. Hank's breath came ragged and uneven, blood oozing from a cut on his forehead and dripping through his reddish eyebrows.

Even though the gun was empty, she leveled it at the strange man and commanded in a firm voice, "Turn around real slow. If you don't want to lose anything vital."

"Annie, it's all right, he came to help," Hank panted in a strained voice, spitting out blood into the dirt at his feet.

The tall, broad-shouldered stranger, wearing a long, linen duster that looked somehow familiar, lifted his arms. He slowly spun around so she could see his face.

"You!"

Annabelle recognized the man as the one she'd bumped into at Dawson's store. Up close she studied his weathered face, the dark brown hair graying at the temples, a neatly trimmed dark beard. But it was those piercing blue eyes that took her breath away. Annabelle felt a rush of heat on her face, realizing those eyes could see every curve of her body in the thin nightgown.

"What are you doing here?" She spoke with bitter resentment. "Why did you bring those men here?" Annabelle realized she spoke with a sharper tongue than he deserved. In truth, the man had done nothing wrong.

It's just my stubborn nature not to depend on anyone else.

Hank shook his head, reached a trembling hand up to his lips where blood gushed. "No, Annie, this is John Wilder, he used to be the sheriff in Pecos River. He tried to help me, but those goons punched him in the gut."

John Wilder.

Annabelle seemed to remember Clara telling her that she and Thomas lived near a former sheriff. When Thomas was alive, she had no need to know, although it seemed he had expressed relief.

Now that she got a good, up-close look at him, when he wasn't riled up over wearing her flour, Annabelle noticed John was right handsome. Even with a grimace of pain on his face.

She lowered the gun, leaned it against the barn, embarrassed. *He probably knows it's not loaded anyway.*

"Oh, I'm sorry again," she managed a shaky grin, folding her arms over her chest while he slowly lowered his raised hands.

Why did I run out here in my nightgown? "When I heard Hank holler, all I could think of was helping him."

"Understandable," John muttered, one hand going to his stomach as he let out a groan. "Maybe, if you could find him something to staunch the blood. And ma'am, I wouldn't mind a hot cup of coffee if you'd be obliged."

Embarrassed by the man's obvious ploy to let her get back into the house, Annabelle gritted her teeth to keep from snapping at him.

He's just trying to help you from being an even bigger fool than you have already been. Stop being so cussed stubborn.

Annabelle took a deep breath. "Surely, it's the least I can do. Hank, you hurt bad?"

"No, I ain't," the older man grumbled, "you go on and make the coffee. We need to talk."

Leaving Thomas's rifle beside the barn, Annabelle hurried into the house. She took time to dip water into the tin coffee pot and sat it on the wood stove. Another couple of minutes to toss in kindling, strike a match, and get a small fire going to heat the water.

She heard Hank and John walking up the steps to the porch. Annabelle hurried into her bedroom, closed the door, and pulled on a wrinkled pink shirtwaist and the brown riding skirt she'd worn the day before. A glance in the mirror over the dresser showed her braid all frowsy and sleep tossed, but she didn't take time to brush it out. John Wilder had already seen her looking at her worst.

And who cares about what he thinks anyway?

When she walked back into the kitchen, she saw John had poured some of the hot water into a basin and found a rag to wipe Hank's face.

Just make yourself at home.

Thankfully, she had enough wisdom to keep her mouth shut before her tongue made her look like a fool again. Seeing Hank taken care of, Annabelle busied herself making the coffee. By the time it had brewed, sending out a rich, warm scent into the room, Hank had a bandage around his head. Annabelle poured coffee into tin mugs and handed them around.

"What did those men want here, Hank?"

In all the time she'd known Hank Dawson, Annabelle knew him as one of the mildest men she'd ever met. Not one to cause men to beat him up. "Why were they beating you?" She pulled out a chair and sat down across from John.

"They didn't plan to kill me, just give me a message." Hank took a sip of coffee, a grim expression on his ruddy face. His tongue probed at the split on his lip. "You might as well hear this too, Sheriff. They're some of Ransom's men."

"Ransom Baxter," John perked up, gripped the tin cup hard enough so that his knuckles turned white. "You're sure?"

Hank nodded. "Told me they were Christopher and Jack Jones."

Annabelle could see the names meant something to John. His blue eyes stared out into the distance, and he gave a startled gasp. "You know who they are?"

At first Annabelle didn't think he'd answer. Then John sighed, loosened the fingers around his coffee cup and spoke in a tight voice. "They're part of Ransom Baxter's gang. Jack is Ransom's second-in-command. If there's something to be done, Ransom trusts him to do it. He's ruthless and he enjoys violence. Christopher is Jack's younger brother. He's about twenty-one. He's almost more dangerous than his older brother. Or so folks say."

"Why's that?" Annabelle asked.

"Christopher's mean enough to steal a fly from a blind spider. Trigger happy too. He shoots first and finds out why later. Anything Ransom tells him to do, he does it. No questions asked. I'm not certain why they'd come *here*."

"Patrick told me Ransom escaped," Hank interrupted. "I'm guessing he's trying to recruit the old gang again. The ones who avoided the noose. An' I can tell you why they came here, Sheriff."

"I'm not the sheriff anymore, Hank, but I'd like to know what they're doing in these parts again."

Hank stared at Annabelle; a spasm of irritation crossed his face. "They came to give us a message. They want you to leave the ranch or else."

"Or else, what?" Confused, she looked at Hank and then to John, seeking an explanation. "Why should they care what *I* do? I've never done anything to them. Or this...what was his name, Ransom Baxter."

Although Hank and Clara had mentioned the Red Hand Gang, Annabelle had never given them much thought. She knew they were outlaws who'd been caught and sent to prison.

"They care because they want this ranch. Ransom does anyway. The Jones boys wanted to tell me if we don't all leave the ranch, we'll die just like Thomas."

Annabelle gasped. Her heart leapt in shock. "Then, maybe his death wasn't an accident?"

Was that why Thomas was killed? Had those men come to ask him to sell and he wouldn't?

Annabelle had known her husband or thought she did. What if those men had come when she had gone to town, pushed Thomas off the ladder, and waited for him to die?

It never stood to reason that a man as careful and surefooted as a mountain goat, could topple off a ladder and hit his head hard enough to die. The gash in his head had looked suspicious to Annabelle, although once she knew he was dead, she couldn't look again. Sheriff Crane had listened to her doubts, but didn't seem inclined to do much.

"I'm sure it's just a tragic accident, Miz Hollis," he'd told her in his mournful hangdog voice, "these things happen on a ranch. Had me a cousin who died falling into a pigpen, got stomped by a sow. Turrible tragedy."

"Then, do you think they're saying they had something to do with Thomas's death? That they killed him and they'll kill me too?"

Hank shook his head, unable to answer.

Annabelle turned toward John. Surely, even a former sheriff could tell her something. "What do you think, Mr. Wilder? Do you think they killed Thomas? Will they try to kill me to get the ranch?"

She could tell he didn't want to answer; her questions caused him to shift and avoid looking at her. "I need to know. Please, tell me something."

"Miz Hollis," the look he gave her was one of pity, his voice quiet and strained, "I don't rightly know what Ransom or his men will do. If he's gone so far as to send a warning, then he wants this place bad. Bad enough to kill and keep on killing."

"Why?"

John shook his head, "Maybe for the same reason Isaac Glover wants to buy up land. To sell it to the railroad at a profit. There's speculation the Texas Pacific Railways want to lay more tracks in the next couple of years. I've heard Glover say if he can buy up land cheap, he can make a killing selling it back to the railroad at a higher cost."

"Enough profit to kill Thomas and...me?"

Annabelle's heart sank when he gave her a nod.

What am I going to do?

Chapter Five

Pecos River

What is she going to do?

It worried John to leave Annabelle and Hank alone on the ranch. But the way Hank figured, the Jones boys had already had their fun. They'd lie low for a while to see if Annabelle heeded their message. Then...John didn't like to think about what might happen. He'd had plenty of dealings with Ransom Baxter before. If the man had killed Thomas Hollis, then he'd think nothing of getting Annabelle out of the way too.

"Not sure how I can stop them," John said out loud to his patient, plodding horse. Like always, Ranger didn't reply.

Reckon I'd be mighty shocked if he did.

After leaving Annabelle's ranch, John rode toward home, his stomach tied up in knots. If he ever got his hands on the Jones boy who'd kicked him, he'd give him what for back. Throughout his years as sheriff, he'd been beaten, stabbed, shot at, and mauled, but after a few days recovering, he'd been none the worse for wear. Today every breath sent knife-sharp daggers through his lungs and his leg ached so badly, tears came to his eyes. Maybe he was getting too old for all this fighting.

As he rode at an easy lope, he thought about what had happened since he woke up this morning.

Now that he knew it was Jones, Ransom's henchman, John had to wonder. Why did they want to mess up his ranch like that? Was it a message? A warning they were coming after him like they'd gone after Sam? Did Ransom want his ranch too, just like he wanted Annabelle's? And if he did, had Ransom killed Sam? Why? None of it made any sense.

Sam and his kids were living on their ranch, as peaceable as could be. As far as John knew, the railroad didn't have any plans to head over to the town where Sam lived. Why kill Sam?

Is there a target on my back too? Does someone want my ranch?

John didn't like to think about such things. He'd spent years *not* thinking or worrying about an outlaw coming after him. Ada had done enough of that. His wife's constant fear had finally sent her packing back east.

"I can't live with it, John," she'd told him the morning she caught the stage for El Paso. "Never knowing when you leave the house if you'll come riding home, or they'll carry you out in a box. You can either keep being a sheriff and lose me, or quit."

There wasn't any choice. The law was his life, and he owed it to the folks who'd elected him to do a good job. Sure, he missed Ada powerful bad at first, but then the pain eased.

He'd been ashamed to admit Ada's leaving made life easier. He didn't have to worry when he went into a shootout or trapped an outlaw band in a hideout. If Ada had been around when he and Sam finally caught Ransom and the Red Hand Gang, she'd have left for sure anyway.

John had taken two bullets, one to the back that laid him low for months. The second bullet ripped out part of his thigh and did something to his leg. He'd carry the gimpy leg as a scar for the rest of his life. If not for Sam and his kids' careful nursing, he'd never have survived.

And now, Ransom and his gang are back in action.

Even though he knew he should set his ranch to rights, John rode on past and headed toward Pecos River. Maybe it was time Sheriff Crane knew about the attacks on his ranch and Annabelle's. He also needed to know Ransom and his gang were back in town if he didn't already.

Sighing, John headed Ranger toward town. It was past noon when he came in sight of the dusty street and wooden buildings of the town, busy with people, horses, and noise.

The jail sat a few doors down from Dawson's Mercantile. The tinkly piano in Malone's Saloon jangled as the batwing doors swung open and closed. John knew some of the men who worked at the stockyards went there for a beer lunch instead of Millie's Café.

Looked like Millie's was bustling too, horses were tied up to the hitching posts and one buggy stood along the alley, loaded down with split logs and a keg of nails. A scent of roasting beef and baking bread caused his stomach to rumble. No wonder. All he'd had all morning was the cup of coffee at Annabelle Hollis's house. Maybe after he talked to the sheriff, he'd treat himself to lunch in town.

John tied Ranger to a post, stepped onto the boardwalk, and headed into the jail. "Sheriff Crane," he called as he entered the dim room, blinking as he left the bright sun behind.

Strange how just being back in the old jail felt as comfortable as slipping on a pair of well-worn moccasins. The same scents of musty wood, smoke from the stove, and rancid coffee hours brewed. Just the way the floor creaked beneath his boots welcomed him home. The rustle of posters tacked up to the walls, as familiar as the sound of his own breath.

"Howdy there, John," Sheriff Crane's crusty voice welcomed him. "Come on in and set a spell. Grab a mug of coffee off the stove. I'm just finishing up my lunch."

From past experience, John knew Millie always provided the sheriff and deputy with a plated lunch, sent over on a silver tray. As he remembered, Millie's special on Wednesday was pot roast, he caught a whiff from Sheriff Crane's desk as he walked toward the potbellied stove. Even with the spring heat outside, the potbellied stove rarely went out, the coffee pot sat on top and turned the dregs into a bitter brew.

"Old enough to stand up without the pot," Sam used to joke.

Rest in peace, Sam.

A wave of nostalgia settled over John as he poured a cup of coffee, the familiar shape of the battered tin pot bringing back a lot of memories, good and bad.

"What brings you into town? Saw you yesterday at Dawson's and thought you'd stop around."

Tobias Crane was a small man, many said too short to do a good job. He stood just over five feet four inches in his leather boots, ordered fancy from somewhere in San Antonio.

He had a few graying strands of hair brushed over an egg-shaped head. Not that folks usually noticed his hair. Even indoors, like now, he kept his balding head covered with a tan, wide brimmed hat. A strip of rawhide circled the brim and Tobias often stuck in a feather like an eastern dandy.

His weathered face had seen plenty of trouble, but his solemn brown eyes looked at the world with quiet, some said lazy, patience.

"He won't make the best sheriff," Sam groused when John took off his badge for good, "but I guess he'll get the job done."

Sheriff Crane had been elected the year John decided to hang up his guns and settle for a quiet life on the ranch.

John hooked one boot tip beneath a chair and slid it around in front of the sheriff's desk. As he sat down, he winced from the pain in his gut.

When I get that guy...

"Sorry I didn't stop by yesterday. Had a lot of work to do on the ranch."

"How you like being retired from the jail?" Crane asked as he spooned up a gravy-covered potato and put the succulent morsel in his mouth.

Again, John's stomach grumbled. Everybody in town knew if you didn't get to Millie's by two o'clock, the Wednesday pot roast was long gone.

"Well, I can't say it was an easy decision, but after that last gunfight with the Red Hand Gang, I figured it was time. Better I quit than harm somebody else because I'm too old for the job."

"You won't ever be too old, John. Best sheriff Pecos River ever had an' that includes me. Can't never live up to your reputation."

Embarrassed, John quickly changed the subject. "The main reason I wanted to stop by is to confirm a rumor I heard from Patrick."

"What rumor is that?"

"I heard Ransom Baxter escaped from prison. That he's been seen trying to round up the old gang."

The sheriff took a bite of his roast, chewed and chewed and chewed, before he nodded. Once he swallowed, he spoke the words John dreaded. "It's true. Somewhere..." Crane shifted a pile of WANTED posters scattered across the same old scarred desk John had used. After a minute of searching, he found the broadsheet and stabbed it with a gravy-spattered fork. A flake of carrot drifted down to land on Ransom Baxter's nose. "Got that poster just the other day."

WANTED DEAD OR ALIVE

John read the bold words across the top of the poster. Ransom's ugly face had been drawn fairly true to life. "Has he been seen around here? Are you going to look for him?"

Crane shook his head, picked up one of Millie's flaky biscuits and yanked a bite out of it. Butter oozed down his fingers and chin. "Far as I heard, he's not been around here. If someone sees him, then I'll get up a posse. It's not your concern, John. You aren't the sheriff anymore." He licked the butter from his fingers, sighed and patted his ample stomach. "Nothing like Millie's biscuits. A man could think he'd died and gone on to heaven."

"How do you know Ransom isn't back in this area?"

"Now, John," Crane shifted in his seat and reached for a tin mug of coffee. "You just go back to your quiet life and leave the law to me and my deputy. You spent years keeping the town safe. Now, it's my job."

"Did you hear Sam Garrett was killed?"

"Yes, sad business. But Sam didn't live here anymore." Crane said with an annoyed look in his eyes. "That's Sheriff North's business. If I can help him out, I will, but he hasn't asked me yet. As far as he figures, Sam's death was an accident."

"Like Thomas Hollis?" Even though he hadn't been sheriff when Annabelle Hollis's husband died, John remembered the talk around Malone's. How the man fell off a ladder. It seemed suspicious then, and even more so now that someone had attacked her ranch.

"Why? You got some idea it wasn't an accident?"

"Not really," John shifted on the creaky chair, having a hard time sitting still. He itched to do something. "I don't know that much about it. But a couple of masked men came out to my ranch this morning and caused a bunch of trouble. After that, they headed to Hollis's ranch and just about beat Hank Dawson to a pulp...If I hadn't come along—"

"Hank? Is he all right?" Crane sat up, alert, fingering the silver star on the right shoulder of his black leather vest.

"He'll live, but he's banged up a lot. Miz Hollis was tending to him when I left. Guess I best go tell Clara he got hurt when I leave here."

"Why would anyone beat up Hank? Did you see who they were?"

John realized the whole morning was too hard to explain. He kept events short as he relayed the facts to Crane. "Well, I know two of them, Christopher and Jack Jones, from Ransom's old gang. There were four who attacked my ranch this morning, and woke me up. Not sure where the other two went, but those two headed to Hollis's. "

"They do any damage?" Crane's eyes widened with recognition at the names. He whistled through his two front teeth, staring hard at John's face.

"Not really, mostly just whooping it up and knocking stuff over. Chased Bossie into my garden, knocked over the rain barrel, stuff like that. They wore masks so I wouldn't know them by sight. Though it's been a few years since I've laid eyes on them."

"You sure it was some of Ransom's men? Sounds more like a couple of young boys just bein' rowdy. How'd you know it was them if they wore masks?"

"After they left my place," John answered, "I decided to follow them. Tracked them toward the Hollis Ranch and heard a woman hollering for help. It was Annabelle Hollis and two of the men were there beating up on Hank. After we chased them off..." John left off the crucial fact about his being punched and kicked, being too ashamed to admit it. "Well, Hank said they'd told him their names and left a message."

"What kind of message?"

"Hank said Jack told him that anyone who lived on her ranch might die, just like Thomas did."

"What did Miz Hollis say to that?"

John thought of Annabelle Hollis, the fear in those spell-binding green eyes, the crimp of worry around her lips. *She's frightened.* He didn't share his thoughts with Crane. Instead, he shrugged and chose his words carefully. "Not much she could say, was there? It did make her question Thomas's death. You went out there when he died. What do you think happened?"

It was the hesitation of Crane's that made John suspicious. The sheriff was trying to hide something, but what?

Chapter Six

"Accident, pure an' simple," Crane stated firmly, nostrils flaring. "He got clumsy and fell, all there was to it. I didn't see any sign a gang had been around."

John kept his concerns to himself. No matter what he thought about Crane, the man was sheriff now. It wouldn't do to antagonize him. Not until he had proof that he'd somehow hid facts about Thomas Hollis's death. "If you're sure…"

"Now, John, you gotta remember Miz Hollis was grieving. Sure, she didn't want to think Thomas could be so clumsy that he'd fall off a ladder. But I investigated. Didn't find anything to tell me anyone had a hand in his death."

There was no way to know for sure at this late date. Still, John probed a little harder. "Well, let's say some of the Red Hand Gang were around then. Could it have been them? Do you know where the Jones boys ended up when Ransom got sent up to prison? They weren't with the men Sam and I captured."

As expected, Crane shook his head, the tan hat snug over his bald head. "There wasn't any idea of them being around. Although I did hear lately that they got away from the law over near San Antonio."

The bigger town wasn't too far for a determined rider or two. *Not if they wanted to come back here for some reason.*

"I guess I best find time to talk to Miz Hollis and Hank," Crane said, pushing himself out of the desk chair. It scraped across the floor, leaving more marks in the grooves he and Sam had worn on the planks. "If the Red Hand Gang's been seen in this area, Ransom might be around somewhere. Sure hope he goes to greener pastures and don't come around here. Tried to keep the town peaceful, sure would like it to stay that way."

"I'd be glad to give you a hand," John offered, setting the tin cup on the edge of the desk, his stomach already protesting over the bitter brew he'd drunk. Hopefully, Millie still had some pot roast to dish up.

"Now, John, you sure you want to give up your nice, quiet life to go chasin' after the bad guys again? You let me handle it." Sheriff Crane gave him a superior look, his brown eyes twinkling.

It went against the grain, but John said his goodbyes and left. He started toward Dawson's but then saw Annabelle's buggy with Hank slowly stepping over the side. Relieved, he didn't have to break the news to Clara, John untied Ranger and headed to Millie's Café. As he opened the door into the noisy room, he heard Sheriff Crane call out to Hank and walk toward the mercantile.

Guess Annabelle saved him a ride.

After a tasty lunch of pot roast and flaky biscuits, John headed back to the ranch. There were chores to do.

At home, he unsaddled the horse and went to work. Bossie's fence needed mending to keep her inside the pasture. There was the rain barrel to set to rights. Just picking up the ripped sheets and stuff tossed from the clothesline took more than an hour. When he got done, John ached all over, especially his gimpy leg and his stomach. He settled for cornbread and milk for supper, took care of the evening chores, and settled into bed early.

Although he seldom locked the cabin doors, he pulled in the latch string, checked to make sure the Winchester was loaded and under the bed. Then, feeling like a fool, he tucked the Colt under his pillow, just in case. He'd never been fearful before but maybe what happened to Sam and this morning's attack had spooked him.

As he lay in bed, one arm cradled under his head, John watched the moonlight shadows glide across the whitewashed ceiling. It worried him about Sheriff Crane. The man didn't seem all too eager to find out about Ransom or his gang. Maybe he was even afraid to go up against them. John had seen plenty of lawmen with limp spines, afeared to go far from the protection of town and jail. Although he'd had plenty of encounters where he felt fear, he'd never let it overcome his ability to do the job. Sheriff Crane might not be made of the same stuff.

***

John slept in fits and starts, jolted awake more than once, his heart hammering. Sound thrummed in his ears, but once he stopped to calm himself down, he heard only the chirping of insects or the rustle of a branch alongside the house.

At about dawn, he got up, unable to sleep. After taking care of the morning chores, he decided to go see Sam's kids. He hadn't felt right since their last visit. Maybe it was time to clear the air and see if they knew anything else about Sam's so-called "accident."

Mighty peculiar there were so many "accidents" lately—Sam and Thomas Hollis.

The town where Sam had settled after he'd left off being a deputy, was only a couple of hours ride away. John wished now he'd gone to see Sam more. When they worked together at the jail, they'd seen one another every day. They ate together, slept in the jail sometimes when prisoners were around, or trailed off after some varmint or another. They were seldom apart. After they hung up their guns, they'd gone their separate ways. Sam figured it was time to settle down with Ethan and

Lily, a place they could make their own instead of living at the boardinghouse. John wished now he hadn't let so much time go by without visiting his best friend.

Shouldn't a been that way. I sure miss Sam.

Now, there was no time to visit again, to sit on Sam's porch, their booted feet up on the rail, spinning tall tales, and sipping the cold lemonade Lily made.

I should have made more time for Sam. Now it's too late.

Maybe he'd visit Sam's grave after he saw the kids.

It took three hours to ride the distance to the tiny settlement of Crawfordsville where Sam had made his home. John had joked it was little more than a watering spot on the road.

Sure wish Sam was around so I could hear his hearty chuckle.

It was near noon when John turned off the narrow path leading into Sam's ranch. Sam had lost his wife, Lucy, a few years after Lily was born. He'd inherited the rundown cabin and forty acres from his father-in-law—a no-account drunk who never had cared to keep the land up.

Often, when he and Lucy were married, Sam would confess how badly she felt about her pa's disgraceful habit. Still, when old man Carrington died, Sam was grateful enough to get the property with Lucy gone. After he quit being a deputy and moved to Crawfordsville, Sam had rebuilt the cabin, shored up the tipsy barn, and put a lot of elbow grease into getting the fields in plowing order. Ethan and Lily had a place to take pride in now, a real homeplace.

As he rode Ranger toward the house, John saw a wisp of smoke curling from the chimney. Red-and-white-striped curtains blew at the parlor windows, open to let in the fresh air. The sturdy log cabin looked the same as it had the last time he'd visited Sam.

Chickens clucked and pecked in the dusty yard. An orange kitten noticed his approach and dropped from the porch railing to dart beneath the floorboards. A whiskered nose peeked out, too curious to stay hidden. The sound of the windmill creaked near the barn, bringing up the life-giving water into a weathered tin stock tank.

Along with the scents of hen droppings and cows, a tantalizing aroma of pie tickled John's nose. It seemed like hours since he'd drank a cup of coffee and eaten a couple of stale bread crusts.

Come to think of it, it had been.

"Sher...Uncle John!" Lily came across the yard barefoot, with the apron of her blue dress held up like a basket. Her brown curls were caught up in a kerchief and her brown eyes sparkled with delight to welcome him. Pink cheeked, she offered him a smile that crinkled her freckled nose. As she got close enough, he could see the apron filled with eggs. She blushed. "I'm just getting caught up with my chores this morning. Come on in the house. Ethan's out in the south pasture. We've got a bull that keeps breaking out of the fence."

Glad she'd gone back to calling him uncle, John climbed out of the saddle, tied Ranger to a porch railing, and followed Lily into the tidy cabin.

It was much the same as he remembered from his last visit too long ago. There were two big rooms across the front of the cabin, a parlor with a store-bought settee and franklin stove blackened to a shine. The other side of the room held a cook stove, an oak table, and several chairs. All clean and tidy, from a sampler Lucy had stitched hanging on the wall, down to the scrubbed wood plank floors. It startled him to see Sam's wide-brimmed black hat still hanging on a peg beside the door.

Lily noticed his glance. "It didn't seem right to take it off there. I tried but the peg seemed kind of..." she flushed, blinking back tears, "lonesome without Pa's hat."

John nodded, watching while she put the eggs in a bowl and opened the oven door. The scent of dried cherry pie filled the room with sweet perfume. "That pie smells better than anything I've had in a long time," he said to cover up the couple of minutes when she swiped at her eyes with a dish towel.

"Even your oatmeal raisin cookies," Lily joked.

"You're probably a better baker than I am any day of the week." John agreed. "And those cookies are about the only thing I can bake besides cornbread."

"Oh, I don't know about that but sit down. I'll cut a slice while it's warm. Unless you're still full of breakfast?" She lifted her brows in a question and John had to laugh.

"Didn't have any breakfast to speak of and that pie is calling my name."

Lily grinned, so much like Sam it squeezed John's heart in a fist of pain. "You want coffee?"

"I wouldn't say no."

In a few minutes, John sat at the table, eating Lily's pie and trying not to groan in pleasure. He smacked his lips a few times at the tart, sweet cherries and flaky crust. After he'd eaten most of the piece, Lily pulled out a chair and sat across from him. "So, what brings you out here? I'm sorry we left your place the other day so..." At a loss for words, Lily just raised her hands in a gesture of giving up.

"It's all right, I understand. Guess I should have been more understanding. I'm kind of coming around to your and Ethan's way of thinking about your pa. Why do you think he was killed?"

"Well, we don't know for sure, but Pa—he'd been all riled up for a few months before he died. Guess he couldn't give up being a lawman."

John smiled and took a sip of the coffee. "Sounds like Sam. He always said being a lawman got in the blood. Do you know what had him riled up?"

Lily's brown eyes wore a perplexed look. "I'm not real sure. A couple of times he talked about the railroad. How they weren't entitled to some of the land they were using. Pa said something about the railroad being corrupt. I remember once, after I asked what he meant, he said there were people taking over land and not giving the owner's the rightful value. It seemed to upset him awful bad."

John knew how Sam could get his teeth into something he saw as unjust. Like a starving dog with a bone. "Do you remember if he talked about anyone specific? Any names?"

Even though he expected the answer, John was disappointed when Lily shook her head.

"Not really. He didn't say a lot—maybe he told Ethan more. A couple of times he just said someone told him something and it bothered him. He'd ride off for hours, asking questions. It worried me. Maybe all his questions put a target on his back and got him killed? That's what Ethan thinks."

"Is that what you think?"

She kneaded her hands together. "I'm not certain. Once he said he had a lead on a man he wanted to follow. Someone who'd cheated a landowner out of their ranch. When I asked who it was, Pa wouldn't tell me. He said it was safer that I didn't know."

A thread of suspicion crawled up John's spine. The sense of wariness he'd relied on as a sheriff. Sam always called it an 'inner knowing' of something wrong.

"Is that what he said? You were safer not knowing the man's name?"

What did Sam know? Was it something that got him killed?

He was startled out of the thought when the door to the cabin burst open.

Chapter Seven

"I thought I recognized Ranger out there," Ethan came in, yanking off his wide-brimmed hat and fanning his sunburnt face. "What brings you here, Sheriff?"

"Now, Ethan, I just got Lily calling me Uncle John again. You aren't going to go back to calling me sheriff and making me feel old, are you?"

Thankfully, Ethan gave a rueful grin. He reached out to accept the cup of coffee Lily hurried to pour for him. "Guess we owe you an apology for running out the other day. We were just awful," he swallowed hard, glanced at Sam's hat on the peg, tears glistening in his gray–brown eyes. "It's been hard without Pa. Seems like nothing's gone right. Some days, I wonder if we shouldn't try to sell the ranch and do something else."

"Reckon I'm the one who should be saying sorry," John answered, gripping the fork tight. "I should have been here for you when you buried your pa, if I'd have known ..."

"We're real sorry about that, Uncle John," Lily said. "It happened so fast and then the neighbors came to help with the grave. There just wasn't time to get word to you."

John understood how it must have been, but it didn't soothe him to know they'd had no one to lean on.

"Those were real hard days," Ethan spoke in a broken voice. It looked like he was trying hard to hold back tears.

"Sit down and have some pie, Ethan," Lily soothed her brother. "I've been telling Uncle John about Pa. But you can probably explain it all better than I can."

After Ethan pulled out a chair and sat down, Lily placed a plate with pie in front of him. When she glanced at John's empty plate, she scooped up another slice for him too.

"Lily told me that Sam was searching out railroad investors or maybe corrupt buyers? You know anything about that?"

"That's right," Ethan agreed. "Pa got to where he rode out three or four hours a week, talking to people. Then he'd get a worried look on his face and wouldn't tell us what he'd been doing, or who he'd talked to." Ethan stopped to chew some of the pie, wiping the cherry juice that trickled down his chin. "Good pie, Lily." After swallowing some coffee, Ethan continued. "Pa did tell me he was over in Pecos River about a month ago. He said he thought he recognized some men he'd known."

"He said he *thought* he recognized them," Lily interrupted. "He told us he wanted to talk to you about it, but he wanted to be certain first."

"You didn't know who the men were?" John asked.

"No, but ..." Ethan began, and John had a familiar sensation in his gut. "I've been doing some searching on my own. Asking around."

"That could be dangerous," John said, trying to keep his voice from sounding too condemning to the young man. It was clear from Ethan's attitude he'd been asking questions, following the same trail Sam had. Whatever it had been, had got Sam killed. John didn't want to see that happen to Ethan too. The boy was too young and inexperienced to know what he might be up against. "There's some word around Pecos River that Ransom Baxter's been up to his old devilment."

"Ransom Baxter!"

Lily's cheeks paled and she clenched her China coffee cup tight. Ethan didn't react in quite the same way. Maybe he had his suspicions, but he laid down his fork and gave John a level glance. "I've heard that. Some say maybe the Red Hand Gang is stirring up trouble too."

"Oh, Ethan, tell me you haven't been trying to find those men?" Lily asked with a beseeching look at her brother. "If they're the ones who killed Pa, then you don't stand a chance. He was a lawman. You can't even handle a gun that well."

"She's right," John agreed, noting the stubborn way Ethan clenched his jaw. *He's not going to listen.* "If even an experienced lawman like Sam got killed, they'll step on you like a bug."

"What am I supposed to do, Uncle John? Sit around and hope justice is done? Pa would expect me to get the men who killed him."

John shook his head. "Revenge is never easy or right, Ethan. Surely your pa taught you that. We never went after anyone with that aim in mind. If you'll let me, I can see what I can find out. Maybe …"

"Why you? You aren't the sheriff anymore and Sheriff North says Pa's death was an accident. I've talked to Sheriff Crane too. He's too scared to go after the Red Hand Gang. If nobody else is going to see justice is done, then I'm aiming to."

John could see he'd have his hands full trying to convince Ethan to back away. Sam's son was a lot like he'd been, full of vinegar and persistent as a flea. If there was any trail to follow, Ethan wouldn't rest until he'd either found justice or got himself killed. Even though he didn't want to worry the pair, John knew he'd have to come clean about the attack on him and Annabelle.

"One of the reasons I came to visit was because of something that happened yesterday. A bunch of masked men came and ransacked my ranch."

Lily gasped in shock and put a hand over her mouth.

"It's all right. Nothing much got broke or ruined. Bossie wasn't too happy." He made a small joke, hoping to wipe the distress from Lily's eyes. "I'm not sure if you ever heard mention of a woman named Annabelle Hollis?"

Both Lily and Ethan shook their heads.

"Well, no reason you should. She lives a few ranches over from mine. Her husband, Thomas, died awhile back, in kind of a strange way like your Pa."

"What do you mean?" Ethan asked.

Might as well tell it all.

"Thomas Hollis fell of a ladder and hit his head. It killed him."

A gasp came from Lily and her eyes widened. "Almost like Pa."

John nodded agreement. "Kind of...except Sheriff Crane called it an accident. Said Thomas fell and hit his head. His wife, Annabelle, figured that's how it happened until yesterday. Right after those men tore up my ranch, I decided to follow them. Tracked them to the Hollis ranch and found two of them beating up her hired hand.

"You know Hank Dawson? His wife Clara runs the mercantile in Pecos River,"

When they both showed they remembered, John continued his story. "Hank's all right, just banged up a little, but the men gave him their names. They were the Jones brothers, part of the Red Hand Gang. Ransom's men." He took a deep breath before sharing the worst part. "The men gave Hank a message. They told him that Annabelle needs to leave the ranch, or she'll die, just like Thomas."

"Oh, no!" Lily moaned.

"That does it!" Ethan slammed a fist down on the oak table, the plates clattered, and his coffee sloshed from the cup. "If they're coming back around, then somehow Pa must have found out. Maybe those men killed the Hollis man and Pa."

"Maybe, but why?"

John figured it was all connected, but how? "We need to know why the gang killed Thomas, maybe your pa and why they're so all-fired on getting Annabelle off the ranch."

"They want the land," Ethan shoved back his chair and stormed around the room, his face flushed and breathing hard. "And I'm going to find a way to stop them."

That was exactly what John feared the most. Sam's son riding out on a revenge trail and getting himself killed.

Sam would never forgive me.

Maybe it was time to think like a sheriff again. To forget how old and tired he felt and find out what the devil was going on. Before it was too late.

Chapter Eight

Hollis Ranch

Annabelle was sorry to see John Wilder leave. Not that he'd done so much, but still it made her feel a little safer. Once he'd ridden off with a promise to "look into things," she tried to get Hank to go on back to town. It worried her the way he struggled for breath and kept reaching up to his head like it ached.

"Let me take you home, Hank. You need to rest and heal."

He didn't want to leave her alone. "Dang it all, Annie," he argued, "If I can't do a few chores limping around, then I'm not fit for nothing. Do you know how many times I've had to care for my cows so stoved up I had to practically drag myself out to the barn?"

"I'm sure you've managed fine, Hank, but you might be hurt inside. Those men gave you a beating. If not for Mr. Wilder coming along, they might have killed you."

Stubborn, Hank shook his head. "Not without leaving their message, they wouldn't. They wanted to send a warning, not kill me. Not yet anyway. And what will you do if I leave, and they come back? You might be an independent woman and capable of taking care of yourself, but still if those men mean business…"

The thought frightened her more than she let on, but Annabelle was used to trusting her instincts. Today, she figured the men wouldn't come back anytime soon. Not until they'd left another warning.

I hope.

"I'll be as sweet as pie and tell them if they want the land that bad, I'll leave. If I do what they want, why should they harm me?"

"Well," he tried to grin and winced instead. Even though John had bandaged the cut on his forehead, Annabelle could see it was all Hank could do to keep his body upright. His lips were bruised and swollen, there was a black eye forming over his right eye and his nose tilted sideways like a lump of raw meat. "I reckon that might keep them confused for a spell."

"I have my rifle too," she reminded him, "and I'm a good shot. You know that."

It took a bit more persuasion, but finally Annabelle got Hank to agree. He hitched up the buggy, slowly and not without a few grunts of pain, and allowed himself to be driven into town.

As she drew the buggy to a stop in front of the mercantile, Sheriff Crane hollered out to Hank.

"Hank! Wait a minute!"

"What's that fool want?" Hank muttered, but only so Annabelle could hear. He leaned heavily against the hitching post, waiting.

Sherrif Crane strode up, fingering the brim of his hat, a perplexed expression on his face. "John Wilder told me you'd been attacked out at the Hollis place." As if remembering his manners, he barely tipped the hat from his bald head and nodded in Annabelle's direction. "Morning, Miz Hollis. You hurt?"

"No, Sheriff, the men just wanted to beat up my hired hand and leave a message."

"So, I heard." The sheriff sighed long and deep. Rubbing his chin, he gave them both an annoyed look, almost like they were the ones who'd brought trouble to the town. "I reckon I'll have to ask around, see if I can find out where those Jones brothers were headed after they left your ranch. Bad business if the Red Hand Gang is back in these parts. I try to keep a peaceful town."

Well, it's not my fault! Annabelle wanted to snap, but crimped her lips shut instead. Ever since Thomas's death, she and the sheriff hadn't seen eye to eye. It was certainly better to stay on his good side, if he had one.

"Won't do you no good," Hank muttered, speaking his mind. "If that gang's hiding out somewhere, they won't let you find them."

"Maybe so," Sheriff Crane answered, a scowl on his weathered face. He hitched up his trousers and snapped a black suspender. "But I'll do my best. Glad you weren't hurt worse. They leave anymore messages, you let me know."

The sheriff turned and walked away before Hank spat out a mouthful of blood in the dirt behind him. "Sorry, Annie," he apologized, "but when John Wilder left the jail, he turned it over to a mighty poor lawman." He leaned heavily against her shoulder. "Now, if you can help me inside, I'm about done in. Hate to admit it, but them boys worked me over worse'n I thought."

Annabelle dreaded having Clara see him. The Dawsons had been so good about helping her since Thomas died and now this...what would Clara think? She didn't have to wait long. The bell over the door tinkled when Annabelle pushed it open with her foot and eased Hank through.

Clara glanced up from behind the counter where she'd been sorting spools of thread.

"Hank!" Clara screamed when she caught sight of his face as he limped into the mercantile, leaning strongly against Annabelle's shoulder. "What happened? Was it the bull?"

"No, Clara," Annabelle answered while Hank struggled to get his breath. Just walking up the two porch steps to the front door of the store had winded him. Hank slumped down on top of a keg of nails, breathing like a runaway stallion, a hand to the wound on his head. "A couple of men attacked him at my ranch. If it hadn't been for John Wilder coming to the rescue, well, I'm not sure what they would have done."

Annabelle didn't want to admit the men might easily have killed Hank. He wasn't young and if they were the same ones who'd overpowered a younger, stronger man like Thomas, he could easily have died. A horrible thought.

"Hank, you go right on back to the bedroom and lie down," Clara insisted, flustered, flapping his hands like she'd shoo chickens. Worry lines creased her forehead. "I'm going to send for Doc Matthews and have him look you over."

"All this fuss..." Hank muttered, but Annabelle could see he was in more pain than he'd let on. It took her and Clara both to help him stand from the keg, then Clara and their son, Herbert, helped him through the red baize curtain that divided the store from the living quarters.

Annabelle waited. She looked out of the door and noticed John Wilder heading into Millie's Café.

I should thank him for helping. Especially after acting so badly. But the truth was, Annabelle felt shaken by the events of the morning herself. After she got Hank settled, she planned to go home and...what?

Ever since Thomas's death, Annabelle had been lonely many days but never afraid. Even to herself she didn't want to admit today she *did* feel fearful. *What if the men came back?*

Herbert pushed through the red curtains. "Ma said thank you for bringing Papa home. She said you're welcome to stay if you want. I'm going for the doc and she's going to close the mercantile for the afternoon."

"Oh!" The idea of staying was tempting, but Annabelle knew she couldn't abandon her animals. "Thank her anyway, but I'll go back home. I've got chores. Can you tell your mama I'm sorry?"

"Are you sure, Mrs. Hollis? Maybe I can ride out later to make certain you're all right."

The idea lifted a weight from her shoulders. "I'd appreciate that Herbert, if you can. I'll bake a peach pie just in case."

She knew peach was Herbert's favorite and Clara couldn't bake it because it made her break out in hives. The grin across his face told Annabelle she'd have a supper guest.

A short time later, Annabelle had the buggy turned toward home and snapped the reins. Cletus, the buggy horse, trotted along at a fast pace, almost too fast. The closer she got to the ranch, the worse Annabelle's heart raced. She touched the Colt revolver at her waist, reassured. If she could get a clear shot, she wasn't afraid. And like Hank had told John Wilder, surely the men wouldn't come back and attack so soon. They'd give her time to leave, wouldn't they?

The ranch lay quiet and peaceful in the afternoon sunshine. A few dark clouds lay low on the horizon, promising a thunderstorm later. Annabelle always welcomed the rain to fill her stock tank and rain barrels, but today it might keep those outlaws somewhere else too.

Funny how being alone had never bothered her until that day. All the wide-open country, stretching for miles from the ranch house always seemed comforting before. Like no one could sneak up on her without being seen a mile away. This afternoon, it felt threatening somehow—too wide and open—too frightening.

Annabelle hurried through the chores, putting the animals in the barn early, and then locking the cabin door once she got inside. True to his word, Herbert Dawson arrived near supper with good news. "Papa says I'm to stay in the barn tonight and keep watch. So don't you worry none, Mrs. Hollis. I'll be around and I'm a good shot. Won the shooting contest at the county fair three years in a row."

"Thank you, Herbert, I hate to put you to the bother, but I'm sure glad you came." Herbert might only be thirteen, but he'd reached his full growth. The boy stood as tall and sturdy as a full-grown man.

She served up a supper of fried ham and potatoes, green beans, and the promised peach pie. Afterward, they sat beside the crackling fire for a while, visiting. "Doc says Papa got beat up really good, but he's going to be fine in a few days, just mighty sore."

"That's good news."

A weight lifted from her heart. She owed a debt of gratitude to the Dawsons. Hank had started to help with the chores just as a favor, after Thomas died. It wasn't like she could pay him, except in home baked bread and pies. Clara appreciated her baking because she had little time to cook while running the store.

At least I'm not taking advantage of Hank's generous nature.

"Doc asked Papa why somebody would want to beat him up. Papa said it might be because of people wanting land for the railroad. A lot of people in town are saying men like Mr. Glover are buying land, maybe even forcing folks to sell who don't want to." Herbert said.

A log snapped and crackled in the fireplace, sending out orange and gold sparks. Annabelle grasped the arms of her rocking chair, almost afraid to ask the question.

"Who told you that?"

The young man shrugged and yawned. "I just hear things at the store. Guess I'll head on out to the barn now. You be sure to pull the latch string in once I'm outside."

"Yes, thank you, Herbert, I will."

She wished him goodnight, trying to keep her voice calm and steady. Inside her body quivered and shook with fear. If powerful men like Isaac Glover were involved in grabbing land, how could anyone fight him?

Chapter Nine

Although she tried to sleep, Annabelle jolted awake at every sound. At about midnight, thunder crashed overhead and shook the small house like a baby with a ragdoll. Brilliant flashes of lightning lit up the room like daylight. Tonight, Annabelle almost welcomed the piercing brilliance of the lightning. Each bolt showed her clearly there was no one in her bedroom.

Pulling the patchwork wedding quilt up under her chin, she lay in bed and listened to the pattering and then hammering as the storm moved across the sky, playing a tune on her shingled roof. Drowsy, heavy-eyed, she finally felt herself falling asleep as water gushed and gurgled from the rain barrel.

As the pink rays of the sun lit up the room, Annabelle forced herself to rise and start a fire in the kitchen stove. While the kindling took hold, she hurried into the bedroom and changed from her nightgown into a pink lawn dress, sprigged with yellow roses. It had been Thomas's favorite dress—a fact that always gave her comfort. It often grieved her that she and Thomas hadn't been able to have children. He'd looked forward to having a son. But now, maybe it was better she didn't have to worry about anyone but herself.

A knock at the kitchen door ended her musing about life. Annabelle hurried to let Herbert into the kitchen, warming up from the stove's fire. "Good morning. If you'll wait for me to gather a few eggs, I'll fix you up breakfast."

"That's all right, Mrs. Hollis," he said. "I'd best get back on into town. Mama will need my help opening the store and making deliveries."

"You sure you won't even stay for a cup of coffee and another slice of peach pie?"

The eager expression on Herbert's chubby face gave her an answer. Annabelle laughed and went to fill the coffee pot with water. Despite her fears of the night before, it was pleasant to cook a simple meal and enjoy the boy's company.

After her pa's death, when Annabelle was only ten, her mama had become a schoolteacher. She grew up loving books and conversation. Despite Thomas's other fine qualities, he'd never been a very "booky" person. To Annabelle's delight, she found Herbert well-read and eager to talk about the newest book he'd been reading, *An Inland Voyage* by Robert Louis Stevenson.

Was this how it might have been if Thomas and I had a son?

There was little time to wonder.

"Well, thank you again, Mrs. Hollis. I'll be sure to loan you that book when I finish. Papa's not much of a reader and even though Mama loves books as much as I do, she doesn't have much time to read."

"I'll look forward to it," Annabelle told the young man as he clapped on a dark blue cap and headed out the door. She stood on the steps of the back porch, watching as he saddled a stocky mustang and then rode out. "Tell your Mama I'll be in soon," she called and waved goodbye.

Maybe even today.

Now that she was alone, Herbert's conversation came back to haunt her. What if Isaac Glover or even the Red Hand gang were trying to force people off their ranches? Was the attack on Hank just the first step?

I need to know more and not just sit here waiting for something to happen.

Annabelle made short work of the chores, feeding the animals, milking the cows, letting the chickens out of the coop. She mixed up a batch of bread dough and left it on the stove to rise. Then, she quickly hitched Cletus to the buggy and headed toward Pecos River.

As she rode along, clucking to the reluctant horse who balked at the puddles left from last night's storm, Annabelle thought hard. Something Thomas had told her once came to mind. A half-remembered fragment of information.

What was it? Something about a neighbor?

"Step lively, Cletus," she snapped at the horse, "it's just water."

As the horse snorted his displeasure, Annabelle gazed around at the low shrubby bushes that lined the muddy road. A few birds darted from a nearby tree and sailed overhead. This morning, the air smelled fresh and clean from last night's shower. She took a deep breath, inhaling sagebrush and pine. Everywhere she looked, grass waved like water in an ocean-a green sea. Insects chirped and rose up as she and Cletus plodded past, the wagon wheels creaking. As soon as Hank recovered, she'd have to get him to put more axle grease on the back left wheel.

Rumors!

That's what she wanted to remember. Annabelle could recall a conversation with Thomas where he talked about rumors.

"Heard our neighbors about three miles down the road sold out their land and left," he'd said, sitting down to a dinner of beef stew and fresh cornbread.

"Oh, why?" Annabelle remembered she'd been more concerned about how brown the cornbread had been on top. "I'm

sorry it's darker than you like," she apologized. "I was busy with a quilt square and didn't realize it had started to burn."

His calloused hand covered hers and he squeezed, those azure, blue eyes filled with love. "It's fine."

Reassured, she'd finished cutting slices and slid one onto his plate. "Now, what were you saying about the neighbors?"

"They sold their land and left," Thomas said, slathering a forkful of butter across his cornbread. A second later, he gave her a worried frown. "Someone in town said they heard Montgomery's were forced off their land, by railroad speculators. But so far as I know, it's just a rumor."

"Could that happen to us too?"

"Not while I'm alive," Thomas promised.

Cletus snorted and splashed through a good-sized puddle. Some of the muddy water sprinkled up and hit the long skirt of Annabelle's pink dress. Any other time it would have been an annoyance, but not this morning.

Thomas was no longer alive. And now she'd been warned to leave the land.

"Get up, Cletus," she slapped the reins hard, urging the horse to hurry.

Once in town, Annabelle went straight to Dawson's Mercantile. She got out of the buggy, tied Cletus to the post and hurried inside. Thankfully, no customers were in the store. As the bell over the door jingled, she heard Clara call out from the back room, "Be right with you."

Fidgety, Annabelle waited until Clara pushed through the red curtains.

"Annabelle! How are you this morning? I was just talking to Herbert, and he felt bad about leaving you alone. If I didn't need him to make some deliveries for me today, I'd have sent him straight back out."

"I'm fine. How is Hank this morning? I can't tell you how awful I feel for his being hurt."

Clara's warm smile settled Annabelle's deepest fear, that Hank had grown worse in the night. "Now, don't you worry about that. He's going to be fine, and Hank has been hurt a lot worse than that. He just feels terrible about leaving you to fend for yourself, especially since those men…" Clara's words faded off and she bit her lip. She spoke in a cautious, almost whisper, even though they were alone in the store. "Hank told me what they said. It's frightening."

Maybe Clara wasn't as cheerful as Annabelle thought. "You must be terribly upset about Hank."

"Truthfully, I am," Clara kneaded her hands together, wrinkling a black apron she wore over a deep indigo dress. "He's so stubborn, he won't rest. The only reason he's asleep now is because Doc put a dose of laudanum in his coffee. It was the only way to get him to stop and sleep. This whole business worries me to death, Annabelle. Why would those men beat him up? A peaceable soul like Hank. Why he's never even been able to spank Herbert."

"He told you about the message they left. About me leaving the ranch or I'd die like Thomas."

Clara shooed the idea off with her reddened, work-worn hand like it was a pesky fly. "Oh, he told me all that. The whole thing is ridiculous. I just don't understand any of it."

It crossed Annabelle's mind that Clara just might not want to think about it. Maybe it frightened her too much. But she had to know. "Clara, I'm worried. I'm sorry to burden you with it since you must be concerned about Hank. You've both helped me so much and I don't want anything to happen to you but..." She gnawed a corner of her lip before she went on. "Herbert and I were talking about rumors he overheard."

"What kind of rumors?"

"That maybe someone like Mr. Glover is buying up people's property to sell to the railroad at a profit. Maybe the people buying the land aren't doing it legally. As I was driving in, I remembered Thomas telling me one of our neighbors had sold out and left. If the rumors are true, then the men who attacked Hank might truly be sending me a message. They want my land. And Mr. Glover has been awfully persistent about 'helping me out' by buying my land."

Distressed, Clara's eyes took on a haunted look. She twisted her hands harder in the apron. "Oh, dear. I just don't know, Annabelle. This is all so hard to understand. Hank and I have talked about Thomas's death, how maybe it wasn't an accident. Maybe you should talk to Sheriff Crane. He'd know, wouldn't he? Isn't that his job, to find out if something illegal is going on?"

The idea had crossed Annabelle's mind, but she didn't hold out much hope of having Sheriff Crane's help. After Thomas's death, the sheriff had almost patted her head like a puppy and acted like she was a silly widow. He hadn't taken any of her concerns seriously. It didn't seem to bother him that a young, agile man like Thomas could fall off a ladder and die.

But, she didn't want to trouble her friend anymore. Clara had enough problems with Hank's injury and running the store.

"Yes, that's probably what I should do." Annabelle tried to make it seem like Clara's advice had helped. "You let me know if there's anything I can do for you and Hank. It's not much, but I'm going to bake bread later today. I'll send it in if Herbert comes out tonight."

"That would be a blessing." Clara reached across the counter and squeezed Annabelle's hand. Just then, the bell above the door jingled and a woman came in followed by two little girls in yellow sunbonnets. One blonde braided twin gave Annabelle a tooth-gapped grin, while the other stayed shyly beside her mother's long brown skirt. "Good morning Mrs. Vaughn, Annabelle greeted the banker's wife. "How are you, Susie and Sarah?"

"Very well, thank you," the twins chorused and giggled.

"Morning, Mrs. Hollis." All business, she turned to Clara. "I have my shopping list."

Leaving Clara to her customers, Annabelle walked outside and turned toward the jail. Her booted feet dragged down the boardwalk as she headed to talk to Sheriff Crane. *Might as well get it over with.*

Chapter Ten

The jail sat at the corner of an alley and Main Street, a few doors down from the mercantile. As Annabelle walked toward the jail, she noticed the sheriff and John Wilder standing in front of the door. They appeared to be having a heated argument. The raised voices could be heard halfway down the street, even if some of the words were covered over by other sounds—hammering, the loud ringing of iron on an anvil from the livery, a man calling to another.

Unwilling to step into the fray, Annabelle stopped in front of the millinery shop, pretending to study the new bonnets in the sparkling window. There was no way she could imagine herself in the poke bonnet of straw, with frilly pink ribbon ties and white silk daisies around the band, but she stared at it anyway.

There was no polite way *not* to overhear the conversation. Or the bits not drowned out by a busy town's music.

John hollered, "I'm telling you, Sheriff, it's too suspicious not to investigate. Sam's kids told me he'd been talking to people and heard more than rumors about investors cheating people out of their land. If somebody's forcing folks to..." a freight wagon rumbled by and the words were garbled under the sound.

Annabelle gasped. *The very thing I wanted to ask the sheriff!*

The sheriff shouted something back, the words lost behind the rumbling of the wagon, until it passed. "And I'm telling you, there's no proof."

John's face grew red with fury. Doubling up his fists, his lips moved but Annabelle couldn't understand what he said.

"Sam came in here a month before he died," the sheriff's words were clear again. "Said he had proof, and I should talk to one family. I did. Rode out and they were loading their wagons, all set to move. Told me they'd sold the land for a good profit. They were leaving for the wife's health; the air hereabouts was too dry. Said nobody forced them to do anything."

"And you believed them?" John's lips curled in disgust. His blue eyes seethed as he stared at the sheriff. "Maybe they were lying."

"Why?" Another wagon rattled by in the muddy street, the wheels squelching in the muddy puddles, sending up a dirty spray. The sheriff's lips moved but whatever he said was lost, even though Annabelle strained to hear.

"I think you better leave the law to me, Wilder, and go back to your ranch," Sheriff Crane's words were clear again, spoken in a voice as cold as death. "If I see there's something wrong, then I'll take care of it, not you. You aren't the sheriff anymore."

Even from this distance, Annabelle could see John's eyes narrowing in contempt as his face hardened. Without another word, he turned and stormed away.

Sheriff Crane yelled something else and vanished into the jail.

Watching John Wilder head toward Malone's Saloon, Annabelle came to a sudden decision. If John believed something suspicious was going on like she did, maybe he'd have an answer.

All I can do is ask.

Annabelle lifted the hem of her skirts and hurried after him into the muddy streets.

**

"Mr. Wilder! Mr. Wilder!"

Striding along toward Patrick's, John was in a foul mood. He sure didn't want to talk to anyone. As the female voice kept shouting after him, he stopped and turned.

Her!

Annabelle Hollis, wearing a pink dress sprigged with yellow flowers, hurried down the boardwalk, a determined look on her face. "Mr. Wilder, please may I speak to you a moment?"

"What about?" he snapped not even trying to sound agreeable. The conversation with Sheriff Crane had rubbed him the wrong way and he was in no mood to be pleasant.

His frown discouraged her for a minute, but Annabelle Hollis seemed made of sterner stuff. He watched her take a deep breath and stand taller.

"I'm sorry to trouble you," she apologized with a timid smile, "but I wanted to ask for your help. I couldn't...well, I overheard some of your conversation with Sheriff Crane. About people buying land illegally. This morning, I remembered my husband telling me..."

"Look!" John knew he sounded harsh, but his patience was worn thinner than a threadbare rope. "Maybe you should talk to the sheriff yourself, see if he can help you. I've got too much going on right now."

John took a step to walk away, but Annabelle boldly grabbed the sleeve of his linen duster and held on tight. "Please listen to me. Please."

Without yanking his arm away and pushing her off into the muddy street, he had no choice. "What is it you want, Mrs.

Hollis? I'm no longer the sheriff. There's only so much I can do."

"First, I want to thank you for coming to Hank's rescue the other day. Those men might have hurt him worse without your help. I wanted you to know how much I appreciated it."

"Well, I..." embarrassed he felt his cheeks warm. "Anybody would have done the same."

"No, they wouldn't."

For just a minute he stared into those green eyes. They stood so close he noticed a small scar above one dark eyebrow. The thought crossed his mind to wonder how she'd got it, and he almost opened his mouth to ask. Then realized how improper that would be. Ma would turn over in her grave at his lack of manners. Before he could think of anything else to say, Annabelle went on pleading, her voice edged with desperation.

"Please, just listen to me for a minute. My husband was killed, I know it. Sheriff Crane keeps saying it was an accident, but I'm sure now it wasn't. Now that those men have left a message, I believe Thomas was killed because he refused to give up our land."

What she said made sense, not that there was anything he could do. He forced himself to look away from the beseeching gleam in her eyes. "Look, Mrs. Hollis, I'm right sorry for your loss. And you might be right about someone wanting your land. There's a lot of word going around that speculators like Isaac Glover been buying up a lot of land. Legal? I don't know. Sheriff Crane don't seem to care much if it is or not."

"But you think Mr. Glover is involved?"

This time he did jerk his arm free. "I wish I could help you, but I can't. Right now, I'm trying to find out who murdered my former deputy. Now, if you'll excuse me, I've got a lot of people to talk to and a lot of places to go."

"No, listen." She stepped in front of him, forcing him to stop.

Would this woman not give up?

"Mrs. Hollis," he snapped, "let me pass or I just might push you over into the street."

Annabelle glanced into the muddy puddles and gasped. Tossed a long auburn braid over one shoulder and gave him an angry look, those green eyes snapping. "Very well, Mr. Wilder, but let me leave you with something you might not have thought about. What if this Ransom Baxter and his gang are working for Isaac Glover?"

Is it possible?

"What makes you say that?"

"Ever since Thomas's death, Mr. Glover has made it clear he'd be glad to take my ranch off my hands. He wants my place, I can tell. The other day you said those men who beat up Hank were part of this Ransom's gang. Wouldn't it stand to reason they all might be working together?"

It suddenly made more sense than John wanted to believe. He hesitated long enough that Annabelle stepped aside to let him pass with one parting shot.

"All I ask is that you think about it. If you come to any conclusions and decide to help me save my ranch, I'd be most appreciative." Annabelle said. As quickly as she'd waylaid him, the woman turned with a flounce of pink skirt and hurried down the boardwalk.

John stood watching after her. He'd made no promises, but he would think about what she'd said. He'd be thinking about it *real* hard.

Chapter Eleven

"John Wilder needs to die!"

Ransom Baxter's piercing brown eyes narrowed in contempt as he snarled the words. A tall, lean man, his ill-fitting suit of black broadcloth hung on his body. Half-starved from the years in prison, Ransom knew he looked more like a refugee than a feared gunslinger. Life in a cell had paled his skin to pasty white and changed his once abundant coal black hair to a sparse shaved brush on his scalp. He supposed he should be glad to be out of a cell, hair shaved to end the itchy lice and vermin he'd endured.

The thought of Sheriff Wilder and his deputy Sam Garett filled Ransom's heart with a fiery hatred. All the indignities he'd suffered were because of Sheriff Wilder and Deputy Garrett.

They were the ones who'd sent him to prison, stopped his gang, and sent many to die. Now that he was free, his one goal was to kill them both, to see them suffer as he had.

Ransom stared at the three men he trusted sitting around a battered table. They'd just enjoyed a meal and now it was time to plan. He should have planned better before allowing Jack to attack Sam Garrett.

"Garrett should have had to suffer more," he sighed deeply at his plans going awry. "I wanted him to die, but slowly, in agony." Who would figure that a simple blow on the head would end his life so soon? "When we kill Wilder, he will die slowly. Suffering. Maybe I'll keep him prisoner for a while, let him see what I had to endure."

"How we going to do that, Boss?" young Christopher Jones asked. At twenty-one, he had all the makings of a good gunslinger. In many ways, he reminded Ransom of himself at that age. Violent, sadistic, and willing to take chances. Christopher hadn't killed anyone at fourteen like Ransom. Still, he'd come along nicely, willing to take chances.

Maybe that was the most important trait of all, taking chances.

"I'll be thinking about it, Christopher. Jack, Deke, you got any ideas?" Ransom turned to his other trusted men. Jack, he considered his right-hand man, second in command. As Christopher's older brother, he'd been by Ransom's side through all their robberies. Thankfully, the Jones brothers had escaped when Ransom and the rest of the gang were ambushed by Sheriff Wilder and his deputy. Jack helped him escape from prison a few months ago.

The fourth man around the table, Deke Parsons, was new. He'd escaped from the prison camp alongside Ransom and had already proven his worth. If Deke hadn't killed the guard chasing them, Ransom wouldn't have had a second opportunity to get back in business. Deke had a reputation as a gunslinger, unpredictable and dangerous. He fitted right in with the others...if he could be trusted, Ransom planned to keep a wary eye on Deke.

"Could ambush him somewhere," Deke offered. "Learn his habits, where he goes, what he does. Be easy then to shoot him or capture him. No one would be any the wiser."

"That helps," Ransom said, even though just shooting Wilder didn't seem enough. He needed to suffer first, unlike Garrett.

I was too eager to see them gone. I should have attacked Sam myself, not sent a green kid like Jack. No matter how vicious he can be.

Ransom sighed. He stabbed a small sliver of beef now congealing on his plate and slid it into his mouth. The years in prison had soured his taste but his stomach still clenched at the smell of food, any food. He'd have to eat a good many years to make up for lost time.

Christopher looked up from oiling his pride and joy, a long-barreled Winchester rifle. "Could send him a few messages, like we did that Hollis woman. Give him a couple of scares, make him fear what's coming. The boys were just having fun at his ranch the other day. Didn't do more than stir up the cow and trample the garden."

Fear! Yes, that would be good. A way to make Wilder pay for all those nights Ransom had spent trapped in a hot, filthy cell, beaten by guards and given moldy bread for a meal. "What do you have in mind?"

"Let me think about it for a spell," Christopher said, dipping a rag in Neet's foot oil, rubbing it along the barrel of the rifle, "it should be something different than what happened to the Hollis woman's hand."

Ransom agreed. Truthfully, he never should have allowed his men to be used in beating up the old man at the Hollis place. Still, he knew it was all part of the plan. Right now, it was someone else's plan, a way to make a profit from selling to the railroad.

But before long, it will all belong to me. It will be my plan. I'll be the one who tells all the others what to do. No one can tell Ransom Baxter who to attack.

But first…first he had a personal vendetta to take care of by killing John Wilder.

John Wilder is the enemy, and he needs to die.

***

After heading away from Annabelle, John turned toward the saloon. His head ached from the shouted exchange with the sheriff. *Fool man.* The conversation told him one thing. He'd get no help from the law in this town. Not while Tobias Crane was the sheriff.

John had ridden away from Ethan and Lily, intent on finding out a few facts. His hope had been to bring Sheriff Crane to his way of thinking. Sam might have been killed because he'd found out information someone wanted to keep quiet. If Sheriff Crane agreed, maybe he'd deputize John again...just to find some answers.

That idea hadn't gone well. Sheriff Crane accused him of stirring up trouble. On top of the frustration and confusion he'd felt since leaving Sam's kids, John thought he might explode like a keg of dynamite.

Then Annabelle Hollis stopped him in the street, begging for help.

How in blazes does she think I can help her? John didn't see how her husband's death could have anything to do with Sam getting killed. Or had it?

The whole business had his head pounding. Maybe talking to Patrick might help. Through the years, when Sam had been off somewhere, it had helped to have Patrick listen. A good meal might fortify him too. It had been hours since he'd eaten Lily's dried cherry pie. John could always depend on Patrick to supply a decent meal. He'd thought of going to Millie's, but she might frown at the trail dust coating his duster and trousers.

Before he could change his mind, John stepped through the doors of the saloon and headed for the bar. A short time later, he pushed away a dirty plate with a steak bone and potato skins. Stomach full, headache easing, John leaned against the bar with a cup of coffee warming his hands. While he'd eaten, he'd told Patrick about his morning, including everything Sam's kids had shared.

"It's just a puzzle Patrick," John slowly turned the coffee cup in a circle, tracing rings on the scarred top of the bar. "If Sam died because someone thought he knew something, are Ethan and Lily safe over there?"

Patrick wiped a linen cloth inside a mug and sat the clean glass down with a row of others. He shook his mop of red hair, "It's a real knot all right, an' what you say is an eye opener.

Who'd have thought Sam would get himself killed by somebody knocking him in the head? I always figured he'd go in a gunfight, or jumpin' into a burnin' building to save a young'un or some such thing. Not because he was ambushed in his own barn."

"Yeah," John signed deeply and felt a twist in his heart. Another reminder. *Sam's gone.*

He's never coming home.

Patrick set down another clean glass. "If whatcha' sayin' is so, I guess the next question would be, who's buyin' up all this land and trying' to put fear in the folks living on it?"

"I guess if we knew the answer to that..." John began as he stared down at his coffee.

The batwing doors of the saloon swung open, and three men entered. After a quick look over his shoulder, John didn't pay much attention at first. At this time of day, the bar hummed with a normal buzz of sound. Men sat around the tables, laughing, joking, slapping cards on the tops, and forks clanking against the tin plates. Chairs scraped along the hardwood floor, boots pounded, and spurs jangled. There was a musical clink of beer mugs and bottles as the thirsty men from the stockyards plunked them down or pounded for a refill.

Mr. Squire, the dark-skinned piano player, sat at the instrument in a corner, coaxing out lively tunes. He'd fled the south, escaping slave catchers until Patrick had taken him in. Now Mr. Squire, his only name, slept on a cot in the pantry, played the piano, and earned money by helping Patrick clean up.

When the bar filled at night, Mr. Squire's playing added a perky, toe-tapping tune. It was the sudden tinkling of piano keys and then the deep silence that roused John's interest. The bar's usual din suddenly quieted, like distant thunder fading west, or the way birds hushed as darkness fell. A prickly sensation along his spine made John turn around slowly again.

As he did, the trio of men stalked across the floor, their spurs jangling. They passed a few tables where men scraped back their chairs, shuffled up decks of cards, and hurried out of the saloon.

Whoever the men were, John knew they meant only one thing.

Trouble.

Chapter Twelve

The tall, chestnut-haired man in the lead, strode up to the bar to stand beside John. He'd dressed all in black, pants, cotton shirt, and of all things, a black bowler hat. John had seen men wearing them in the bigger cities, but they gave the man a strange appearance out here, set him apart. *Maybe that's what he wants, to be noticed.* A pair of pearl-handled revolvers poked from the snug holster around his waist and he looked like the kind of man who could use them well. The man's hardened lips twisted in a smirk as his dark, intimidating eyes glared around at men seated at different tables. A couple of cowboys stood, shifted away, and hurried from the bar.

The black-clad man leaned against the bar, close enough that John caught of whiff of whiskey on his breath and a powerful stench of sweat.

John felt he should know the men, they looked somewhat familiar, but he didn't. Although, come to think of it, the hair he saw beneath the bowler looked mighty close to one man he'd seen at Annabelle's. *The one who punched me in the stomach.*

In the old days, John would have punched back before he got answers. This afternoon, his body ached and reminded him he wasn't as young as he used to be.

He took a sip of coffee as the man turned, his spurs jangling. "You must be John Wilder." He spoke in a low, menacing voice, his eyebrows arched in black Vs.

Acting as normally as he could, John took another drink of coffee and answered. "That's right. You know my name, how about telling me yours?"

"Reckon you'd like to know."

John shrugged, refusing to play a game of cat and mouse. "Tell me or don't; 'sup to you."

"Don't you recognize us, Sheriff?" a second man taunted, his voice low. "Maybe seen us on a WANTED poster or something."

"Were you on a WANTED poster? You got a bounty on your head?"

Behind the bar, John saw Patrick's right-hand slide down to where he kept a loaded rifle.

"Ain't no need for your gun, bartender," the second, younger man scolded, reaching a freckled hand across the bar to grip Patrick's white shirt sleeve. "We ain't doin' nothing wrong. Far as I know, we ain't ever been on a WANTED poster. 'Course, that could change." He gave an odd, braying laugh.

The younger man had similar coloring to the man in black, a rugged, lean shape. His long and curling hair flowed from beneath a wide-brimmed tan hat—almost the same chestnut–brown John remembered from the attack. *I don't remember hair that long though.*

"Why don't you tell me your names? Unless you're afraid."

"We ain't afraid of nothin'!" the younger man snapped out, his hand reaching for the butt of his Colt.

"Easy, now," the man in black cautioned the younger one. "We aren't here to cause any trouble. Just here to give you a little message, Sheriff."

"I'm not the sheriff anymore," John said, keeping his emotions in check. In the past, he'd have taken a swing and knocked the first man down without hesitating. Then he'd have taught the second boy some manners. The third man, he didn't know about. Ever since they'd entered the bar, the short, stocky man wearing worn trousers and a ripped shirt had stood silently behind the other two. His pale, shallow face gave off the look of someone who'd been in prison for a while. A face that hadn't seen the sun in many a day. A pallor with which John was familiar. *Who is he? Who are they?*

"Go ahead and give me your message anyway."

"You surely remember Ransom Baxter, don't you?"

Patrick gave a sharp intake of breath and clinked a beer mug down on the bar.

Hoping he looked calmer than he felt inside, John nodded. His fingers gripped the coffee mug, and he made a determined effort to loosen them. "Yes, I remember him. He escaped from prison. You know anything about that?"

"That's what I heard too," the man in black taunted, "and it just might be he sent a message to you."

Despite his outward appearance of calm, John kept his voice forceful and steady. "If you men know where Ransom's hiding out, you'd better turn him in. The law won't turn the other cheek if you help him hide."

The younger man snorted. "Is that a fact?"

"It's a fact," John said in a stern voice, eyeing each man in turn. "Ransom is a wanted man. If any of you are working for him, I got to figure you're on the wrong side of the law too."

This time the third man spoke up, slow and easy in a southern drawl. "If that's so, then why don't you arrest us?"

"For what? I'm not the sheriff anymore. Far as I can see, you haven't committed any crimes...yet."

The man dressed in black nodded. "That's so, Wilder. We ain't done nothing you know about. Yet." Another laugh. "We're just here to give you a message from Ransom. He's got plans and he wants you to stay out of his way. Long as you do that, no harm will come to you."

John knew the men expected a reaction, maybe fear or anger. He deliberately kept his hand gripped around the coffee cup and his expression blank. Even if his toes curled in his boots and his stomach twisted in knots, he wouldn't give the men the satisfaction of knowing his tension.

"You gave yer message," Patrick snapped out. "Now be outta my place, before I toss ya out."

What would he have done if the men hadn't followed Patrick's command? John didn't know or much care. He only knew his breath came a little easier as they turned and headed back out of the saloon.

After a few tense moments, sound began to fill the room again. Mr. Squire plunked out *Camptown Races*, and a couple of men began a loud and lively game of poker. Patrick plopped a glass of beer down in front of John. "Drink up, laddy."

"You know what I think, Patrick? Those were Ransom's men giving me a warning. They could have even been the Jones brothers. Hard to tell. They wore masks when they ransacked my ranch and attacked Hank Dawson."

Patrick shrugged. "An' so what if they were? No much you can do without proof."

"It makes me wonder how deep Ransom's reach goes. If he's the one who warned Annabelle to leave and for me to watch out—to stay out of their way—what's coming next?"

"That I canna answer, but I'm sure you'll find out. Despite Sheriff Crane's turning the other cheek to the gang, you'll find the answers."

I'll have to speak to Annabelle about this. Seems like she might be right. Her husband and Sam's death may be related.

"You're right, Patrick. I may not be the sheriff anymore, but I'll clean up this town again if it's the last thing I do. Ransom Baxter won't get away with whatever he's doing. If he killed Sam, he's going to pay."

***

Wilder Ranch

Next Day

"That sheriff is a darned fool," John raged, although the cow staring at him with a mouthful of cud couldn't have cared less. Bossie's brown eyes were wide and limpid. She chewed and looked at him, her mind on nothing more than the hay he tossed off the back of the wagon with a pitchfork. The sun beat down, and John stopped to wipe the sweat from his neck with a red kerchief. As soon as he got this extra hay out to the cattle, he planned to head back to the cabin and sit in the shade for a spell. It might only be spring, but the Texas summer heat had arrived with a vengeance.

The morning had been long, and he'd decided to take some hay to the cattle he hoped to sell later this summer. The grass had started to grow again, but not enough for good grazing. The small herd of longhorns he'd bought would need a lot of fattening up.

"There you go," he tossed the last of the loose hay over the wagon bed, threw down the pitchfork, and headed back to the barn.

As he neared the barnyard, a frightened horse's whinny alerted him. Barney, his wagon horse, returned a reply, stomped and stopped right in the middle of the yard. No matter how much John snapped the reins, the horse refused to move, trying to run back into the field.

"What the...Barney! You fool. Giddup!"

An instant later John saw a plume of gray smoke billowing from the barn window.

The barn's on fire!

"Hya!" He slapped the reins across Barney's back and forced the reluctant horse to move forward.

Barney danced and shied as they got near the barn, his frightened neighs a match for the horses trapped inside. John jumped off the wagon seat and let Barney and the wagon keep heading down the road. At least he'd be safe once he stopped running. Barney was the least of John's worries just then.

He ran to the barn, yanked open the door, and burnt his fingers on the metal latch.

From inside he heard panicky kicks at stalls and the frightened whinnies of Ranger and his other horse, Buttermilk. He'd left them inside this morning until he had time to trim their nails. Both horses were tied on short leads to their stalls.

"I'm coming, fellas!" he hollered, although he didn't know how.

Dense, dark smoke curled from the windows as orange–red flames licked up the wooden sides. The air filled with the scent of burning pine boards. One of the windows cracked from the heat and a crackling tongue of flame licked out to grab the shingles on the roof. The frenzied horses attempt to escape intensified in fearful, almost human-like screams.

Smoke hung in the air, the acrid taste scorching John's lungs as he struggled to get a clean breath. Heat radiated from the barn, so hot that the cotton fabric of John's shirt burnt his skin.

I've got to save the horses!

John ran to the side of the barn, dunked himself in the water trough until he was soaked to the skin. Taking a deep breath, he covered his mouth and nose with a wet kerchief and ran into the burning barn.

The smoke choked him even through the handkerchief. Inside the building, thick, black smoke filled the room until he could barely see in front of his face. Small fires crackled along the floor, eating up bits of straw and chaff. It was so hard to breathe, John coughed as the over-heated air burned down his throat. One hand forward, he felt his way along like a blind man to the first stall—Ranger.

The horse's panic almost knocked John down as he tried to quiet the stallion. Ranger's hooves crashed into the wooden stall, desperate for safety.

"Easy, boy, easy," John shouted to be heard over the snapping, crackling fire. He yanked a knife from his pocket and slashed Ranger's lead rope.

Ranger pranced and jerked away, shoving his rear into a corner of the stall. The horse whinnied in terror as the flames shot across the loose hay on the barn floor.

"Get out!" John went behind the horse, slapped his rump hard and forced the animal into the fire.

Ranger stomped forward, then at the last second, sensing safety, he galloped through the fire and out the barn doors.

John headed to save Buttermilk next—just as a beam fell and blocked part of the door. He cursed under his breath, managed to get to the stall, and slashed Buttermilk's lead rope.

By now the intense heat had almost dried his clothes, the cotton shirt burning against his arms and back. His lungs ached for a breath of fresh air, but John kept on.

The foolish horse would not run as Ranger did, but kept pulling away from the flames and smoke.

Buttermilk bolted, heading to a boxed-in corner of the barn. Another few minutes and they'd both burn to death or smother in the smoke. No matter how much John yelled or tugged at Buttermilk's rope, the horse refused to budge. In the end, John did the only thing he could do to get the stubborn horse moving. He poked him hard in the rump with the knife, just enough to draw blood. Buttermilk took off like a shot out of a cannon, cleared the beam blocking the barn door, and raced to safety.

Coughing, and gasping for air, John limped out of the barn, his gimpy leg screaming in agony. Once outside, he collapsed in a heap a few yards away from the barn, now fully engulfed in flames.

The timber cracked and groaned as the fire ate away the pine boards he'd saved to buy. The heat was so intense, John's face flamed like the worst sunburn he'd ever had. A few hard-breathing minutes later, he realized his eyebrows were singed. He could smell the scorched hair. A sharp pain and the scent of seared flesh startled him. He looked down at his arm to see a fresh burn.

How?

His arm screamed in agony, begging relief but John couldn't do anything but lie in the dirt. Bleary eyed, he coughed, and gulped for air while the barn became a giant fireball. The outline of the building stood glowing, and crackling, the flames twisting in a mad dance. When the shingles caught, blazing under a summer sky, it was all over. The roof caved in, sending out embers to dance in the bright sunshine. Within minutes, the barn was nothing more than a pile of burning sticks, charcoal–black and smoldering as it ran out of fuel.

The two haystacks beside the barn also went up in smoke—feed he'd have to replace for the cows. Summer's harvest gone like dust in the wind.

Ranger and Buttermilk stood out in the field nearby. Both horses had gotten over their fright enough to graze, with occasional glances back to their burning home. Once he caught his breath, he'd have to doctor Buttermilk's wound.

For now, there wasn't a lot to do but watch his barn go up in smoke and wonder.

Was this the message I was supposed to get?

Chapter Thirteen

Hollis Ranch

"This is too much! Just too much!" Annabelle screamed, red-faced, and flinging up her hands like a wild woman.

What a sight I must be!

But she couldn't help it.

Poor Hank, he'd think she was losing her mind if she couldn't control her feelings any better than this. But the discovery this morning really did feel like the last straw.

Sometime during the night, her feed stores were ransacked, the animal food scattered and spoiled. Someone had broken into the small room behind the barn and managed to plunder two barrels of chicken feed, the extra grain she'd bought to fatten up her cattle for slaughter, and another barrel of dried corn she'd saved for the pigs. If it had just been poured out, Annabelle could have swept up the grain and used it. To make certain that didn't happen, an evil hand had poured kerosene over the chicken feed, grain, and corn. The pungent odor of kerosene had crinkled her nose when she opened the feed room door. Nothing could eat it now.

It was just too much. Annabelle felt like it was another blow to shove her off the ranch.

How much more can I take without going under?

Losing a few grains of feed might give her pocketbook a pinch but losing what she'd need for the next few months was devastating. If she had to buy more grain during the winter, she wouldn't make a profit from selling the animals.

Annabelle had to count every penny to make her ranch pay. It took hard work, scrimping, and doing without to buy the animal feed she needed. Even when Thomas had been alive, they'd barely scraped by.

"Why would anyone do this?" she raged at Hank. "An animal might have torn into the barrels and sacks but not poured out kerosene."

Poor man!

Early that morning, Hank had come back to work, despite his injuries. His black eye had turned to shades of purple and green. Hank's lips were still puffy, and he limped through morning chores. Clearly, he hadn't yet recovered from the beating.

"I'm sorry, Hank, I don't mean to take out my anger on you. It's just a big blow. Someone did this deliberately to make me lose money. Maybe they figure if I can't feed my animals, I'll have to sell out and lose the ranch. Or give up altogether."

"Could be," Hank agreed, leaning heavily against a beam of the barn, obviously still in pain. "Guess you'll hear sooner or later. Maybe this is another message from those fellas that were here before."

Annabelle sighed and righted the broken barrel that had once held the chicken feed. "I don't understand what's going on, Hank. Yesterday, I tried to speak to John Wilder about those men. He and the sheriff were having an argument about some of the same questions I'd had."

"What questions would those be?"

"Whether or not Thomas's death was an accident. Or if his death and the death of that deputy, Sam Garrett, were connected somehow. Those men who beat you told me to leave. What if they came by and told Thomas the same thing? He

95

would have told them to go away and not look back. He'd never allowed anyone to intimidate him. They could have knocked him off the ladder. What if someone *is* trying to force people off their land?"

Someone like Isaac Glover.

"Do you think those men came back last night to ruin my feed?"

Even though she liked to think of herself as independent and capable on her own, Annabelle's heart had lifted when Hank rode into the barnyard that morning. The idea of being alone had been frightening. She could only be thankful young Herbert hadn't made it back out last night. What if he'd been in the barn?

Had those men come back while she slept to leave another message? What would she do if they came again and did worse? What if the next time they hurt Hank or Herbert even more badly?

How can I protect myself and the ranch?

"Do you think this was another message from them? If it was, how can I stop them from coming again?"

Although Hank's expression changed, he didn't speak for a few minutes. The rooster crowed from the barnyard. In one of the stalls, a pig snorted and then a piglet squealed. "Guess we got to consider that possible. Since nobody else would be so mean. But I'm not sure how we can stop them, Annie. Not if they want the land that bad."

"I won't sell! They can't force me. There must be a way to keep them away."

This time Hank smiled, the sweet-caring grin that felt like a blessing on his weathered face. "If there is a way, I reckon you'll figure it out, a smart gal like you. Guess for today, all we can do is put one foot in front of the other and think on it.

I'd best get the slop out to them pigs and then milk the cows," he said like any other day. But he still leaned against the barn beam, deep in thought, a furrow of worry on his bruised face.

"Annie, I reckon there's something else you need to know. Yesterday, something happened at Malone's. I heard tell about it from Mr. Johansson at the livery. He was having a friendly game of cards and heard the whole thing. I went to Malone's and spoke to Patrick to get the facts straight."

Annabelle felt a sudden stab of fear clenching her stomach. Twisting her hands in the green-and-white-checked apron, she waited to hear. Afraid to listen but bracing herself anyway. "What?"

"Three men came into Patrick's when John Wilder was there. Patrick said they tried to goad him into a fight, but John kept his calm. The men never gave their names, but they said they had a message from Ransom. Kind of the same message they left for you."

Annabelle's blood chilled. "What did they say? Did they tell him to leave his ranch?"

"Not exactly. Mr. Johansson said Patrick told him they just kinda hinted he better keep his nose out of things. If he knew what was good for him. Or else."

Or else what?

Hank shrugged, going to dump a pail of slop into the feeding trough for the pigs. The squealing porkers came running on their short, stumpy legs to push dirty snouts into the food.

As he fed them, Hank kept up a low-voiced bantering with the animals as he often did. "That's enough of that. You give someone else a chance for some food. You there, with the black spot, shove over."

The normal, everyday sound of Hank's voice, despite being attacked a few days before, eased some of the fear from Annabelle's mind. Until Hank finished with the pigs and turned to face her again.

Biting her lip, Annabelle tried to still the foreboding she felt, seeing the wrinkled brow, hearing the cautious way he spoke, almost like he didn't want to frighten her more. "I'm wondering if it's just some bandits come to town. John always had men trying to pick fights before. Natural thing being a sheriff to have gunfighters want to show the ladies how brave they are. You can't always stop that kind of thing when you're a lawman. Maybe those men yesterday were cut from the same cloth."

"Who did Mr. Wilder think the men were?" Annabelle asked, annoyed at the slight quaver in her voice.

"Patrick didn't know that," Hank answered, setting the pail back on top of a tack box. "Later, I asked Patrick myself if John thought two of the men mighta been the Jones boys. But like Patrick said, it's been a long while since John had any run-ins with Ransom's gang. He knew about the Jones boys, but he hasn't seen them in quite a spell."

"He saw them when they were beating you up."

"True enough," Hank agreed, "but they wore masks. I must be honest, if they hadn't told me their names, I wouldn't have known them either. And John came just in time to get punched and kicked before they took off. They coulda been anybody. The way Patrick figured, even if John knew it was the Jones boys, he couldn't pin anything on them. When Ransom was captured, he was alone. John and Sam had no idea where the rest of the gang had gone."

"You mentioned a third man; any idea who he might have been?" Annabelle held the barn door open as she and Hank walked out into the bright morning sunshine. The crisp, fresh air of a new day filled her lungs, and she breathed deeply.

Somehow, the tragedy with the ransacked feed didn't seem too awful when she looked at the enormous blue sky above.

God's still on the throne, right? It will be all right...somehow. Won't it?

"Now that puzzled Patrick too. Said the third man looked like he'd been in prison for a spell. An' before you ask, there's just a look a man has who's been locked up, away from sunlight."

"Mr. Wilder didn't know the man either? Could it have been Ransom Baxter? He's been in prison for years, hasn't he? Maybe it changed how he looked."

Hank didn't even give it a second thought before he replied. "Wouldn't o' changed him that much. Ransom had a scar along one cheek, from an old knife would. Patrick told me this fella didn't have the scar. So, it most likely wasn't Ransom. Although..." Hank stopped to pick up the milking stool and pail before he opened the corral gate.

Judith, Annabelle's fawn-colored Guernsey cow, stood nearby, her udders full. The gentle creature came to the fence and leaned her head over the top rail. Annabelle stopped to pat her absentmindedly; questions scattered in her mind.

"Although?" she asked, waiting for Hank to finish his thought.

Hank went into the corral and placed the milking stool near Judith. Easing the milk pail under the cow, he sat and began to milk.

"Coulda been a friend of Ransom's—gossip says another prisoner helped him escape. Killed a prison guard. Sheriff Crane said there's a WANTED poster out for a man named Deke somebody, but they didn't draw a picture." Hank lifted one blue shirted shoulder and gave Judith a pat on her side. "Guess it's possible the men were the Jones boys and this Deke fella, but like John told Patrick, he couldn't tell for certain."

Annabelle sighed. They still knew nothing for certain.

"Well, no sense in trying to figure it out, we have chores to do if you're sure you can help. I really wish you'd rest a bit more, Hank. That was quite a beating you took."

"Now, don't you go fussing over me, Annie," he said, smiling despite the battered tilt to his puffy lips. "Soon as I finish milking, I'll head on out to check the fence just like we planned the other day."

Something else to worry about.

The day Hank had been beaten, they'd planned to check all the fencing. "I sure hope nothing's happened to Prince Oxford. I should have tried to check on him earlier."

Annabelle had high hopes for her prized bull. She had groused plenty when Thomas invested too much cash in buying the purebred bull. He'd argued that having an expensive sire would lead to calves they could sell at a higher profit. Annabelle had often teased Thomas about treating Prince Oxford like a cossetted son.

"Now, Annabelle," he'd admonished on more than one occasion, a twinkle in those blue eyes, "it's not like I've given him a gold-plated stall in the barn."

Oh, Thomas, I wish you were still here.

Thomas had built a strong, separate, fenced-in area for Prince Oxford near a sparkling creek, with plenty of shade and grass for grazing. A couple of times, the bull had managed to knock down the gate and gone missing, usually looking for a willing heifer.

"That's been on my mind too," Hank said. "Soon as I finish here, I'll saddle up and ride out to his pasture. Last time we fixed that gate, I think we stopped his wandering off."

"I hope you're right." Annabelle tied her apron tighter around her waist and reached for the willow basket she kept near the barn. "As soon as I've gathered the eggs, I'll come and help you."

Glad she'd worn a loose linen blouse and brown divided skirt, Annabelle hurried into the henhouse. The hens had gifted her with a dozen warm, brown eggs this morning. She carefully placed each one in the basket and took it into the kitchen.

"Annie!" Hank's voice called, just as she put the basket on the kitchen table. "Annie!"

She hurried outside as Hank reined up near the porch, the horse breathing hard from a fast gallop. "You best come."

"What's wrong?" She asked, her heart in her throat. *Not more trouble!* "Prince Oxford?"

Hank nodded, trying to catch his own breath. "I can't find him. The truth is, that gate's open, and he got out."

Annabelle groaned. "How did he manage to open it again? I thought the last time we…"

Even before she'd finished talking, Hank shook his head. "Ain't likely he did it himself. That gate's plumb torn off the hinges. The barbed wire has been cut by a tool; Prince Oxford couldn't do that. No, I'd say somebody stole your bull or let him out on purpose."

First the ruined feed, now a missing purebred bull. Annabelle knew one thing. Somebody or more than one somebody wanted her off her ranch. They might have figured she'd scare easy, but Annabelle knew she had more grit than that. Thomas had paid for this ranch with his life.

They aren't running me off. This is war.

Chapter Fourteen

Wilder Ranch

John stood on the porch the next morning, a tin cup of coffee warming his hands. Pinkish orange rays of sun peeked over the horizon, pointing to the charred remains of the barn.

A few smoldering boards sent out wisps of smoke to foul the freshness of the morning air. Some of the hens pecked close, clucking to one another, finding their favorite roosting place gone. They scattered across the barnyard confused and gossiping in hen talk.

Guess I ought to count my blessings.

It was just a building—wood, nails, and some hay. Probably lost my good milk pail in there, the wooden box grandpappy made to keep his tools in, a little tack, and my best saddle. Still, it could have been worse. Didn't lose any of my horses or other animals. Even the haystacks can be replaced. Reckon everything can except for the toolbox.

The burn on John's arm hurt like blazes this morning, even though he'd rubbed lard on it yesterday. Small price to pay for saving Ranger and Buttermilk. That and his singed eyebrows.

When he'd looked into the small mirror hanging on the bedroom wall, he noticed his face looked strange—the remains of his eyebrows looked like twisted caterpillars perched over his eyes. But if those were the only the injuries he'd got, John knew he had to be grateful.

Wonder if this is the message those men meant to send me? And who was the messenger? Ransom?

John had spent a restless night trying to figure out the meaning behind the barn fire. As a former sheriff, he knew when something was an accident and when it was a clear case of arson. He'd smelled the biting twang of kerosene oil when he ran into the barn to free the horses. Someone had deliberately set this fire. No doubt about that.

"Was it because of me asking questions about Sam's death?" he muttered out loud, used to talking to himself to get answers. A practice Ada used to despise.

"People will think you're a lunatic," Ada used to scold. "Talking to yourself like a crazy person."

"Ethan thought Sam was killed for poking his nose into too much, wanting to know more about the railroad buying land. Was that it?"

The rooster jumped up to perch on the railing of the porch and utter a loud, "Cock a Doodle Doo!"

"Ya don't say, Solomon," John chuckled. "How do you feel about me riding over to the Hollis Ranch? Ask Annabelle if she's heard anything more. I brushed her off a few days ago, but maybe she's got the right idea. Maybe Ransom is in cahoots with somebody like Isaac Glover."

In answer, Solomon preened his feathers and jumped down.

"Figured you'd say that," John teased, "but I'm going anyway." With one more regretful glance at the smoldering barn, he tossed out the dregs of his coffee. Thankfully he'd put his second-best saddle on the porch. He soon had Ranger saddled and ready to ride.

As John rode toward Annabelle's, he passed a small glade of live oak, cedar elm, and a few hackberry and thorn bushes.

Good place to hide, Sam used to tease.

A glint, like sunlight off glass caught John's eye. It was only a flash as he rode along, sitting easy in the saddle.

Someone's watching. The skin at the back of his neck prickled, just as it had so many times before. Sam used to joke John had eyes in the back of his head.

Who are you and what do you want?

Acting casually, John ambled along, whistling a cheery tune. His right hand slid down to touch the grip of his Colt. Slowly, cautiously, he drew it out of the holster. He rode past the person hidden in the brush, then in a sudden move to catch them off guard, he kicked Ranger's side and brought the horse around in a sharp turn behind the shadowy form.

Jumping out of the saddle, he positioned his body behind Ranger and hollered, "Toss out your weapon, then come out with your hands up!"

Curses turned the air blue, but then a long-barreled Winchester sailed out of the bushes. It landed in a puff of dirt near Ranger's hooves. Ranger shied and pranced backward.

"Now, come on out, and if you've got another weapon don't try to use it."

"That's the only one," a young voice said as the man pushed his way out of the brush. Him! It was the long-haired man who'd come into Patrick's saloon a few days before. In one hand, he carried a spyglass.

"Who are you? Why were you spying on me?"

The man glared from chestnut–brown eyes, a scattering of freckles across his nose making him look too boyish to be trouble. Once he spoke his name, John knew otherwise.

"Christopher Jones," he growled. "Can't a man be out hunting if he wants? Ain't no law against it is there?"

John motioned to the spyglass. "Funny way to hunt. What are you hunting with that?"

Christopher shrugged, then a wicked twist crossed his lips. "Maybe hunting ex-sheriffs."

John cocked the Colt and leveled it at Christopher's forehead.

"Hey now, I ain't done anything."

"You got a horse? Get on it, we're going visiting."

"What? You can't."

"I got the gun and I say we're going to the Hollis ranch." John walked over and picked up Christopher's Winchester. "Now, mount up and don't try anything."

Cursing and muttering, Christopher went into the brush and untied a lanky skewbald, chestnut colored with white patches. He pulled himself into the saddle and yanked hard on the reins.

"You first."

John kept the Colt aimed on Christopher's back as they rode toward the Hollis ranch. He didn't remember the horse from the attack at Annabelle's, but a man can change horses and shove long hair up under a hat.

The first person John saw as he came abreast of the house was Annabelle. Dressed in a blue linen shirt, divided brown skirt, and worn, mud-speckled boots, she glared at them with those green eyes. Tossing her auburn braid over one shoulder, she stormed toward the riders. "You happen to see my bull on your way here? He's dark black and...who's this?" She motioned toward Christopher.

"Somebody I picked up along the way," John answered, lowering the Colt and tucking it back in his holster. "Name's Christopher Jones."

"Jones!" Annabelle's eyes narrowed. "You're one of the men who beat up my hired hand the other day."

Christopher shrugged, and gave her a cheeky grin, "Reckon you'd have to prove that."

"You told my hired hand, or somebody did, that Christopher and Jack Jones were leaving a message."

"Can't prove it was me though, can you?" The younger man sat in the saddle without a care in the world. "Anybody can use anybody else's name. An' if a person's wearing a mask, can't rightly tell who they are, can you?"

"How'd you know the men wore masks?" John asked, suspicious all over again.

The younger man didn't answer, just gave them a half smile and shoved back a wide-brimmed hat.

Annabelle's lips pursed in annoyance. Fire in her eyes, she turned her ire on John. "Why'd you bring him here? Are you taking him in to the sheriff?"

I wish.

"Well now, ma'am, I can't," John knew the second the words were out of his mouth Annabelle wouldn't like the answer. "Like he says, anybody can use anybody else's name. An' none of us really saw the men's faces well enough to identify them. Can't prove he had anything to do with my barn getting burnt down... "

"Your barn burned down?" Annabelle interrupted. "When?"

"Yesterday."

She put fingers to her lips. "Oh, no. How awful! Were any of your livestock hurt?"

"No, just the barn and a saddle I was partial to." He tried to make a joke, but it pained him more than he cared to admit.

Grandpappy carved that toolbox. Sure do wish it hadn't turned to ash.

"They've been busy then," Annabelle said, hands on her hips and a scowl on her lips. "Someone broke into my barn and destroyed a bunch of my feed. Then my prized bull got stolen or..."

"Reckon you'll find your bull," Christopher let slip, in a bragging voice. "Probably just got lose when the fence got cu..."

Too late, he realized he'd spoken up when he should have kept quiet. Red-faced, Christopher clamped his mouth shut and tightened his grip on the reins.

"What do you know about it?" Annabelle demanded. "Are you the one who did it? My hired hand's been searching all morning. That bull is worth a lot of money. If you know where he's at, you'd better tell me."

"Don't know nothing," Christopher said. "Probably some of Ransom's gang, like my brother, Jack."

"You know where Ransom's hiding out?" John asked. "If you do, you'd best turn him in and save yourself a hangman's noose."

"What my brother and Ransom do are none of my business. You can't prove I did anything. Can't say I even belong to the gang."

John narrowed his eyes and put on his sternest expression. "Maybe we can't, yet. But, like I said before, Ransom Baxter is a wanted man. If I find out you're involved with him, I'll do everything I can to see you brought to trial. Now, get out of here, but don't let me catch you causing trouble or I'll be on you like a flea on a dog."

"You're letting him go?" Annabelle stared at John like he had three heads. "Why can't you turn him in? Force him to lead you to the gang."

John shook his head. "We got no proof he did anything."

While Annabelle and John argued, Christopher kicked his heel into the skewbald's side and took off down the road. Before John could catch his breath, the man had ridden off in a cloud of dust from the hard-packed road. Within seconds, he was little more than a speck in the distance.

"He's getting away!" Annabelle screamed.

Chapter Fifteen

John sighed, watching as Annabelle took a couple of frustrated steps, like she planned to run after Christopher.

It's going to be hard to explain.

"I can't believe you just let him go!" she shrieked, red-faced and shaking her fist. "He just about admitted he knew something about Prince Oxford being taken. He might have beaten Hank and you! Even if he's done nothing yet, you can't prove he won't now. I don't understand. You could have stopped him. Forced him to tell you where the rest of the gang is hiding." Annabelle finally ran out of steam, tugged the end of her braid, and stared at him. Perplexed. "What kind of a sheriff were you anyway?" she snapped.

"I'd like to think a darned good one, ma'am." He managed a slight grin which she didn't return. Hoping to get back into her good graces, John tried to explain himself. "Like I said, we can't prove Christopher did anything. He's young and inexperienced, that's why he gave away what he knew about your bull. My hope is that he'll head back to Ransom and the gang, tell them we're on to them. It might be a way to draw Ransom out in the open or even scare out Mr. Glover if he's a part of this."

"But..." she sputtered, clearly unable to come up with a reply.

"Guess you just got to trust me on this, Mrs. Hollis. I didn't expect to run into Christopher, but I was coming over to talk to you, if you got the time. I got to thinking about what you said the other day in town—about Ransom and Glover."

This time Annabelle sighed, lifted a hand over her eyes, and glanced up at the sun. "I've got time. Hank is still out trying to find Prince Oxford. I just came home to check on the stew.

Would you like to stay for lunch, Mr. Wilder? It's a bit early but we've been out before dawn."

"I wouldn't want to put you out, Mrs. Hollis," John answered although his stomach grumbled. A heady scent of roasting meat tickled his nose and his appetite. Unless he went to Millie's or Patrick's saloon, most of John's meals were uncooked like milk and canned beans. He'd never been much of a cook, except to bake the oatmeal cookies Lily liked.

"It's no bother. Come on into the house."

John dismounted, tossed Ranger's reins over the porch railing, and followed Annabelle into the house. He followed her into a pleasant, clean parlor, filled with light from a couple of real glass windows. A Seth Thomas clock ticked away the time from a cherrywood mantel over a river stone fireplace. John caught sight of a daguerreotype of a man and woman in a red velvet case. He didn't want to get caught staring but it looked like a wedding photo.

Wonder what happened to the one me and Ada had taken on our wedding day?

"Just sit on down at the table," Annabelle said. "The stew's already made. I just came home to make sure it didn't burn."

He swiped his boots on a rag rug near the front door and walked toward the kitchen end of the room. A round oak table with four store-bought chairs sat beside the large range, gleaming with blacking. He pulled out a chair, took off his hat, and sat down, already tasting the promise of a good meal.

"Let me mix up some biscuits and we can eat soon. I hope Hank comes along. He was trying to repair the fence in case we find Prince Oxford." The despair in her voice tugged at John's heart. "It's just sometimes...it's so...hard."

A strange feeling came over him and John found himself staring at the slight, sunburned woman before him. When those green eyes turned to his, John couldn't help himself from looking back, unable to stop staring. *I'd like to get closer, to know her better, to...whoa, you better stop that kind of thinking right there. Look what happened with Ada. No other woman is going to want you either.*

"Is there something wrong?" She asked, "You're..."

John scooted forward on the chair, scraping it along the floor. He shifted uncomfortably, unsure what to do with his hands or where to put his booted feet. "Um, no, nothing's wrong, I've just been thinking maybe you were right the other day. Mrs. Hollis...what you said..."

"About what? And please, just call me Annabelle. We're neighbors. No need to stand on ceremony." As she talked, Annabelle scooped out a cup of flour and dumped it into a bowl. She fingered up a lump of lard and began to mix it in.

"Well, Annabelle, I been thinking on what you said, how maybe Ransom and Glover are in cahoots. Trying to buy up property for the railroad. I went to visit Sam's kids the other day, my old deputy, Sam Garrett. Don't know as you ever met him?"

She plopped the dough on a floured cabinet top, took a cup, and cut out biscuits. A wrinkle marred her forehead as she thought. "I'm not sure I ever met your deputy. Thomas and I kept to ourselves mostly. Hank told me he'd been killed too, a strange accident almost like my husband."

"That's right, except Sam was hit on the head. Ethan, his son, thinks it happened because Sam asked too many questions, got too nosy about folks losing their land to the railroad."

Annabelle took a few minutes to place the biscuits in a cast iron skillet and slide it into the oven. She added a couple of pieces of kindling to the fire. "So if Ethan is right, his father was killed because he knew too much. That wouldn't explain Thomas's death, unless it happened because he refused to sell our land. It seems so hopeless. How can we fight them—whoever they are?"

The warm, yeasty aroma of freshly baking biscuits distracted John for a minute. That and the beautiful woman who pulled out a chair and sat down across from him. Those clear green eyes looked straight at him, never wavering, hopeful for answers. Or maybe just help.

"Well now, maybe I've got a few ideas..."

If I can stop looking into your eyes and thinking about how I'd like to know you better.

***

Wilder Ranch

"Uncle John! Uncle John!" a fearful voice shouted. "Uncle John?"

John stopped to swipe the sweat off the back of his neck with a red bandana.

"I'm coming," he hollered back as he limped around the side of the cabin to find Ethan.

The young man sat astride a sleek, well-groomed brown Morgan—his young face flushed with the heat and brown eyes filled with fear. "Uncle John! What happened to your barn? When I saw it, I was afraid..."

John sighed and came forward slowly, his leg aching like the devil. After having lunch with Annabelle and Hank, he'd ridden home in time for chores. Annabelle still hadn't found her missing bull, so he'd taken time to help them search. They found hoofprints and a clear path where the bull had walked through a patch of muddy creek bed, but then the trail petered out once the animal got to the grassy meadow. Discouraged, Annabelle thanked him and told him he'd better get home.

It had been a long day. Not being as young as he once was, John's body felt every minute of it.

"Evening, Ethan," he said, "get on down and come in for a cup of coffee. I need to rest my leg, and I'll tell you the whole story."

Ethan dismounted, tied his horse to the porch railing, and followed John into the shady house, a welcome relief from the unrelenting sun.

"Was it an accident?"

"Nope. Deliberate. Smelled the kerosene where somebody set it afire," John limped to the stove, built up a small fire, and dipped a pot of water from the drinking bucket. He set the battered tin coffee pot on the stove and managed to half fall into a chair before his leg gave out. It took every ounce of strength not to clench his teeth.

"Are you all right?" Ethan asked in a sympathetic voice, reaching out, unsure how to help.

Despite the young man's concern, John hid a grimace at the stabbing pains in his leg. "Fine and dandy, just that old leg wound acting up. I'll set a spell, and it will ease up directly. Soon as I get us a cup of coffee ..."

"No." Ethan went to the stove and motioned John to sit. "I'll make the coffee. You just rest. I remember how bad your leg used to pain you after you got shot."

Although John wanted to protest, it felt mighty good to have somebody wait on him. *Kind of like Annabelle this afternoon.* Soon, the rich scent of brewing coffee filled the room as Ethan set out the tin cups and a sugar bowl. As Ethan sat it on the table, he gave John a sheepish grin, a glint of humor in his eyes.

"Sorry, I can't stand coffee without a spoonful of sweet."

"Help yourself, son," John chuckled, glad he kept store-bought sugar for Sam's kids.

Once they both had coffee in front of them, Ethan sat down, put both hands around the cup, and said, "your barn didn't burn by accident, so who burnt it down? Did you see anyone?"

"Wish I knew." John blew on the hot brew then took a cautious sip. "I was out in the field when I smelled smoke. By the time I got back near the barn, it was already in flames. Ranger and Buttermilk were inside, but I managed to get them out. Didn't lose much that can't be replaced."

He was glad he'd pulled down his plaid shirt sleeves, so Ethan couldn't see the scar from the burn.

Ethan's chapped lips set in a hard expression as John spoke, his dark eyes narrowed, forehead wrinkled. "It's most likely the same ones who killed Pa. You know it, Uncle John. Like I said, they need to be stopped, before they do worse. Maybe kill you too."

"Maybe, but I can't rightly prove anything yet, Ethan. Until I do, I can't go around accusing people."

John didn't feel the need to share the fact he'd caught Christopher Jones spying on him. Not yet. Ethan was too hot headed, too intent on revenge. The boy was likely to go off half-cocked and get his head blown off.

"Maybe," Ethan pressed his lips together tight. "All I know is that I'm not gonna let whoever killed Pa get away with it."

A sigh built up in John, but he kept it in. The truth was, he could recognize a lot of Sam and himself in Ethan. The way they were when they'd first started out as lawmen, filled with a keen sense of justice, the hunger to right every wrong. Wisdom only came with learning not everything could be set right with revenge. In fact, most wrongs could be made worse when a man went on a vengeance trail.

Ethan had a reckless streak that needed to be curbed before it was too late.

Chapter Sixteen

"I agree with you; justice needs to be done," John stated, unsure how to help Ethan without pushing him away. "But, Ethan, surely Sam taught you going off all hot-headed is a good way to get yourself killed."

The chair scraped back across the floor as Ethan shoved his tin mug of coffee away. Coffee sloshed out on the table, but John didn't make a move to wipe it up. The fire in Ethan's eyes spelled trouble, sure as anything.

"I don't intend to get myself killed," Ethan snapped, his brown eyes smoldering with resentment, "but I'm sure going to see that someone dies for taking Pa's life."

"How do you plan to do that?" John kept his voice calm and steady, not condemning him.

"That's why I came here," Ethan said, his anger cooling a tad. "I need your help."

John lifted one of his singed eyebrows. "How so?"

A glint of anticipation shone on Ethan's tanned face as he twisted on the chair. "Well, a few days ago, I happened to follow this fella, not sure who he was, but I heard someone call him Christopher."

Christopher? Jones?

"Where'd you see this fella? Hear his name?" It took all John's patience to speak in a calm, slow voice when he wanted to blurt out the questions.

"I was in Pecos River." Ethan leaned over the table, the sleeve of his tan shirt soaking up the spilled coffee. He was so excited to share his news, he didn't notice. "There were a few men hanging around Malone's. One had long, kind of walnut–brown hair down to his shoulders, a holster with a lot of wear. Pa used to say a man who had a worn holster drew his gun a lot."

"Yes, I remember him saying that. Where'd you follow this fella?"

Ethan didn't answer right away but went on with his story while John fidgeted with impatience. "I'll tell you in a minute. Anyway, Mr. Malone didn't appear too happy they were there. He served them a beer, but they didn't stay long. When they left town, I followed them."

Dangerous, stupid fool thing to do!

Although John wanted to shake some sense into Ethan, he kept quiet. Whatever he'd done a few days before, Ethan sat across the table unharmed. "Where'd you follow them?"

"Up into the hills, but I stayed way back and didn't let anyone see me. I had on some old clothes that day. I'd been to town to buy nails. So, I figured if anybody stopped me, I'd ask directions like I got lost. Just a dumb farmer."

Thank the Lord for small favors!

John's blood ran cold at the idea of Ethan facing off against somebody like Christopher Jones. It'd be like a rattler against a rabbit—Ethan wouldn't have a chance. "You should have come and told me. It was awful risky."

"I know." Ethan had the grace to lower his eyes like a reluctant schoolboy. A sheepish grin flickered across his face. "Anyway, Uncle John, I followed the man named Christopher. He started out with another man but, after a few miles, they split up. Not sure why, but I stuck with Christopher. Before they split up, they stopped and talked about guns."

"What about guns?"

Ethan shrugged and bit a corner of his lip. "I'm not sure. They were too far away for me to hear everything they said. Just something about making sure the guns were safe. Christopher went on alone and stopped at an abandoned cabin. He went inside, came out a few minutes later and rode off. I gave him plenty of time to get away before I rode here."

The sense of unease John felt at the news made the hair at the back of his neck stand on end. He didn't like the sound of this one bit. Ransom's gang had been known to stockpile weapons before. "Well, you did something right anyway," John knew he sounded gruff, but Ethan had to learn to look before he leaped. "You didn't try to look in that cabin alone...or did you?"

"No," Ethan shook his head and lifted his hand in an angry gesture. Red splotches colored his cheeks—either embarrassment or fear. John didn't know which. "I thought maybe you'd go with me to check it out. I remembered someone saying the Jones brothers were part of Ransom's gang. I know you think I'm young, Uncle John, but I've got some sense. I wasn't about to get trapped in that cabin alone."

John didn't want to move from the kitchen chair. Resting, the pain in his leg had eased up some, but he knew if he didn't go with Ethan, the young man would strike out on his own. Maybe get himself killed. "How far is this cabin? Should we wait for morning?"

A decisive shake of his head. Ethan's words were full of fire. "No. I couldn't get a whole lot of what the men were saying, but the one named Christopher said something about meeting on Wednesday around noon."

Wednesday. The day after tomorrow.

"How far is this cabin?"

"Maybe two hours…" Ethan guessed, squinting his eyes and staring up at the ceiling. "I came straight from there to tell you. If we go now, we should make it before dark. From what I heard, no one will be around tonight. It's not like they were guarding it or anything."

John sighed. *If I don't go, he'll go back there on his own. No telling what trouble he'll find.*

"Let me milk Bossie before we leave, then I'll saddle up. We best take some lanterns along…got a couple out on the back porch."

Eager to be on the way, Ethan jumped up. "You milk the cow, and I'll round up the lanterns and saddle Ranger." At the door, Ethan stopped and turned to grin at John. "Thanks, Uncle John, for believing me."

John gave him a two-fingered salute and formed a smile with his lips. Truth was, he'd rather do half a dozen other things instead, including wrestling a nest of snakes, than follow Ethan into what might be a trap. Still…if Ethan had heard right, Christopher Jones and some other members of the gang had weapons hidden.

What did they plan to do with them? That was the most troubling thought of all.

***

As they rode into the foothills, dusk settled over the land, shrouding it like a purple blanket. A low hum of insects filled the evening with a chittering of sound, along with the faint rustle of leaves from the oaks they passed. The rich, ripe odor of horseflesh filled John's nostrils, along with the earthy aroma of mud puddles they plodded through. The horses' hooves alternately splashed and clopped, walking through puddles and then hard-packed dirt. John hoped only the night birds and scurrying animals were listening.

"The cabin is up around the next bend," Ethan whispered as they drew closer to the place. "It looked abandoned to me, the roof's caving in; scraps of curtains hanging over the windows."

"Let's leave the horses here and go in on foot anyway," John answered. "Grab a lantern." He dismounted, tied Ranger to a nearby red elm, and pulled out his Colt. Ethan did the same, unhooking the lantern from his saddle horn. He didn't light it. With his weapon in his right hand, John led the way through a faint path in the underbrush. It looked like someone had walked toward the cabin, but not often. Feeling assured that no one lived there, John studied the cabin as they walked stealthily closer.

No lights shone in the ramshackle building as they approached. The cabin's walls showed wide gaps where the chinking had fallen out. As they stepped closer, a small animal, too dark to tell what, scurried out of the opening where a door would have been. It hurried into the brush with a terrified squeal. A slight breeze tugged the faded scraps of cloth that might have served as curtains over the window openings. They blew like long, dark ghosts, almost as if the house were breathing in and out.

"Go ahead and light the lantern," John spoke in a normal voice.

There was the scritch of a match, a nose pinch of sulfur, then the flame as Ethan touched the lamp's wick. He placed the globe back on and held the lamp up higher. Deep shadows lay across the rickety steps to a porch; the floorboards were rotten and gaping.

"Watch your step," John whispered, although it was apparent the place was deserted.

Stepping gingerly over the holes, John led the way into the cabin, the porch boards creaking at his entrance. It appeared to be one large room, filled with drooping cobwebs, a dozen summers of dirt and leaves blown in. In one corner, a dangling piece of stovepipe led down to the rusted remains of a pot-bellied stove. Patches of old newspapers covered a couple of the holes in the wall and one lone whiskey bottle rolled away from John's boot as he stepped onto the hard, dirt floor. The skittering and scrabbling of small feet indicated some residents.

"Doesn't look like anybody's been here in a long time," Ethan said, lifting the lantern, slashing long, black slashes of shadows over the dusty walls. "Except for that…"

He pointed toward a long, wooden crate, covered with a moldy, gray blanket. A new wooden crate.

"I see that." John holstered the Colt and stepped toward it. "Guess we best see what's inside."

Someone had taken the nails out of the crate's lid. John had no trouble lifting the wooden slab. As Ethan held the lantern, he let out a long whoosh of breath. "Rifles."

John clenched his teeth.

The wooden crate held at least ten new Winchester rifles.

"What do we do now, Uncle John?" Ethan asked, sounding more like the nineteen-year-old boy he was, rather than the hot-headed vigilante he wanted to be.

"Only thing we can do." John bent over, picked up a couple of the rifles, and motioned for Ethan to do the same. "We take the guns and set the place on fire. If they planned this spot as a supply line for something, it cuts them off."

"Won't they know someone was here?"

"Maybe. Or maybe they'll think lightning struck, or somebody got careless. It won't do much to stop them, but it's a start."

Ethan reached for the rifles, then stopped. "It doesn't seem like much."

"Maybe not," John answered, "but if Ransom's got something planned, this will set him back and make him spitting mad. When that happens, we need to be ready."

"Ready for what?"

"The fight of our lives."

Chapter Seventeen

Wilder Ranch

Solomon crowed the tiding of dawn long before John was ready to open his bleary eyes the next morning. He hadn't gotten home the night before until somewhere around two o'clock. After he and Ethan had taken all the rifles from the crate, John splashed lamp oil around the floor and then stuck a match. Just like he expected, the rundown cabin went up like a tinder-dry pile of wood. Flames crackled and shot up into the night sky, announcing the fire for miles around.

"Let's get out of here," he'd told Ethan, "Just in case someone is watching."

They had no idea where the Red Hand Gang might be hiding out. As far as they knew, some of them were nearby guarding the cabin. Thankfully, no one sounded an alarm or chased them. John only drew a deep breath when he and Ethan made it back to his ranch without being followed.

"Safest place to hide the rifles is down in the root cellar," John said after they'd taken care of the horses.

Fighting sleep, weary down to his bones, John helped Ethan store the rifles under the floorboard of his kitchen in the root cellar. Too tired to ride home, Ethan agreed to bed down on a pallet in front of the fireplace. After that, a cyclone could have blown the place down and neither of them would have woken up.

"Ra roo!" Solomon shrilled again, just as John's eyes drifted closed again.

Might as well get up.

He muttered a curse, dragged himself out of bed, and yawned. John gathered his dirty clothes and dressed, shoving his feet into stiff boots. They'd scrambled through more than one muddy puddle last night on the trips to stash the rifles in their saddlebags.

Outside, he heard Bossie's usual morning moos, issuing the demand to be milked. Pale filtered dawn touched rosy fingers in the parlor and landed on Ethan's mop of dark hair. Still yawning, John stepped over the sleeping boy and headed out into the dew speckled morning.

"I'm coming, Bossie, I'm coming. Sure named you right, didn't I? Bossy as any other female."

Although maybe not Annabelle Hollis. A slight smile curved John's lips.

He grabbed up the milking stool and pail from the porch and walked out to the lean-to he'd fashioned for the cow. Once the barn burned, he'd figured Bossie needed a temporary home to keep her safe from the weather. He'd taken some boards and leaned them against the chicken coop, a fact the hens seemed to resent.

"Maroo..." Bossie called again.

The cackling hens scolded her and the red-feathered one he'd named Delilah pecked at the cow's hoof.

"Here, now, you stop that!" John scolded around another yawn. Tugging a suspender strap over the shoulder of his plaid shirt, he stomped a foot at Delilah. "You keep that up, you won't get any pepper mash."

A chill breeze blew through the barnyard, stirring up the scents of manure, sour milk, and the hen house. Another job waiting to be done. Clean the hen house, build a new barn, scout out the Red Hand Gang...all in a day's work. John let out a snort.

He'd just perched on the milking stool when he heard a rider coming fast. Cursing under his breath for not wearing a weapon, he glanced from around the edge of the lean-to. *Trouble?*

A second later, he breathed a sigh of relief. Just the Dawson boy, Herbert, galloping along on a dappled gray horse. Although why he rode so fast, the horse lathered up and breathing hard, John couldn't imagine. Maybe trouble after all?

"Sheriff Wilder!"

I'm not the sheriff.

"What is it, son?"

"Sheriff, um, Mr. Wilder, Ma sent me out. She wanted to know if you can come into town right quick."

Why would Clara Dawson ask him to come into town? John couldn't think of any good reason. "Why? Is Sheriff Crane..." *Hurt? Dead?*

Red faced, panting as hard as the horse, Herbert's chubby cheeks showed the traces of tears. He gulped, sputtered over words. "Somebody robbed the store last night. Tore up a lot of supplies, broke out the big window in front an' Ma had to send to San Antonio to get glass that big. Whoever it was took a lot of meat, canned goods, and ammunition. Stole money out of the cash drawer too."

"Isn't Sheriff Crane around? He'd have to investigate a robbery like that."

Herbert sneered, wrinkling his nose like he'd sniffed a bad smell. "Oh, he came by, said probably just some kids for a dare

126

or bein' mean. Ma's awful upset. Said he wasn't worth the powder it would take to blow him out of the jail. An' Ma don't ever talk like that. She sent me out to see if you'd come, maybe figure out who did it."

John sighed, reluctant to step on Sheriff Crane's toes. It didn't take much imagination to know how Tobias would take his interference and suggest he go home to his "nice, quiet, ranch."

He didn't realize Ethan had come up behind him until the boy spoke. "He'll come or I will."

"Tell your ma I'll be in as soon as I can," John agreed, unwilling to have Ethan take up the challenge on his own. "Got to finish my morning chores and put on clean clothes."

"Thank you, sir!" His mission accomplished, Herbert turned the gray around and headed back down the road toward town.

Ethan stared off at the retreating figure, forehead wrinkled. "You think the gang did something because we burnt the cabin last night?"

John shrugged, tugging Bossie's udders to spritz milk into the pail. "Don't see why they would. They'd attack me or you, not Clara Dawson's store. But you heard the boy. They took food and cash. It figures the gang needs supplies. Won't know until I get into town. It don't seem likely the gang would know anything about the cabin yet."

A dart of worry crossed his mind, "What are you planning to do today?" John wanted to warn the boy not to go off hot headed...but he bit his lip. When he was a young brash upstart—words like that would have sent him right off to do the worst. "You coming along to town too?"

"Don't worry, Uncle John." Ethan spoke in a placating tone, like he had to keep the old man from being anxious. "I need to go back to the ranch and check on Lily. We hired a couple of boys to help, but I need to make sure things are all right. We just planted our wheat before I came here. Thanks for going with me yesterday."

Only way to keep you from getting your fool self shot.

"I'm glad we went too, Ethan. If you hear anything else, you come to me. Don't go against that gang on your own. We haven't proven yet they had anything to do with your pa's death."

"Maybe..." Ethan muttered, leaving John with a weight of worry on his mind.

***

Pecos River

"What do you mean there's nothing you can do?" John railed at Sheriff Crane, who was sitting behind the desk forking up Millie's meatloaf and stuffing his face.

"Look, John, somebody robbed the store. I'm looking into it. Far as I can tell, it was a bunch of kids takin' a dare or..."

John wanted to slam his fist on the desk, or shove off the silver tray with the meatloaf, and fluffy mashed potatoes swimming in brown gravy, hiding a mound of peas. Instead, he curbed his temper. "Listen, Crane, I don't care if it was kids. You're letting criminals get away with a crime. If they're bold enough to rob Dawson's Mercantile, they'll get worse unless somebody takes a strong hand with them now."

And if it's the Red Hand Gang, you need to know that, too.

"As far as I can see," Sheriff Crane scooped up a forkful of peas and put them in his mouth. He chewed, swallowed, and said, "none of it's your concern, John. Why don't you go on back to..."

Before the sheriff could say another word, John stomped across the hardwood floor and out the door of the jail. He resisted the urge to slam the door on his way out. John walked down to the mercantile, distressed to see the boards covering the usual sparkling windows. Shattered shards of glass covered the front step, and the destruction spilled out with each step he took. A bucket of brooms were snapped in two, scattered among a barrel of pickles that spilled vinegar-scented brine down the steps. Apples were stomped into a gooey mush and just to be mean, a mischievous hand had smeared jam all over the front of the whitewashed doors.

The doors were locked. John knocked, waited, and saw the curtains part open the merest slit. A second later, he heard the bolt sliding and Clara motioned him through the door. "Oh, John, please come in! I'm so glad you came."

"Of course, I came..." he started to say until he stepped into a disaster.

Chapter Eighteen

The destruction was unimaginable. John had seen summer cyclones do less damage than what he saw in the mercantile. Stepping inside, his boots crunched glass and slid in a mess of cracked eggs. The scent of vinegar, kerosene, and hard candy turned his stomach.

If the scene outside hadn't prepared him, John's heart might have quailed at the evidence of destruction inside. Shelves were overturned, bolts of fabric soiled and ripped beyond repair. Other barrels of goods were tipped upside down, cornmeal mixed with kerosene, flour coating every available surface, and a keg of nails grinding underfoot. Someone had tossed canned beans against a wall where they dripped slowly down the whitewash.

"Just...watch where you step," Clara lifted a weary hand and led him back toward the rear of the store, toward the family's living quarters. "I don't even know where to begin. Hank went over to the hardware store to buy some nails. He and Herbert will have to rebuild some of the shelves...Sit down and I'll get you a cup of tea. We have no coffee...it's all..." she gulped, and wiped tears from her eyes.

"Who could have done this, Clara?" he asked. The family slept in the second-floor bedrooms, but surely, they'd have heard something. "Didn't you hear anything last night?"

"No, sad to say. Herbert slept over at Annabelle's again. Hank's pain was bothering him, so I slipped some sleeping powders in his milk, kept him snoring all night. I guess I was just worn out from it all and slept like a top. Then, at about dawn I heard glass breaking, figured that's when they smashed the window. I shook Hank awake and we came downstairs, but by then whoever it was had got away. Guess now we'll listen to Herbert and get one of those pups from Doc. His dog just had a new litter an' our boy's been pining for one. If a dog had barked, we might have stopped all this."

John didn't tell her that a dog might bark, but it could also be shot or poisoned by someone determined to keep it quiet. "Too bad you didn't see anyone. Might have given you an idea."

Clara shrugged, handed him a fresh brewed cup of tea, then wiped away another tear. "I truly have no idea. Sheriff Crane..." her lips crimped, and she didn't speak again until she took a deep breath. "He thinks it's just young boys but Hank's not so sure. Not after those Jones boys beat him up and left that message for Annabelle. Hank thinks maybe they're angry she hasn't left the ranch yet, and are taking it out on us. Why, I don't know. It's not like we can tell her what to do."

"Do you think Annabelle will leave her ranch?" John knew what he thought, but truthfully, he didn't know her all that well.

"Maybe if they kill her, like Thomas..." Clara said. She sat down heavily on a chintz chaise lounge with walnut arms. "Annabelle Hollis is one of the strongest, most determined women I know. No matter how desperate things have been since she lost her husband, she's not about to leave her ranch. No. They'd have to kill her to get her off that land."

"Had she and her husband lived here long, when he got killed?" he asked, hoping to get the pained look off Clara's face and distract her from the mess.

"Four, maybe five years." Clara took a sip of tea. "They came from Missouri. Grasshoppers wiped out their crop first year they married. But the way Annabelle tells it, you'd never know the hardships they faced. Lost their horses halfway here and ended up walking, pushing carts with the goods they had left. She's been a good friend."

John didn't know what to say to that, although it gave him more reason to admire the green-eyed beauty.

I'd sure like to know her better. If she's not still grieving her husband.

Outside, the town began to wake up. Wagons rolled by in the street, squelching in the mud from the rain the day before. Men shouted and a loud clang came from the Blacksmith's shop. "I don't suppose we'll do any business today," Clara mourned, pushing back a limp strand of her dark hair. "Unless Annabelle has some ideas about how we can sell what's not broken or torn or..."

Tears dripped unchecked from Clara's eyes. "Hank was going to ask her later if she'd come and help, but I don't like to be beholden to her..."

Unable to watch the woman's distress, John stood and reached for a broom. "Why don't I start helping you clean up? I'm not doing much on the ranch right now."

"Oh! No, I can't ask you to do that. It was selfish of me to send for you, but I thought, maybe you'd have some idea of tracking down who did this. But how would I ever get them to pay for the damage if Sheriff Crane won't arrest anyone? I'm just so confused, John! I wish you were still the sheriff."

I don't.

"Clara, why don't you go rest for a spell? I'll let you know when Hank gets back. You let me start to sweep up. I don't mind at all."

It took a bit more persuading, but eventually he wore Clara's refusals down. John brought her another cup of tea, a warm green shawl, and hurried back into the mercantile. Grabbing up the broom again, he stomped over broken glass, a child's toy top, crunched through an upturned barrel of sugar, and plunged in.

He couldn't help it. The more he heard about Annabelle Hollis, the more he admired her. She didn't seem the kind to up and leave like Ada had...simply because life got too hard.

***

Hollis Ranch

The knock on the door came just as Annabelle tied a piece of string to the length of her long braid. "I'm coming," she called out, hurrying from the bedroom. As she crossed through the kitchen, Annabelle tugged the waist of her black riding skirt and tucked in the hem of a yellow blouse she favored.

Probably Hank, ready to find out what chores she had for him today. The first would be searching for Prince Oxford again.

"I'm glad you came ear..." the words died on her lips as she opened the door to a stranger.

A tall, lean man who put her in mind of the late President Lincoln, stood on the porch. At the door's opening, he swept a bowler off his head and gave her a courteous bow from the waist. "Mrs. Hollis? My name is Alexander Dumont. I'm a lawyer representing Mr. Isaac Glover. I believe you are acquainted with him."

"Yes."

Annabelle crimped her lips and didn't invite him inside. "What do you want?"

"Perhaps we could discuss this in your parlor."

"Whatever you want, the answer is no." Annabelle started to close the door.

A flicker of annoyance crossed his face, but he quickly hid it behind a false smile. "Mrs. Hollis, if you will please hear me out. Mr. Glover has asked me to come here to offer you a generous sum to buy your ranch. He feels that, as a woman alone, it's just too much to have a profitable ranch and—as such—he's willing to give you more than he would any other seller. All you need to do is accept this bank draft..."

He pulled a slip of paper from a leather portfolio and dangled it before her eyes.

Annabelle gasped at the number written on the check. Mr. Dumont hadn't lied. It was a generous sum.

"I don't know." What would Thomas have her do? "It's a lot to think about."

"It surely is, Mrs. Hollis, but Mr. Glover is quite anxious to buy this ranch. He feels his offer is most generous. I'm to tell you that if you accept now, today, he can also see to your protection. It's come to his attention that other... shall we say... parties have retaliated against you because you won't leave."

Annabelle stiffened her back and clenched her hands alongside her skirt. *So I sell the ranch, take Glover's generous offer, walk away with a fortune and my life. Is this what they offered Thomas? Is this why he died?*

"You can tell Mr. Glover I'll have to think about it," Annabelle put a puzzled expression on her face, like she might be too dumb to figure it out. "Maybe if I took time to read the contract, see what he's asking me to do."

Mr. Dumont stared at her with suspicion. "Hmm, well, this is most irregular. It's a simple contract offering to buy this land. I was told to get your signature, but I suppose...well it would be all right if you read the contract before you turn over the deed to your land. Might I ask when you'll have an answer for Mr. Glover?"

"Um, well...can you give me a couple of hours?" Annabelle asked. "I was on my way to help a sick neighbor," she lied. "I'd really like to read this before I sign. Mind you, I'm not refusing Mr. Glover's offer outright. As you say, it is extremely generous and a woman alone, like myself, does find it difficult trying to make a ranch profitable."

"That is exactly what Mr. Glover said." He pulled a sheaf of papers from the portfolio and handed them to Annabelle. "This will be our little secret," he winked. "I won't speak to Mr. Glover until later today. Might I call again this evening? You can sign the papers and tomorrow you can put your bank draft in the bank. We will give you ample time to pack your belongings."

"Yes, that would be fine. Now, if you'll excuse me..." Annabelle kept her hand on the door as Mr. Dumont bowed again and went back to a shiny black buggy sitting before her porch.

"When you come back, I'll make coffee and pie," she promised, smiling until he snapped the reins and the high stepping horse led him out of the barnyard.

Annabelle resisted the urge to slam the door behind him.

"If you think I'll sell my land to you, Glover, you can think again!"

She tossed the papers on the walnut table and went to build up a cook fire. It puzzled her that Hank hadn't shown up yet. She and Herbert had finished breakfast hours ago and the boy had headed back to town. Although she wanted to toss the papers in the fire, she stopped. Mr. Dumont hadn't wanted to give her the papers.

Why? What secrets did they hold?

Chapter Nineteen

A few hours later, Annabelle had her answer, and a growing knot of dread settled in her stomach.

The papers the lawyer had given her told too many of Glover's secrets. It was a contract all right, but mixed up in between all the legal papers was a crudely drawn map and notes. *Glover's handwriting?* Annabelle didn't know. What she now knew was why Glover—and maybe Ransom Baxter—were so eager to get her land.

The map showed different ranches where Glover wanted to buy up land. It didn't take a lawyer to understand that, if the railroad could purchase that land, they wouldn't have to build a trestle over two different rivers. She could see why it might be tempting. But no one from the Texas Pacific had ever tried to buy her out. Maybe they figured they'd just build the trestles. Unless someone like Glover managed to buy up the land...and offer it for sale at a higher price than he'd bought it.

Annabelle frowned, holding the pages so tightly that her fingers cramped. A second hand-drawn map showed plots of land running in a straight line—a few parcels were blacked out while others—like her ranch were still open. *No, that can't be right...*

The page showed plots leading in a straight line to take in much of the town of Pecos River.

"They can't do that!"

Distressed at seeing how many of her friends and neighbors—including the Dawson's, would lose their land, Annabelle stood up and paced around the kitchen. *It's not right.* Her heart thumped beneath the yellow blouse. A tension headache pounded in her head.

She and Thomas had only lived in Texas for five years. They'd come from Missouri after Mama died. Even though they weren't old timers, like the Dawson's or even John Wilder, they'd grown to love and cherish the town and its people.

If Glover's scheme went through, he'd uproot lives and destroy the town.

Annabelle stared at the amount Glover had written on the bank draft. Yesterday, when she felt so discouraged about Prince Oxford, she might have been tempted to accept it. Waved goodbye to all the heartache. Today, she knew she couldn't.

I can't leave here. Thomas gave his life for this ranch. I've got to stay.

The rest of the afternoon, Annabelle busied herself with chores, wondering where Hank was. It wasn't like him not to come or send word if he was too busy to help her out. Herbert had gone home right after breakfast, but it was getting toward late afternoon, and he hadn't shown up again.

It's childish to depend on Herbert coming to stay here with me. I'm a grown woman. She thought of the implications in Glover's offer. *If I accept and sell him the ranch, then I don't have to worry about any more messages—from him or Ransom. Does that mean they are working together?*

It was all too much to think about. She needed someone with a clearer head to help her figure it out.

Annabelle bit a corner of her lip, undecided about who she could talk to.

"I take too much of Hank's time," she said out loud to the empty kitchen, "and I sure don't want to be here when Mr. Dumont comes back to help me sign the papers."

If she hitched up the buggy and headed toward town, she was almost certain to pass the lawyer coming back. But, if she went in a different direction, maybe toward John Wilder's ranch, he'd have an idea. Annabelle took heart at remembering how John had listened the day he came to help search for Prince Oxford. A spark of hope eased her fears. *I'll talk to John. But, what if Hank or Herbert come looking for me?*

Annabelle scribbled a hasty note and tacked it to the front door with a knife. Thinking of Mr. Dumont and not wanting him to know where she'd gone, she wrote:

Went to visit friend. Will talk to you tomorrow. Annabelle Hollis.

That done, she hurried to saddle Cletus, with a worried look at the dark clouds massing in the sky.

As she swung her leg over the saddle, a flicker of lightning forked down like an ominous warning.

***

It had been a long, difficult day. John had stayed to help Hank and Herbert hammer in some new shelves at the mercantile. Together, they'd managed to sweep out a lot of the wreckage and find anything still in one piece. Clara had rallied and got them mopping and wiping down the worst of the spilled mess. By the time they all settled at Millie's Café for lunch, the worst was behind them.

"I can't thank you enough, John," Clara said as he mounted Ranger to leave. "If you find out who did this, maybe you can force Sheriff Crane to make them pay for the damages."

He tipped his hat, keeping a pleasant expression on his face although his leg screamed in agony. "I'll do that, ma'am."

It took all he could do to ride home, conscious of the dark clouds gathering in the east.

"Gonna be a heck of a storm tonight, Ranger," he told the horse as they plodded along.

To John's surprise, he found Annabelle Hollis in front of his porch when he got home. "Miz Hollis... Annabelle... what brings you out here? It's fixing to come up a storm."

"Is it?" She turned a distracted eye to the rolling blue black clouds massing in the west. "I guess I didn't think. I need to talk to you about something that's happened."

"Another attack?" John got out of the saddle faster than he thought he could, going to

stand by her side. "Are you hurt?"

"Oh, no, nothing like that," she shook her head, her auburn braid flopping across the shoulders of a yellow blouse. "A lawyer came today from Isaac Glover. Well, it's a long story. Maybe I should head home, and we can talk tomorrow."

The wind picked up, sending leaves and branches skittering across the dusty yard. Dirt swirled in circles along the ground, and from the distance came a loud crack of thunder. Bossie mooed her distress, the chickens ran for cover, clucking.

"No, listen," John said, fearing for her safety, "go on in the house and put on some coffee. Wait out the storm at least. I got to talk to you, too. Clara Dawson sent a message."

Clara had told him to give word to Annabelle that neither Hank nor Herbert would be coming that night.

"What about?"

John shook his head, "It's too long to explain. We can talk once I put the horses under cover. Guess I'll have to lead them back to the old shed. Might take me a couple of minutes to get out there. I'll take your mount, too."

"Cletus," she said, with an upturned grin, "that's his name. I sure don't want to put you out."

At first, he thought she might refuse, but then Annabelle shrugged, sighed, and went inside. "Maybe just until the storm's over."

It took longer than he thought to unsaddle the horses and lead them out to the shed. Ranger balked at sharing the space with Cletus. Thankfully, he'd left Buttermilk there earlier. By the time he had them all groomed, watered, and fed, the sky had turned as black as coal. Rolling masses of clouds covered the sky in an ominous warning.

Thunder shook the ground, and a loud snap of lightning lit up the sky.

John made short work of milking Bossie and saw she was as sheltered as possible in her lean to. The chickens needed no urging to cower in the coop. John ran for the cabin, milk pail in hand, as the first spattering raindrops thumped him on the back.

Inside, his house smelled better than it had since before Ada left. A pot simmered on the black stove, sending out an aroma to rumble his stomach. The mouth-watering scent of ham and beans. "I hope you don't mind," Annabelle said, a pretty flush on her face, and one of his tattered dish towels tied around the waist of her black riding skirt. "I figured you'd be hungry, and with this storm, I probably need to stay here a spell."

"It's turned into a gully washer out there," John agreed. "You're welcome to stay the night if you need to. You can have the bedroom, and I can put a pallet on the floor. If you won't feel it's too improper."

Annabelle laughed and it was like the sun coming out on a dreary day. "We can talk about that after we do justice to this ham and bean soup. You're soaking wet, why don't you get changed and we can eat first."

John hurried into his bedroom, shut the door, and made fast work of putting on clean clothes. A quick glance around showed him just how much he lived like a pig. Clothes were strewn all over, the sheets were dirty, cobwebs dangled over the one lamp. Thinking about Annabelle seeing the mess, he took a few minutes to shove dirty trousers under the bed, smack at the cobwebs, and pull the faded patchwork quilt up like he actually made the bed.

By the time he got back to the kitchen, Annabelle had dished up a savory soup and pulled a pan of biscuits from the oven. "Wash up and we can eat when you're ready."

He didn't need to be reminded twice. It warmed him to see she'd heated the water for the wash bowl and set out a cake of lye soap. Or maybe she figured he was so dirty he could use a good cleaning. Wouldn't be wrong there, not after the day he'd spent at the mercantile.

"What message did Clara send me?" Annabelle asked when they were both seated at his rickety table, dipping spoons into a savory meal. "Is everything all right?"

After a big swallow of ham, John shook his head, not knowing where to start. "Well, nobody got hurt, but the mercantile was robbed last night. She wanted you to know Herbert couldn't come tonight and Hank would be sticking close to town for a while."

"The store was robbed?" Annabelle's green eyes filled with concern. Her spoon dropped onto the tin plate with a clang. "Who would do such a thing? You sure they aren't hurt?"

John shook his head again, unable to talk with his mouth full of biscuits. He swallowed. "No, Clara and Hank slept through the whole thing until they heard glass breaking. When they went to check, they didn't find anyone. Don't have any idea who caused it. Wasn't just robbed; whoever did it wrecked the store. That's where I've been most of the day, helping them clean up. They won't be able to open again anytime soon." John told her about the destruction, watching as her tanned face paled.

"Oh, my! Poor Clara. She takes such pride in her store. What did the sheriff say?"

"Him!" John kept the word he wanted to use for the sheriff behind pressed lips. "They got him over there, but he wasn't much help. Figured it's just mischief. Maybe young boys out for a lark."

"And you don't?" she asked, dishing him another ladle of bean soup and placing another flaky biscuit on his plate.

"No, I figure it's got something to do with the Red Hand Gang. If Ransom's around, he's got a plan. I can see him robbing the place for food and cash. There's something else too..."

As they ate the meal, he told her about finding the rifles with Ethan. "We took the rifles, and set fire to the cabin, but if Ransom and his men have got something planned, they'll figure out a way."

"It gets worse and worse, doesn't it?"

Annabelle went to the stove and brought the coffee pot to refill their cups. "That's why I came over to talk to you. A lawyer was on my porch this morning. He had an offer from Isaac Glover for my land. Glover's been pressuring me to sell for months now. Maybe he's tired of waiting. The lawyer told me if I sold, they'd make sure I was protected."

Protected? From who?

"What do you plan to do?"

Chapter Twenty

Until she answered, John didn't realize he'd been holding his breath.

The fiery force of her words both reassured and worried him.

Annabelle Hollis is one determined redhead.

"I'm not selling to him, that's for sure. But I'm not sure what to do. I told the lawyer I wanted to read through the papers. When I looked through them, I found maps showing all the land Glover wants. He's out to destroy the whole town." Annabelle pulled a sheaf of papers from the pocket of her dark riding skirt and handed them to John. One of her hands brushed against his and set John's heart racing.

He stared at the map, watching as her long, slender finger pointed to the different parcels of land and the local landmarks. "You can see here where he's trying to save the railroad from having to build trestles. I'm sure they'd jump at the offer if they could buy the land that's flat."

He kept his fingers tight around the warm cup of coffee. It was the only way to stop himself from reaching out to grab her hand.

Get a grip on yourself. You'll be scaring her out of here in the storm. Pretty woman like that wouldn't be interested in an old worn-out lawman like you.

Forcing his mind back to the maps, John narrowed his eyes and peered at the evidence.

"It makes me think Ransom's involved in all this too."

John leaned back in the chair, his heart racing as he caught the sweet scent of violets from her hair. "I can just see them

Jones boys pulling a stunt like the mess at the mercantile. Not that I know much about Jack and Christopher. When Ransom and his gang rode together before, they were other men I knew better. But, just the sneaky way I caught Christopher spying on me, then letting slip they had something to do with your bull going missing..."

Thankfully, Annabelle didn't remind him she'd wanted him to take Christopher into the sheriff. "Guess maybe you figure I should have turned him in. Maybe he wouldn't have had time to smash up the store?"

Annabelle shrugged and tossed her braid over one slim shoulder. If she figured he'd had bad judgement, she didn't say. "You didn't know, and you still don't, that it was him. Like you said yesterday, he hadn't done anything. Can't see Sheriff Crane being likely to do anything about it."

A piece of wood snapped in the black range. Outside, a gust of wind banged against the window, startling them both. A spattering of rain hit the tin roof of the porch, followed by a boom of thunder.

"Sure sounds bad out there," John murmured, glad he'd made it over the creek before it flooded.

"You and Sam Garrett must have been after Ransom Baxter for a long time." Annabelle said after they'd listened to the sounds of the storm for a few minutes. She twisted the tin cup of coffee in her hands. "Hank mentioned you were shot?"

John nodded, taking a sip of coffee. *The woman made mighty good coffee.*

"Yup, in that last standoff. Ransom and some of his men had us pinned down in a canyon. Didn't think me an' Sam would make it out alive. Even today it puzzles me how we did it. Guess the Almighty was on our side that day." He gave a short laugh. "I remember thinkin' when we got out, and had Ransom and some of his men behind bars, I was sure glad I didn't have to try to explain anything to Ada. She'd have raised a fuss."

"Ada?"

"My wife."

"Your…wife?" Did he detect a touch of disappointment in Annabelle's voice. A warmth spread through his body, even though she pulled back with a frown on her lips.

Could it be she felt a spark of interest too?

"That was Ada. We were married about ten years when she finally told me she was done. Never knowing if I'd come home alive, or they'd ask her to pick out my buryin' clothes. Poor Ada. She went to El Paso, and worked for a lawyer for a while. Got a letter maybe two years ago to say she'd died of a fever."

Annabelle sat a little straighter.

Was it his imagination or did the news about Ada's death reassure her somehow?

"My condolences. I know how you feel since I lost a spouse too. So, you're a widower now?"

"Reckon. But, didn't figure I was married once Ada left. She just didn't cotton to me being a sheriff."

They sat quietly, listening to the sound of wood popping and dropping into the coals. Outside the wind howled and rain slashed against the house. It sure wasn't a night to be outside.

John stood stiffly, his bad leg hurting him. He clamped his teeth while he stood long enough to get some feeling back in the limb. "Ransom left me with a reminder from that last showdown. I sure don't like the idea of going up against him again."

"Do you think it will come to that?" Annabelle asked in her gentle voice. "Can't you just catch him and the gang and send them back to prison?"

He chuckled before he realized she might think he was making fun of her. "That would be the best outcome, I guess. Well, I reckon I'd best check the animals before the storm gets worse. Like I said, you're welcome to the bedroom. It's got a sturdy lock on the door. Ada insisted when she was here alone. Sorry it's not any cleaner but guess men just don't think about that when there's not a woman around."

"Thank you," she said, "I really don't like to put you out, but I'm sure the creek is flooded. I'd rather live to see another day. Let me do up these dishes first." Annabelle stood and stepped to the dry sink, her hands full of tin plates.

Hoping to be helpful, John grabbed up the coffee pot to fill with water from the drinking bucket on a stool. He stood right behind her, so closely he caught another whiff of violets from her hair. When she turned, her warm breath blew across his cheek. She stood so near he could see the tiny scar above her eyebrow, the flecks of brown in her green eyes.

"I...um..." John gulped, wondered if she felt the rapid beating of his heart.

Annabelle stood quietly, inches away from him, and their sleeves brushed.

John stared into her tempting eyes, felt her sweet breath caress his cheek, and had the sudden urge to kiss her in the worst way. He moistened his lips, and tried to form words, but found himself unable to speak. Without thinking, his boots slid across the floor until they stood toe to toe.

His heart yammered harder and harder; he couldn't help the wild yearning inside. Any second, he expected Annabelle to smack his face, to call him a name, to run away, but she didn't.

Did she desire his lips as much as he wanted hers? John bent his head, leaning closer to her pink lips, parted, waiting.

"Annie," he whispered, lowering his face until he felt the soft, sweet silkiness of her lips.

BANG!

The gunshot startled them both. Their bodies jumped backward, Annabelle hitting the edge of the dry sink, while John slammed into a chair.

"Hey in there, Sheriff Wilder!" a voice hollered. "Come out, come out wherever you are!"

The command was followed by a booming clap of thunder.

What in the...

"Howdy, Sheriff Wilder! Remember me? Ransom Baxter! How'd you like it if I shoot up this purty little house you got?"

From outside came a bright flash of lightning. A gunshot hit the parlor window and shattered it. Ada's prized lace curtains, long since grown dusty and torn, fluttered inward on a gust of raindrops.

John pulled his Colt from the holster hanging on the back of the kitchen chair. A round of bullets hit the side of the house, not enough to pierce the thick, log walls but enough to be heard. "You need to hide!" John jerked Annabelle down to the floor, "Quick, into the root cellar and stay there."

"No!" she protested. "Give me a gun and I can help you."

"I don't know what he plans," he argued back, easing up the trapdoor in the floor. "You need to be safe. Go on, do as I say and don't come out. No matter what."

149

If Ransom had the notion to kill him, John hoped Annabelle wouldn't be found. Just in case, he crawled into the bedroom, took the Winchester from under the bed and forced it into her hands. "If he comes in..."

John didn't need to say more. Annabelle opened her lips like she might protest, then with a flick of her braid, she nodded. With one final glance, Annabelle took the rifle, turned and headed into the cellar. After shutting the trapdoor, John took a deep breath, lifted the Colt, and walked toward the front door.

Time to stop Ransom...again. Or die trying.

Chapter Twenty-One

What am I doing down here?

Annabelle didn't want to hide; it wasn't in her nature. Even as a child, she'd never run away from trouble. Mama used to say she'd take on any bully in the schoolyard rather than back down.

I should be trying to help, not hiding like a helpless female.

"Stay safe," John said as he dropped the trapdoor and headed after Ransom.

A faint line of lamplight showed around the edges of the door. Standing on the damp, musty earth, Annabelle shivered in the cold. The thought crossed her mind that this must be what it felt like to be buried.

What a gruesome thought.

From her underground hiding place, Annabelle heard a faint sound of gunshots followed by loud rumbles of thunder. A drip came from nearby, coursing a muddy stream down one of the walls.

Annabelle listened to the sound of John's boots as he crossed the parlor floor. The sound of a door scraping open and then John's voice. "Ransom Baxter! Show your face and fight like a man."

There was another spattering of gunfire, further off, drowned out again by thunder and the frantic pounding of rain. A cold draft of air blew across Annabelle's neck like ghostly fingers. Standing with her hands clenched tight around the rifle, Annabelle realized she was holding her breath, almost stiff with fear.

Please, don't let John be hurt...

She didn't know if she was praying or hoping.

What's happening?

Unable to stand the agony of waiting any longer, Annabelle decided to ignore John's order. Legs quivering, she climbed up the short ladder, flipped open the trapdoor and scrabbled into the kitchen. The lamplight had grown dim, the wick sputtering. A coal dropped in the stove, sending out a whiff of smoke. In the parlor, the shattered window let in a spattering of raindrops, the lace curtains blowing in and out.

Winchester in hand, Annabelle walked toward the cabin door just as it banged open.

John!

"Are you hurt? Shot?"

Water streamed from his dark hair and dripped off the end of his nose onto his short beard. His brown shirt and dark trousers were soaked through, and with every step, his boots squelched. "What happened? Where's Ransom?"

Shaking his head, a puzzled look in his eyes, John sat down heavily on a kitchen chair. "Gone. Vanished."

"Gone? But I heard gunfire. I thought for sure maybe he'd killed you." She laid the rifle on the table, glad she hadn't needed to use it.

"Don't know what he had in mind. Maybe playing with me before he kills me? I don't know. He took some shots, but it wasn't like he planned to shoot me just yet. Rode around on a horse and played cat and mouse. By the time I got outside, he was already riding away."

"I was so frightened."

Annabelle could never figure out where the fear came from, her body shook so hard, she could barely stand. Wrapping her arms around herself, she trembled.

"Here now, it's over, he's gone," John stood and put his arms around her, getting her wet too. He gave her an awkward pat on the back. "You're safe here. I'll sit up in case he comes back. You best go on into bed, and mind you lock the door."

Although it felt pleasant to have John's arms comforting her, Annabelle realized she needed to step away. "Thank you, I think I will go to bed. Did you need to get dry clothes?"

He shook his head. "Gonna build up a fire and dry out. You go ahead. Goodnight."

"Goodnight." Annabelle managed to walk into the bedroom, lock the door and collapse on the bed.

Don't you go having feelings for John Wilder now, her mind warned her, but she had a feeling her heart wasn't about to listen.

***

Hollis Ranch

A Few Days Later

Annabelle rode Cletus into the barnyard. She'd spent a long morning checking her fence. Thankfully there had been no further damage, although Prince Oxford had yet to return. Hank was still out checking the fences on a different part of the property. Hopefully, he would find everything well too. It was about time something went right.

It had been a few days since Annabelle had ridden to John Wilder's ranch to talk to him about Glover's offer. When she left to come home, John advised her to tell Glover's lawyer she needed more time to think it over. Annabelle had been prepared to do just that, but Mr. Dumont had never come back.

A day after the storm and Ransom Baxter's nighttime attack on John's ranch, Hank had come back to work. Annabelle would never tell anyone how relived she'd been to have a man around the place again, even if only for a few hours.

"Clara's got the mercantile back open," Hank reported, grinning. The bruises on his face had faded from purple to a sickly yellow green, but he walked with a perkier step and announced himself healed.

Even though worry dodged her footsteps, Annabelle tried to push it aside and get back to work. With Hank ready for chores, they rolled up their sleeves and got back to the work at hand.

"Now, who the devil is that?" Annabelle whispered to Cletus as she rode into the barnyard a few hours later.

A strange horse stood tied to the porch railing, a dark–brown mustang with a blondish–white mane. The horse lifted one leg and stomped down into the mud.

Annabelle reached for the Colt she kept in a holster, as she rode closer to the house. A strange man stood from one of the rocking chairs and walked to the edge of the step.

"Who are you, and what do you want?" she demanded, sitting astride Cletus. If needs be, she could ride away and hope to escape.

"Mrs. Hollis, I presume," the man spoke in a gravelly voice.

A tall, lean man, who looked half-starved, stared at her with piercing brown eyes. A deep scar slashed down his right cheek.

His skin, a sickly pale pallor, had begun to darken under the Texas sun, and his black, ill-fitting suit draped over his body like a garden scarecrow. His black hair topped his head in a short scruffy mat like a shorn field. In one hand, he held a new tan hat, the brim curled up at the edges. "I'm Ransom Baxter. Maybe you've heard of me."

The outlaw!

"I've heard of you."

He glared at her...taking stock?

Annabelle wasn't sure but she kept her grip tight on the Colt. Her pulse roared in her ears and her skin grew clammy.

"Then I'm sure you'll take the message I've been sent to give you seriously. Mr. Glover is very...shall we say...distressed that you haven't accepted his generous offer to buy your ranch. He wants you to know something. Being a fair man, he's decided to give you another chance. If you don't sell the ranch, things will get worse. The small incidents that have happened so far were just the beginning. A little feed can be replaced. Another bull can be bought. Minor mishaps. Just warnings."

"What about my husband's death? Was that a warning too?" Annabelle snapped, trembling with a mixture of fear and rage.

He shrugged one scrawny shoulder, a smirk on his face. "That I can't say. I'm just here now to give you another warning. Sell up, and nothing more will happen to you."

A cold fist closed over her heart. She'd had enough. She pulled the Colt from the holster, and aimed it right at Ransom's heart, although she doubted, he had one. "Get out of here, now." Her voice sounded high and hysterical to her ears. "Before I shoot you where you stand."

He was probably armed, but she didn't care. To her relief, he took his time walking down her porch steps, mounting up on the mustang and turning back toward the hills. "As you wish, but this isn't the last you'll be hearing from me."

Only when he'd become a mere speck on the horizon did Annabelle lower the Colt. Her hands were shaking, her knees quaking, and she struggled to swallow a lump in her throat.

What am I going to do?

She hadn't backed down, but the meeting had left her rattled. The message was clear. Glover wanted her land, and Ransom was helping him run her off. Just like she'd suspected. The thought crossed her mind that John would have to believe her now. *I've got to tell him soon.*

Cletus nickered as another horse came into the yard.

Annabelle turned, fearful, then relaxed to see Hank coming toward her.

"Annie, I checked the fence along the south pasture and everything's fine down there. We might need to run some more wire...what's wrong?" Hank asked as he rode up, a coil of barbed wire around his saddle horn, leather gloves tight on the reins. "You look pale as a sheet."

"It was him," she managed to whisper. "Ransom Baxter. He came to give me a warning."

"What kind of a warning?"

It was all Annabelle could do not to break down and sob. She swallowed past a lump of fear in her throat. "He said Glover wanted to warn me. I can either leave or else more bad things will happen."

Hank's usual placid face grew drawn and pinched. Grumbling, he dismounted and held out a hand to help her off

156

Cletus. "Guess he's clear enough about who's behind all the mischief around here. I won't abandon you, Annie, but I gotta say this is hard news to hear."

As Hank helped her from the saddle, Annabelle clung to his hand.

What if Hank leaves me? He isn't young. What if he leaves and I have no one to help work the ranch, even if I can keep it out of Glover's clutches?

"What are we going to do, Hank? Maybe I *should* sell to Glover. If I don't, how can I fight him?"

John had cautioned her not to tell anyone else what she'd found in the maps Mr. Dumont had mistakenly given her. Annabelle wanted to tell Hank, but she didn't dare. Not yet. John had warned that it was better to keep the information under their hats for now. No sense in letting Glover know they'd figured out his scheme.

If I don't fight Glover, people like Hank and Clara will lose their home and business. If Glover's scheme goes through, he'll take over the whole town and sell it to the railroad.

"I sure don't know," Hank answered, a worried look crossing his face. Deep in thought, he took a few minutes to answer. "Glover's a powerful man. An' from what I hear about Ransom Baxter and his Red Hand Gang, they're a force to be reckoned with. It's worrisome, for sure."

Maybe Hank was thinking about the destruction of the mercantile. Annabelle didn't want to ask. She wouldn't blame him if he was. From what Hank had told her, they'd lost more than they could afford. What if Ransom's threat was the final straw to force Hank away?

"I'm scared, Hank. I wish I knew what to do."

Chapter Twenty-Two

Pecos River

John tied Ranger to a hitching post in front of Patrick's saloon, brushed the trail dust from his duster, and stepped into the cool, dim room. Mr. Squire was at the piano, playing a spritely tune. Several other men sat around the tables, drinking, joshing and enjoying the evening. John envied them their relaxed, almost carefree life.

My life seems like a runaway wagon about now.

"Evening, Patrick," he greeted his friend as he stepped up to the bar. "I'll have a beer."

"Comin' right up, laddy," Patrick filled a mug and slid it across the scarred bar. "What's got you so down in the mouth? More troubles out at the ranch?"

John waved a careless hand, not sure he could even begin to explain. The events of the past week were too unbelievable. "Just a lot of things." He sighed and looked down into his beer, wishing he could get drunk enough to forget.

When he didn't speak again, Patrick shrugged and went to the end of the bar to talk to someone friendlier. Soon, the men's laughing and good-natured ribbing about another man's fishing catch irritated him. John took a big gulp of warm beer and turned his back on the merriment.

As he glanced around the dim, smoke-filled saloon, John noticed a man sitting alone in the corner. It was a face he recognized—one he'd rather not see.

Isaac Glover.

Glover sat behind a plate with a broiled steak, smug and content. As John watched, he cut the steak into neat, bite-sized pieces and ate with obvious relish, savoring each forkful. Remembering Annabelle's run in with Glover's lawyer, John seethed inside.

He didn't often get angry, but when he did, John knew better than to let his temper out. Tonight, he didn't care. He sat the beer mug on the bar, strode over to Glover, and stared down at the man.

"Hello, Wilder, is there some reason you're glowering at me tonight?" Glover lifted a linen napkin and dabbed at the corners of his lips, still the fine gentleman he pretended to be.

John wanted to wipe the simpering smile from Glover's face with a fist. Instead, he clenched his hands to his side and glared down. For the first time in a long time, he almost wished he were sheriff again. Although there was no crime, he could charge Glover with.

"Don't deny it, Glover. I know Ransom's working for you. He's trying to run people off their land so you can buy it up cheap and make a profit selling it to the railroad."

Glover carved another bite of meat and put it in his mouth. Chewed and dabbed at his lips with the napkin. "You can't prove anything like that, Wilder." Even though he denied it, Glover's lips curved up in a smirk.

John clenched his hands until his nails bit into his palms. *I'd like to wipe that grin off your face for good.* "Maybe I can't prove it yet, but you mark my words, I will. You won't get away with it."

"What's goin' on here?" Patrick came up with a damp dishtowel slung over one shoulder. "John, let's not have any unpleasantness now. Ya hear me."

"Tell that to him." John pointed at Isaac, who'd finished off the steak and laid his knife and fork across the white china plate.

Glover stood without a care in the world. While they watched, he reached for a broadcloth suit jacket and put it on, straightened his string tie, and grinned at John.

"Nothing to tell me, Mr. Malone. If Wilder has a problem, it belongs to him alone. Thank you for the fine meal. My compliments to Mr. Squire, as well." He tossed the coins to pay for his food on the table.

Enraged by the man's careless attitude, John stepped in front of Glover and grasped the front of his white linen shirt in one fist.

"You listen good, Glover. I know you're behind all this with the railroad. You sent that lawyer to threaten Annabelle to sell..."

"I offered Mrs. Hollis a reasonable price. There were no threats."

John twisted the shirt, taking pleasure in seeing Glover's face redden. "You threatened her. Admit it."

"That's enough," For such a short, pudgy man, Patrick could raise his voice loud when he wanted. "I'll have none of that in here. The both of youse out. Now! No fighting in my saloon."

Glover jerked from John's grip, tugged at his shirt, and headed toward the door in a casual strut. "I'm just leaving."

After one backward, annoyed glance at Patrick, John followed Glover through the swinging doors.

I should get in a few punches, make him see I mean business.

A second later he realized how stupid that would be. If Glover had Ransom on his payroll, it wouldn't be wise to pick a fight now.

Outside in the last rays of the sun, Glover had the nerve to tip his black wide-brimmed hat before sauntering off to his house.

Frustrated, John unhitched Ranger, mounted up and headed out of town. As he rode along, he let his anger cool somewhat. *I should have just talked to Glover, tried to see what he knew about Ransom. He might have told me something if I'd just talked civil to him.*

Dusk came on slowly. The sagebrush along the road sent long, dark strips of shadow over the dusty road. Evening bird song filled the night, along with the steady clops of Ranger's hooves. About a half a mile outside of town, the hair at the back of John's neck stood up. One of the long, lengthy shadows striping the road had the shape more of a man than a tree trunk.

As he rode closer, John's eyes made out the shadow of both a horse and a tall, slim man standing along the side of the road.

John put his hand over the Colt in his holster. Wary, he squinted his eyes but couldn't make out a face in the murky purplish twilight.

"Who's there?" he called in a stern voice.

The shadow man lifted both hands up in a gesture of surrender, but it could be a trap. "I'm not armed."

Something sounded familiar about the voice, but it wasn't until John drew Ranger to a stop near the shadow that he caught a good look at the face.

Christopher Jones.

"Sheriff Wilder?"

I'm not the sheriff.

"Crane's the sheriff now, not me. What do you want?"

It could be a trap. John looked slowly around but the woods were too dark and shadowed to offer him much hope of spotting an ambush. "What do you want, Jones?" he snapped in a commanding voice, his hand tight on the grip of the Colt. "Where's your brother and your friends?"

Christopher shook his head and moved into a patch of light from the fading sunset. "I don't know where they're at. I wanted to talk to you, if you've got time to listen."

"I'm listening."

He still didn't trust Christopher, but he might have useful information to use against Ransom.

"I've been thinking. The other day, when I was spying on you, that day you could have killed me. Wouldn't have been anybody to know or care. Maybe my brother, Jack, but it's not like I'd be missed. Jack, Ransom and the others, they've got a plan and a lot of times I feel like they use me to get what they want. Ransom says I'm a person who's willing to take chances. But, you know," Christopher looked off toward the last rays of the sun as it sunk beyond the horizon, leaving his face in shadow. "I don't know that's how I want to be anymore."

Was he drunk? Loco?

John didn't know what to think. This Christopher was a different boy than the smirking, wise-cracking one he'd met the other day. "What are you talking about?"

"It's just I've been thinking. Guess you never knew but when the rest of the Red Hand Gang went to the gallows, me an' Jack, we watched." A shudder seemed to pass through Christopher's slim body, his long dark hair wafted around his shoulders like a shroud. "I ain't never seen a man…" he gulped and swallowed hard. "Hanged before."

John thought of all the men he'd seen hang. "It's not a pretty sight." It could be sobering if a man was in the right frame of mind.

"No, it's not." Again, Christopher trembled like he might be trying to shake off the memory. "The other day when you caught me, you could have shot me down. But you let me go and spared my life."

He shuffled a step back and his piebald horse snorted. Christopher reached up a hand to rub down the stallion's nose. "It got me to thinking. Used to be, I wanted to be just like Ransom. I admired him, all the crimes he committed, the men he'd killed. But then I thought, what was it all for? Guess you figured the Red Hand Gang mucked up that store the other night. I wanted you to know I didn't have no part in that. Yeah, I stood watch on the outskirts of town, but I didn't destroy those people's property. That woman, Miz Clara, once when I was younger, I went in there staring at those toy tops she had. There was a purty one all painted with red and yellow stripes. Jack, for sure, wouldn't buy me a toy, but that woman, she slipped it into my hand."

John couldn't figure if this was a confession or if Christopher was drunk, crazy or a little bit of both. "I'm not sure what…"

"Yeah, I know you think I'm talking out of my head, but I'm trying to explain. Here lately, the stuff Jack and Ransom are doing rubs me the wrong way. If all they do gets a rope around their neck, then, that's not how I want to live. And I wanted you to know that."

163

"Well," John didn't know what he was supposed to say. It was good Christopher wanted to turn over a new leaf, but what if he was still a wanted man somewhere? John had only a scant knowledge of the Jones brothers' activities, including beating up Hank Dawson.

"A few weeks back, beating up that old man, Hank, well, that kind of done me in. Can't take back what I did, but I'm kinda hopeful you'll let me make amends somehow. If you'd let me help you."

"Help me!" John didn't mean to sound so shrill, but the shock of Christopher's words startled him. "How could you help me?"

"By telling you everything you need to know about Ransom and the gang. Then helping you catch them."

John stared down at the young man standing by Ranger's snout, the palest of moonlight shining across his freckled face. "Why would you do that? What's in it for you, Jones?"

He tossed his long brown hair back and looked off down the road. When he turned to answer, John could hear the sincerity in the young man's words. "Maybe living past twenty without dangling from a rope around my neck."

For many years, John had trusted his gut reaction to things people said and did. Sam used to taunt him about being able to read people's hearts. Whatever it was, a gift or curse, John had learned long ago to trust the still, small voice inside his head. Christopher Jones knew the gang. He'd lived with them and had a clear idea of Ransom's next move. Maybe, he even had a notion about Glover's plans for the town.

"What do you say? If I leave the gang, can you protect me and let me help?"

"Yes," John agreed hoping it wasn't a mistake.

Chapter Twenty-Three

Wilder Ranch

Next Day

Early the next morning, John rode out along his property line, checking the fences. It was a chore he tried to do once a week to make sure none of his market cattle had managed to escape. Every head of cattle was money in the bank, and if any went missing, it meant less profit. With all the uproar lately over Ransom Baxter's return, John had neglected some of his ranch chores. He wanted to help Annabelle save her ranch, find justice for Sam, and keep his kids safe. But, first, he needed to make sure not to neglect the way to put food on his own table next winter.

After he'd milked Bossie and scattered feed for the chickens, John saddled up Ranger and headed toward the north pasture. The barbed wire there had been a bit loose last time he'd ventured that way. He made sure to take along a hammer and a coil of new wire, just in case.

As he crossed one ridge and rode easily down into a small valley, John uttered a couple of curses as he hopped out of the saddle. It didn't take a second look to see someone had deliberately knocked over two fence posts, taken wire snips to the barbed wire and made a big mess of one whole section of fence. It would take him a good two or three hours to repair the damage and hope, just hope, none of the cattle had gone through already.

"Dang it all, Ranger! I wonder if that's another warning from Ransom or Glover."

First the barn and now this mess.

Maybe I was too hasty accepting Christopher's offer to help. Could be he hightailed it back to Ransom and told him I'm still on the trail of whoever killed Sam.

Last night, after the meeting with Christopher, John spent an uneasy night wondering if he'd done the right thing. He told Christopher to go back into Pecos River and tell Patrick he needed a place to stay.

"It's not safe for you to go back to Ransom now," John told him. "If he finds out you're willing to help, he'll kill you. Patrick can keep you safe until we figure out a way for you to help."

For the first time, Christopher had looked as young as he was, a frightened freckled-faced boy, not an outlaw in the making.

This morning, John wondered if he'd done the right thing in sending Christopher to Patrick. While he didn't doubt his old friend could handle Ransom and other members of the Red Hand Gang, he wished now he'd gone back to town along with the boy.

Had someone discovered Chistopher's change of heart? Were the broken fences another warning to stop his nose sticking where it didn't belong?

John led Ranger toward the lopsided fence post. He looped the reins around the post and scouted around the area.

"What have we got here?" he muttered to himself, walking along the fence line.

Thankfully, he didn't notice any cattle prints in the soft mud near one post hole. What he did see were a lot of horse prints leading off into the hills. It looked like someone didn't care if they left a trail. On purpose or carelessness?

Leaving Ranger to graze in the new shoots of grass, John pulled out his Colt and followed the prints. He held the Colt in an easy grip, ready to use it if necessary. John stepped cautiously over the horse prints and trailed them up the other bank of a nearby creek. It looked like two or three riders; one of the horse's shoes had an odd shaped nail that looked almost like a heart. Wouldn't that be proof if he found the horse?

The sun rose higher and hotter in the sky as John walked along, stopping every so often to wait and listen. He had no idea if the fence busters had done the deed last night or early this morning. For all he knew, members of the Red Hand Gang could be lying in wait, hoping for him to come along. John tightened his grip on the Colt, ready to fire if needed.

Careful to walk as silently as an Indian scout, his boots took soft, careful steps over the leaf-strewn path. After a few hundred yards from the path, he found fewer and fewer horse prints. The mud had dried and only a print here or there, or a broken branch signaled the direction in which the men had gone.

John stopped, wiped the sweat from his forehead with a red bandana and squinted up at the sky. He'd been following the prints for about forty minutes. *Maybe just over that rocky outcropping and then I'll turn back.*

Coming out of the wooded path, John climbed over a pile of gray shale and made a grim discovery.

What the...?

Shocked, John stood and stared, Colt held steady in his right hand. Nestled in a small, sheltered glade of elm and pine, sat the burnt-out shell of a wagon. Scattered around the wagon were household goods—a washboard, cast iron Dutch ovens, a keg of some grain swarming with ants. A weathered wooden trunk had busted open, spilling clothes that were bleached and tattered by the constant winds. As John took a closer step, he startled a bird who'd built a nest in the charred hunk of wood that was once a wagon bed.

The bird's irate *caw caw* sounded an alarm. Smaller animals rustled out from under the twisted metal of the wagon wheels and scurried into the woods.

Near the shallow edge of a creek, John noticed a mound of dirt that looked suspiciously like a grave. Three more mounds were nearby. They'd each been dug in haste, one mound burrowed open by wild animals. It took a pile of strong, heavy rocks to keep out the varmints, but not everyone took the time. Or didn't care. Looks like whoever buried these folks didn't care.

John walked over for a closer look, then wished he hadn't. A man's long skeletal fingers reached out like he was trying to crawl out. Even though he'd seen a lot as a sheriff, John felt bile rise in his throat.

He turned to study the wagon. Someone had attacked it from the looks of the scattered belongings, then set it on fire. As far as he knew, most of the native Indians were peaceful enough. Sometimes there were rogue gangs who came up from Mexico, but not often. If it had been them, they'd have taken most of the goods, not torn them and scattered them to the winds. They would have just left the bodies to rot or for the buzzards.

Someone had buried the bodies in the hopes they wouldn't be found for a while.

Why?

The wagon was a total loss, charred down to the metal rims of the wheels. Parts of the wagon bed were still there, enough to make out the shape. Anything inside had turned to ash in the inferno. The fire looked to have happened a few months ago, perhaps around the time of Sam's death.

John scouted around, poking a boot here and there in the dirt, hoping to find a clue as to the identity of the people in the graves. He'd almost given up when he saw a glint of dull metal half buried in the dirt. With the tip of his boot, he scraped off the caked-on mud and bent to pick up a long, tarnished gold buckle. TM was engraved on it, surrounded by a carving of twisted rope.

Travis Montgomery.

John would recognize that belt buckle anywhere. It had belonged to Travis, a neighboring rancher. He and Sam had met the man while tracking down a horse thief one summer. A broad, jovial man, he'd raised thoroughbreds for the army on a tidy plot of land along the Pecos River. John could remember when he'd heard from Sheriff Crane that Montgomery was selling out because of his wife's health. What was it Crane had said? Montgomery told him the air was too dry; they were leaving. It hadn't puzzled him then, but it did now.

Standing beside the burnt-out wagon, a slight scent of fire still in the air, John rubbed his fingers over the belt buckle.

If the Montgomerys were leaving, settling elsewhere, who had made sure they didn't make it there? Or was someone like Ransom or Glover afraid that once the Montgomerys left, they wouldn't hesitate to make trouble.

Had they been forced off their land? Wasn't that what Sam believed? Ethan said his pa spent a lot of time questioning people, that he almost had proof some families hadn't left willingly.

What if Ransom wasn't just threatening people or forcing them off their property? What if he was making sure they disappeared too?

Thomas Hollis and Sam Garrett hadn't disappeared, but they had ended up dead. Was it all part of Glover or Ransom's plan? To get rid of anyone who opposed them or stood in their way.

John had seen enough. Only birds followed him as he turned and headed back to Ranger. If this is what the Red Hand Gang had planned for others who went against them, it was time to stop them now. Before there was no turning back.

Chapter Twenty-Four

Hollis Ranch

"John," Annabelle greeted him as he drew Ranger near her small porch and reined him to a stop. "What brings you out here? Have you heard anything more in town?"

He shook his head and dropped out of the saddle, frustrated and tired. After the discovery of the burnt-out wagon, he'd felt the need to talk to Annabelle. *We're in this together.* Although he'd rather just be working on his ranch, John had to admit getting to the bottom of Ransom's plans set his blood racing. *Maybe I miss being a sheriff more than I thought. And maybe I just like spending more time with Annabelle.*

"No, but there's a lot I need to talk to you about. If you got time?"

Annabelle lifted a weary hand and motioned him into the cool house. "I've got time. There's something you need to know too. Come in and have a cup of coffee. I've got pie."

For the first time in a couple of days, John felt his lips lift in a smile. "I never say no to pie," he chuckled, glad to talk of normal things for a few minutes.

Once they were in the house, seated around the kitchen table with dried apple pie and tin cups, Annabelle shared a morsel of startling news.

"He came here. Ransom Baxter."

"What!" John dropped the fork; it clattered on the plate sending flakes of pie crusts across the table. "Did he threaten you?"

Annabelle shrugged, but he could see it had shaken her more than she cared to admit. The woman's hands trembled as she poured him a cup of coffee. "Yes, I suppose he did." She sighed, sat down the coffee pot, and shifted her long auburn braid over the shoulder of a green-striped dress. "He told me I should accept Glover's offer or more bad things would happen. I don't want to admit it, but...he frightened me."

He didn't stop to think about the gesture. It felt right to put one of his rough hands over her hand lying on the table. Warmth spread through his veins at the small, but work-worn hand beneath his. It surprised him when she turned the hand and clasped his, tight, like she wanted his comfort.

Well now...

Unaccustomed to any show of emotion, John cleared his throat, gave her hand a warm clasp and released it. His hand shook as he picked up his fork. Been a long time since he held a woman's hand.

"I don't like him coming here," John stabbed a bite of apple, put it in his mouth, and chewed. The sweet taste of cinnamon caressed his taste buds like a kiss. It took a struggle to pull his mind back to the distasteful conversation. "I went into town like I told you I would. Had a run in with Glover at the saloon. Told him I knew he was in it with Ransom. Guess this proves they're in cahoots. Whatever it is they're doing."

A fearful look passed over Annabelle's face, her green eyes staring off at a problem he couldn't see. "They want people off their property. Ransom almost admitted it. Hank and I talked later and I'm afraid he might leave if it gets too dangerous here." Annabelle sighed. One finger followed the rim of her coffee cup as she looked around her home with a wistful expression. "Maybe I should go ahead and sell out. Maybe it's not worth trying to hang on here. They've beaten Hank. Torn down my fences. Maybe even killed Thomas. I should give up."

172

"Don't do that."

John didn't mean to sound so forceful, but the memory of those shallow graves haunted him. *What if Annabelle sold out and ended up the same way? Selling was no guarantee to stay alive.*

"This morning, I found something—a burnt-out wagon, and I think what's left of the Montgomery family."

"The Montgomerys?" Annabelle narrowed her eyes in thought and pursed her lips. After a few minutes, she shoved away her cup and snapped her fingers. "I remember them. They lived near the river. Wasn't he the one who bred horses for the army?"

John nodded.

"Clara mentioned they sold out and left because of Violet Montgomery's health. But whenever I saw the woman, she seemed as strong as an ox. "You say you found what's..." He saw realization in Annabelle's eyes when she understood his meaning.

Eyes wide with horror, she whispered, "What's...left of them. Th-they're dead? How?"

"Maybe why's a better question. They'd already sold out to Glover, and were leaving. Why kill them unless somebody feared they might cause trouble once they were gone? Most men don't like being cheated. Travis Montgomery strikes me as the kind who'd raise a fuss if he lost out to somebody like Glover. All I can figure is that someone—Glover, Ransom or the gang—wanted to make certain that Travis could never tell the railroad they were forced off their land."

"They had children." Annabelle looked sick at the thought.

John laid down his fork, unable to stomach another morsel of the delicious pie. He'd tried not to think of Montgomery's three sons. The small graves reminded him again about Ethan. He hadn't heard from him since the day after they'd set fire to the cabin and hid the rifles. Maybe it was time to check up on Ethan again.

Thinking of Ethan reminded him of another young man. Christopher.

"There's something else you need to know."

Annabelle sat up straighter, like she might be steeling her body for more bad news. "I suppose it can't be any worse than what's already happened."

"I'm not sure it's good or bad." He told her about running into Christopher Jones the night before and his offer to help.

"And you said he could?" Those green eyes pinned him down like a knife. For just a second, he remembered how stern Ada could be when he'd done something she didn't agree with. "Are you sure that's a good idea, John? What if he's being used by the gang to trick you? I can see Glover or Ransom using him. Especially now they know you've figured out they're mixed up in this land grab together."

"I thought of that too." John shifted in the chair, doubting himself all over again. "but I got a feeling the boy's sincere. That he does want to help. I guess I'll find out shortly. Last night I sent him in to stay with Patrick at the saloon. I figured I'd ride over here and talk to you, then go on into town."

At some point, he needed to find time to check on Ethan too. So much for what Sheriff Crane thought of as his "nice, quiet, life on the ranch."

"Well, I thank you for the pie and coffee." He shoved back the chair and stood, ignoring the shooting pains up his leg. "Is

Hank going to be around if Ransom comes back? I don't like to leave you here alone."

She nodded. "He's out looking for Prince Oxford again, but he's going to stay in the barn until..." she opened her hands and made a hopeless gesture.

"We'll straighten it out," John promised, "and find a way to live in peace again. I may not be the sheriff anymore, but I still want to see justice done. For Sam, the Montgomerys, and Thomas."

The smile she gave him warmed him clear down to his toes. "Thank you, John. I know you will."

***

Wilder Ranch

Next Day

"Uncle John! Uncle John!"

The frantic pounding on his door woke John early the next morning. Despite his intention of heading into town after leaving Annabelle's the afternoon before, he'd had to give up the idea. It was all he could do to pull himself up into the saddle and lead Ranger back to the ranch. His leg often took time to go into spasms, and he knew it would be foolhardy to ride any farther than necessary.

He made it back to the ranch, limped around doing chores, breathing hard, and collapsed on his bed before the sun set. After a painful night, he'd managed to fall into a troubled sleep near dawn.

Now this...

"I'm coming," he groaned, pulling himself out of his rumpled bed. Thankfully, this morning, his leg pain had gone from a roar to a dull throb.

He yanked on a pair of pants over his long johns, pulled up a limp suspender and hurried to open the door.

"Lily? What are you doing out here so early?"

"Oh, Uncle John, it's Ethan."

His heart stopped for a beat, breath frozen. *Ethan's dead.*

"Is he?" John forced the words past numb lips.

"I don't know. I don't know what's become of him." Lily wailed, red eyed and weeping. She threw herself into his arms.

As John patted her back, trying to comfort the girl, she told him what she knew. "No one has seen him since early yesterday. He didn't come home last night. I'm so frightened. Please help me, Uncle John."

"Come on in and sit down. I'll fix us a pot of coffee, and you can tell me what you know." He gave her another reassuring pat on the back, wiped a calloused finger under one eye to brush away the tears. Despite his own fears, he managed a shaky smile of comfort. "Maybe it's not as bad as it seems. Ethan's a great one to stay out hunting all night."

Once he got Lily settled on a chair, he put on water for coffee, building up a small fire in the stove. John hurried into the bedroom to put on clean clothes; a worn pair of brown trousers and a dark brown cotton shirt Ada had made one Christmas.

Barefoot, he came back into the kitchen to find Lily twisting a damp handkerchief and staring off into the distance. "I'm so frightened," she repeated.

John sat down across from her at the table and took her hand. "Now, tell me what you know, Lily. When did you last see Ethan?"

The fire crackled in the stove, sending out puffs of wood smoke. Soon, the brewing coffee added a comforting scent into the kitchen and John got up to pour them both a tin cup.

"Yesterday, Ethan said he was going out to check the wheat field. A couple of the hands went with him. Everything was fine when they all came in at dinnertime."

He nudged the cup of coffee closer to her and felt a sense of relief when she lifted it to her lips and took a sip, cradling the warm cup in her hands. "Okay, that's fine. Then what happened?"

"About suppertime, the hands came in. They said Ethan told them he had somewhere to go, and he'd be along later."

"Did he say where?"

Lily shook her head; fresh tears coursed down her cheeks. "I kept thinking he just lost track of time and he'd be in during the night. But he..." she gulped, "Ethan never came home. Something's happened to him. I just know it."

Chapter Twenty-Five

A hollow feeling settled in John's stomach as he listened to Lily. None of this sounded good. "Does anyone know where he planned to go? Any of your hands say they saw the direction he headed."

Lily shook her head. "Benny, one of the boys, said Ethan mentioned going to scout along the Pecos River, near the old ferry. But he couldn't remember if that was yesterday or another time. I'm so scared, Uncle John. What if Ethan found out what happened to Pa and decided to go after the gang?"

Even though he'd had the same thought, John didn't want her to worry more than she already was. "Look, Lily, I'll find him."

John didn't know what to do with her in the meantime. Sending her home might not be wise.

"You ride along with me until we get to town. It doesn't seem safe for you to be on your own right now."

"You think something's happened to Ethan? Like Pa? Oh, Uncle John! What will I do if he's gone too?" This brought on a fresh burst of tears.

"Now, stop that kind of talk. Let me put on my boots and we'll head into town. You can stay with Miz Dawson. I'll find him, Lily." *Or die trying.*

As soon as John got Lily into town, he took her to Dawson's Mercantile. Impatient to be searching, he took the time to explain to Clara what was going on and to ask if Lily could stay. As he thought, Clara was glad of the company and help with sorting out the rest of their damaged merchandise.

"You just leave her with me, John," Clara said as he put Lily into her capable hands. Clara put a comforting arm around Lily and drew her into the store. It took a load off John's mind. Lily would be safe, and Clara would find a way to keep her thoughts from worrying about Ethan.

I'll do enough of that for both of us.

John had no real destination in mind as he turned Ranger toward the river. Even though Ethan had mentioned the old ferry dock, John didn't head there straight away. It wasn't a place where someone could disappear. Too many cattlemen used the low spots in the river to herd cattle across at that place.

As John rode past Patrick's saloon, he thought of stopping in to see if his friend had seen Ethan. This early, the doors were closed and shuttered, so he decided against it, although he was curious to know if Christopher was still there.

Time for that later. Right now, Ethan's life might be in danger. *If he's still alive...*

John took his time riding up and down the few streets of the town. It was early enough most places of business were just waking up. He passed Mr. Johansson at the blacksmith shop, heating up the fire in his forge. After a wave of greeting, John hurried on. Millie from the café passed him with a market basket perched on one ample hip of a pink-striped dress. Her ruddy, plump cheeks grinned as she headed toward her kitchen. A couple of young boys—freshly washed faces, cowlicks slicked down—raced toward the school at the edge of town. Too early for school so they must be up to some shenanigans. They gave him a wary glance as John rode past.

John came to the edge of town and headed toward the Pecos River. There were plenty of places for a person to hide along the banks. Or for someone to drop a body, if it came to that.

As he had when he was sheriff, John tied Ranger to a nearby maple branch and got down to scout along the edge of the woods.

He'd just about given up hope of finding anything when he noticed a lone horse, riderless, wandering aimlessly near a grove of trees, cropping off leaves. The empty saddle, reins dragging clutched John's heart. *Ethan?*

It looked like the stout Morgan Ethan had ridden the night they burnt down the cabin. The horse shied, whinnied, and sidestepped away when John walked closer. "Easy there, fella, easy. Where's your rider?"

The Morgan snorted, tossed back his head, and stepped toward the trees. Just before he could run, John caught the reins and held tight. The horse stepped back into a soft patch of mud.

Plenty of horse prints, some boot prints, others too stomped out to look like more than indents in the mud. There was enough of a story left in the dirt to show a scuffle of some kind, deep imprints, broken branches. There was even a long, smooth path, like maybe a man had been dragged a short distance.

Stepping to the side, careful not to erase the path, John followed the drag marks into a small glade. A pile of rocks had drops of dark liquid on them … blood. John put his finger down to touch one spot and came up with blood. Recently shed blood. He took a step back and felt a pebble or something under his boot.

Lifting his foot, he spied a single gun casing. John picked it up and clenched it in his hand.

Someone had waylaid Ethan here. Maybe shot to frighten the horse or make a point. Or given Ethan a flesh wound to force him to dismount. The drops of blood weren't enough to indicate a man had been seriously wounded or killed. *Not yet.*

The bullet casing told him worse news than that.

Ransom had captured Ethan.

***

"Hank, there you are," Annabelle couldn't help the relief she felt to see the older man ride into the barnyard later that afternoon. "I thought for sure you'd be out earlier this morning."

And how long am I going to keep depending on him? He's got his own life with Clara and his cattle—how can I keep presuming he will be a free ranch hand for the rest of his life? Maybe I'm fooling myself, that I can run a profitable ranch alone. "I know I rely on you too much, Hank, please forgive me. It's just, with all that's been going on, I was worried."

"Well now, Annie, I woulda been out sooner, but there's lots going on in town. I ran into John. He was going to the saloon to get Patrick to help him do a little tracking."

"Tracking?"

"It's young Ethan, Sam Garrett's boy. He's missing. John thinks Ethan tried to go after Ransom himself and now he's certain the gang has him. John found Ethan's horse and a bullet casing along the riverbank."

She lifted a hand to her lip. "How awful! Maybe you'd rather be helping them track down the gang."

Hank laughed. "Annie, I'd be like a one-armed man in a rope-tying contest trying to help John Wilder and Patrick Malone do anything. Best I stay here and help you. If they need me, they'll ask. I figured to go look for Prince Oxford again this afternoon."

She couldn't help feeling part of this was her fault, but when she said as much to Hank, he shook his head of white hair. "And how you figure that? You ain't done nothing but try to stay peaceable on your ranch."

"It just feels like things are getting worse. Ethan wanted justice for his pa, John told me. What if something happens to him too? Maybe if I'd have sold out to Glover, he'd have left the young boy alone."

"Don't see how." Hank scratched his head in puzzlement. "If Ransom has Ethan, it's because the boy went out looking to capture him, not because of you keeping your ranch."

Annabelle knew she couldn't explain, but maybe she could find a way to help. "Hank? Would you mind if I rode into town? There are some errands I need to run."

As expected, Hank didn't mind at all. "Let me hitch up the buggy for you," he offered. "And don't you worry about a thing while you're gone. I'm going to find that bull today!"

It didn't take long for Annabelle to ride into town. Her first thought was to see if she could find John and ask him about Ethan, but she didn't see him or Mr. Malone. As she drove Cletus past Millie's Café, she saw Miz Millie sweeping the front of the boardwalk before the restaurant.

"Good afternoon, Millie. Have you seen John Wilder around?"

To Annabelle's surprise, Millie gave her a scowl, turned her back, and refused to answer.

"Have I done something to offend you, Millie?" she asked, unsure what it might have been.

The woman didn't answer, just went inside the café and slammed the door behind her. Hard.

Wonder what's wrong with her? Clara will know, surely.

Annabelle pulled back the wagon brake in front of the mercantile, looped the reins over the wagon seat and jumped down. As she reached the top step and stopped to open the door, Mrs. Vaughn came out, a market basket tucked through one arm. "Good afternoon, Mrs. Vaughn. How are you today?"

To Annabelle's shock, the banker's wife glared at her just as Millie had, twisted her head to look in the other direction, and hurried past.

Now what's all that about?

Annabelle opened the door, heard the pleasant tinkle of the bell and waited for Clara to come from behind the baize curtains. "Oh, Annabelle, what brings you into town? Hank said he was going out to the ranch. Nothing's happened, has it?"

"No, everything is fine. Hank is there," she answered, relieved her friend didn't react as the other women in town had. "I had a couple of errands to do and thought now was a good time while someone was home to watch the ranch. Clara, tell me something? Why are people treating me strangely today?"

"Strangely?" Clara asked, but not as if it were a big surprise. Almost like Clara knew what she meant. "How do you mean?"

Annabelle explained about Millie and Mrs. Vaughn. "Have I done something to offend them?"

"It's not that..." Clara twisted her hands in the pale blue apron around her waist. Looking around as if she didn't want to be overheard, she leaned across the wooden counter and motioned Annabelle to come closer. In a voice just above a whisper, she said, "It's Mr. Glover. It's his doing."

"What's his doing?"

183

"He's been going all over town, spreading vicious rumors about you. Saying things about you and John Wilder that... well...I don't believe a word of it, mind you, but others aren't so sensible."

"What kind of rumors?" A chill ran up and down Annabelle's arms.

Clara looked near tears. "Oh, dear, I'd rather not say. He's just spreading all kinds of lies about you, so people won't sell to you or help you...or do anything. He came in here this morning and told me I should tell Hank not to help you at all! And he just about ordered me not to sell you anything from the mercantile. Or else."

"Or else what?" Annabelle pressed, sick to her stomach at this revelation. Poor Clara looked like she'd burst out crying any second, and if she kept wringing her apron in her hands, the fabric would rip in two.

"I'm not certain. Oh, Annabelle, he's such a powerful person in town. Even if we know the rumors aren't true, some people will believe them. Mrs. Vaughn told me her husband is going to ask you to close your account at the bank and go elsewhere."

"He can't do that!"

Or maybe he could.

A sinking sensation settled in Annabelle's middle. Isaac Glover was powerful enough to have his way in Pecos River. To run her out of town with his rumors and insinuations.

Maybe I should sell him the ranch and just leave town.

Chapter Twenty-Six

Near Pecos River

"I'm hoping we can get Ethan back before sundown," John said as he rode along the riverbank with Patrick and Christopher. "If we can't..." He left off before speaking about his fears. The longer Ransom kept Ethan, the less likely they were to rescue him alive.

After finding the blood and bullet casing, John had gone straight to Patrick's saloon. As he'd often done in the past, he asked Patrick to step in and help him track down the gang. For years before opening the saloon, Patrick was one of the best bounty hunters John had ever known. In all his years as sheriff, there had been more than a dozen times Patrick rode with him and Sam to hunt down an outlaw. Today, John was grateful to have Patrick and Christopher by his side.

Thankfully, Christopher had been with Patrick, still willing to help and leave the gang. Without Christopher's help, they wouldn't have known to travel toward a canyon about fifteen miles up in the hills.

"He's not always there," Christopher hastened to tell them as they rode along the hard-packed road, three abreast, "but a lot of time the gang hides out there after they've done something close to town. We can try there anyway. If they aren't there, I can show you some other places. Ransom likes to keep moving around so's we don't get caught."

Patrick leaned over on his sturdy gray mule and spit over the saddle. "You best be tellin' the truth boy, or you'll have the devil to pay and a curse on ye."

Christopher paled a second but then sat up taller in the saddle. "I can't guarantee they'll be there, Mr. Malone, but they go there often. It's one of the places we've been to. That's all I'm saying."

"Good a place as any to look," John agreed as he gripped the reins in a tight hand. When his knuckles ached, he tried to relax but then grew tense again. *There's so much at stake! I've got to save Sam's boy.*

"I gave up long ago trying to guess the Red Hand Gang's whereabouts," he said, hoping his voice sounded steadier than his quivering insides.

"Well, this direction leads kinda in the way of the tracks from where we saw the scuffle," Christopher said. "And we've found some horseshoe prints since then. So maybe it's where they took Ethan."

"Let's keep going then," John said.

It was mid-afternoon when they approached the hills. "Up there." Christopher pointed to a gray rock sticking up like a finger pointing to the sky. "See where the lone pine grows out of the crevice? If you go past that, there's a narrow opening into the canyon. They'll likely have a guard there. I could go first; they won't know that I've decided to ride with you. They'll just think I've been off somewhere."

John thought about it. Wondering if Christopher had led them into a trap after all. "No, I'll ride along alone. See how it feels. You and Patrick hold back until you see if I need your help."

"Are ya sure?" Patrick asked.

John nodded. He eased Ranger down the path, heading up toward the pinnacle of rock. Small rocks covered the dusty path, but a clear track of horse prints showed riders not long ago. Nothing stirred in the quiet afternoon. The warm sun beat down across the shoulders of his plaid shirt, up ahead a bird called to its mate from a branch of sagebrush. As John neared the opening an uneasy feeling came over him, a prickling along the back of his neck, like all the hair was standing on end. *A warning?*

"Whoa, Ranger," he muttered, pulling the horse back to a slower pace.

John went a little farther along the road. A slide of rock moved under Ranger's shoe and scattered down a small cliff. The sounds of rock hitting rock were as loud as explosions. If the gang were unaware he was inching closer, the rocks would have alerted them by now.

A shadow moved by the lone pine a second before John heard the retort echo through the hills.

Gunfire!

A trap!

They watched us coming!

John yanked the Colt from his holster and fired blindly toward the pine.

Patrick and Christopher galloped up alongside him, weapons firing to give him backup. The fire from the rocks came in an unrelenting stream of pot shots, hitting and chipping off pieces of rock, or chunking out dirt in front of the horses' hooves. John managed to take cover behind a large boulder. From the corner of his eye, he noticed Christopher drop from the saddle and scurry, belly down into a crevice.

Seconds later, he heard a yelp from Patrick. The old mule brayed in either fright or anger, dancing circles in the dust. As

John turned around, he saw blood streaming into the wind from a wound on Patrick's shoulder.

"Blast ya varmints!" Patrick yelled, showing the wound must not be too serious. It hadn't seemed to stop him from coming forward, a sawn-off shotgun in the other outstretched hand.

"Patrick, get back! Go!" John hollered over the sound of gunshots.

Not listening, Patrick kept urging the reluctant mule toward the fight.

Darn stubborn fool! He's gonna get himself killed.

Thankfully, the mule had more sense than Patrick. As a bullet grazed his flank, the mule gave one bellow of outrage, turned and ran back down the road faster than John had ever seen it move. Patrick had all he could do to control the frantic animal, and they were soon out of sight around a bend in the road.

"Christopher!" John called to the younger man. "We're pinned down. Probably outnumbered. Let's retreat!"

Bullets pelted around thick and fast. John figured any second, they'd both be dead from either a well-aimed or lucky shot. Ranger, used to gunfights, reared and whinnied.

"You sure?" Christopher asked, leaning against a rock, long hair fanned around a sweaty face.

John nodded, grabbed the reins of Christopher's Morgan, and led the horse to his hiding place. Christopher pulled himself into the saddle and needed no urging to head back to town.

"You think they'll follow us?" Christopher asked as they raced toward Pecos River.

John kept looking over his shoulder as he slapped the ends of the reins on Ranger's side to keep the horse heading toward safety. They rode a couple of miles before it became clear no one had followed them.

It wasn't until they came within sight of the town John could relax. The tension left his body, and he realized he'd gripped the reins so tight his nails bit into his palms. "They didn't follow us," he said to Christopher.

"That's good," the young man said, "but you gotta wonder why. Now they know we can find them again."

That wasn't John's only concern right then. "What's worse is they know we're looking to rescue Ethan. If he's still alive."

***

Furious at how the rescue had fallen apart, John rode into town feeling like a whipped pup.

"What do you want to do now, Mr. Wilder?" Christopher asked.

"I'm going to make sure Patrick is all right, then figure something out. We can't afford to make another mistake. Not with Ethan's life at stake. You have any idea what the gang might do?"

Christopher shook his head, brushed the sweaty strands of hair off his dusty face and peered toward the edge of town. "It's hard to say. I never knew Ransom to take a prisoner before. Usually, he just goes ahead and kil..."

John knew Christopher stopped short at saying Ransom usually killed his captives. *Not that I didn't know that already.* "Looks like Patrick's mule is in front of the saloon. Let's stop and see how badly he got shot."

They hitched their horses in front of the saloon and went into the dim, cool room. Normally, a crowd would have been gathered, but today only Patrick and Mr. Squire were seated at one of the tables, a basin of bloody water and stained linen towels on top. Patrick's ruddy face had paled but he only winced as Mr. Squire pressed on the wound.

"How bad is it?" John asked, pulling out a chair across from Patrick.

Christopher stood around the edge of the table, staring at the men but not speaking.

Mr. Squire's dark cheeks turned up into a grin. "It take more'n a bullet to stop Mr. Patrick," he said in his southern accent. His short, capable hands twisted a length of bandage across the upper part of Patrick's arm. "It hit him in the fat part of the shoulder—just be a graze. He be as good as new iffen he lets it heal."

"All right, all right," Patrick shoved away Mr. Squire's hand and yanked his shirt back over the shoulder. His hairy chest had dried blood but other than the bandage, Patrick looked unharmed. "Durn fool tore a hole in me new shirt," he fumed, poking his finger into the jagged rip. "Cost me fifty cents too."

"I'm glad that's all they tore a hole in, Patrick," John said. "What did you think you were doing out there? I told you to wait until I'd had a look."

Patrick snorted. "A fine thing, laddy, me holdin' back when the gunfire started. An' what was gonna happen to you? I was tryin' to rescue young Ethan, like you were."

"I know but..." John didn't get to finish his through before the batwing doors of the saloon swung open and Annabelle ran into the room.

"John? I saw you ride into town and need to talk to you...what happened?" She asked, catching sight of Patrick with the blood-soaked shirt draped over one shoulder and his hairy chest exposed. "Are you hurt, Mr. Malone?"

Patrick flushed to the roots of his white hair and attempted to pull the edges of the shirt to cover his bare chest. "Tis just a flesh wound," Patrick assured her, "an' when this man here gets done jerking my arm around, I'll be just fine."

Mr. Squire gave a chuckle and winked at Annabelle, as he gave Patrick's bandage a final twist and tied the edges together. "It just be a flesh wound, bleed a lot. He be sore for a few days, but he be fine."

She turned those green eyes at John. "What happened? Clara said you'd gone to search for Ethan, that he's missing. Did you find him?"

"Not yet," John sighed, already feeling it might be too late for Sam's boy. "We tracked the gang to a place in the hills, but they ambushed us. Patrick got shot so me an' Christopher came on back to town. We're gonna need help."

"Oh, dear," the words came out of Annabelle in a tired moan. She sat down heavily in a chair and looked around like she had more troubles too.

"Did something else happen at the ranch? Hank told me he was going out there today."

"No, nothing happened. I just came into town and..." a quick glance at the other men and she clamped her lips together. Clearly, Annabelle didn't want to share anything with him in front of Patrick, Christopher, or Mr. Squire.

"You all just set down," Mr. Squire said, as he stood up, gathering the bloody basin of water and the used strips of cloth. "Let me rustle up a meal an' some hot coffee. You all got plans to make to catch them outlaws."

John wanted to tell him not to bother—they didn't have time to eat—but then thought better of it. It was true. They did need to talk and plan, not go off half-cocked and try to ramrod into Ransom's lair. Ethan's life depended on it.

Chapter Twenty-Seven

"I'll go take care of the horses and the mule," Christopher offered and left the room. His spurs jangled as he crossed the floor and let himself out the door.

That left John, Annabelle, and Patrick around the battered table. Although the saloon should be full at that time of the day, Mr. Squire put up a sign on the door—*Closed for Repairs.* Patrick waved a weary hand and didn't try to stop him. Maybe the flesh wound was bothering him more than John thought. Patrick wasn't a young man anymore.

While they waited for the meal, no one talked much. Annabelle looked like she had troubles on her mind, but didn't speak them. Mr. Squire hurried in with hot cups of coffee and a pitcher of cream. In a few minutes, there was a good aroma of frying ham and potatoes mixed with the scent of stale tobacco in the saloon. John was surprised when his stomach rumbled, embarrassed to be thinking of food when Ethan was still missing.

Patrick must have sensed his distress. "We got ta keep up our strength, laddy, to find the boy. Nothing to be ashamed about."

Soon, Mr. Squire had set plates of fried ham, potatoes, and black-eyed peas before them all. Christopher, back inside from taking care of the horses, joined them. Everyone ate with little talk, although Annabelle mostly played with the food on her plate, only taking a bite or two.

Something's wrong. I need to find out what.

With his stomach full, John felt more capable of finding Ethan. "We need a better plan. Ransom has had Ethan, probably since last night. Anyone have any ideas?"

He looked first at Annabelle; she had dark circles under her eyes and a worried furrow on her forehead. She kept clutching the long, auburn braid and twisting the end between her fingers. "Maybe we should see if Sheriff Crane can do anything?" she suggested. "Couldn't he stop Glover and Ransom?"

Patrick gave a low chuckle. "Could if he would."

Although he figured it might not do any good, John realized there was some sense in asking Crane. "It's not such a bad idea, Patrick. He is the sheriff, and Ethan went missing from his town. I think I'll head over there and talk to him."

No one else wanted to go with him. Patrick had no use for the sheriff, considering him a fool. Christopher feared the sheriff might recognize him and put him in jail. As for Annabelle, she looked like a stiff wind might knock her down. "Maybe I'd better wait here," she muttered, "then I need to head home."

As soon as he had a talk with Sheriff Crane, he needed to talk to Annabelle and find out what troubled her.

***

"What do you mean you can't do anything?" John had planned to keep his temper when he spoke to Crane. From the last couple of times he'd talked to the man, he knew how quickly things could end up in a shouting argument.

"I'm telling you, Ransom's taken Ethan. He disappeared in your town, seems like that makes you responsible for helping find him." John leaned the palms of his hands flat on the desk and glared a few feet from the sheriff's face.

This afternoon, Sheriff Crane didn't have a tray of food on his desk. All he had in his hand was a mug of bitter-smelling coffee. As John explained the events of finding Ethan's riderless horse, the bullet casing, and going to track down the outlaws, Sheriff Crane kept a steely eyed glance on him. Not once did the man nod or grimace or even shove back his chair, ready for action.

"There's nothing I can do." It was the second time he'd repeated the statement that made John's blood boil. "You got no proof Ransom's responsible for taking Ethan. Or even that he's involved. I can't go off on a wild goose chase just because you think you've figured it out."

John wanted to punch the man in his stupid face. Instead, he leaned over the desk, breathing hard, staring in shock at the small man before him. "I don't got a signed confession from Ransom that he took Ethan, but it's pretty clear to me he's the one to blame. Ethan didn't make a secret of the fact he's been trying to find out who killed Sam."

"Says you."

"You're a fool, Crane!" John exploded. "I can't believe you'd ignore the evidence and let Ethan die."

"What evidence? You got a bullet casing and a horse without a rider. Maybe the boy got thrown. Maybe he got in a fight and somebody shot at him. Maybe he ran off. You ain't got no proof Ransom did anything."

John could feel himself getting angrier by the second. If he stayed there another minute, he'd pummel Sheriff Crane into the hardwood floor—and who would that profit? "You won't do anything at all?" he asked in what he hoped was a civil voice. "Not even look around or go out to that canyon with me?"

"Look, John, I don't want a target on my back too. If there's no real proof..."

The words told him all he needed to hear. Sheriff Crane was too afraid to do anything to bring down Ransom and the Red Hand Gang. If he wanted to save Ethan and bring down the gang, he'd have to do it himself.

***

Hollis Ranch

I should have gone back out and searched for Ethan on my own. Not let Crane's foolishness or anything else stop me.

John lay on Annabelle Hollis's parlor sofa, his long legs draped over one hard wooden arm of the boughten piece of furniture. It sure would have been more comfortable sleeping on the floor, but she'd insisted the sofa would be softer. *Ha!*

It had been a few hours since the disappointing, but not unexpected, meeting with Sheriff Crane. The man had proved before that he didn't want to go up against the Red Hand Gang if he could find a way out of it. Sam would have had a few choice words for Crane. A man who shirked his duty was a coward as far as Sam was concerned.

Not like me and Sam. John cradled his arm under his neck and sighed. *I hope Ethan is still alive to save.* It grated on his mind that he hadn't been able to keep searching.

When John returned to the saloon, he found that despite Patrick's telling him the wound was "nothing," it had brought on a fever and shakes. Mr. Squire had helped his boss to bed with Christopher's help.

Although John wanted to go right back on the trail after Ethan, he knew better than to ride out alone. Now that Ransom knew he might be coming for him, he'd ride into an ambush for sure.

If I get myself killed, there won't be anyone to help Ethan or Annabelle.

When Annabelle said she needed to get back to her ranch to feed her animals, John knew he should head home too. Whatever else happened, he had a ranch full of animals to care for.

"As soon as I get my animals fed and watered," he promised as they rode home, "I'll come stay the night at your place. You shouldn't be alone now that Ransom knows I'm after Ethan."

"Why should that affect me?" she asked. "Although Clara did say she couldn't send Herbert out tonight and I'm not sure Hank plans to stay…not after Glover's spreading gossip."

"Then it's best I make certain you're safe," John said. As they rode along, Annabelle had told him what Clara had said about Glover spreading rumors. "It's mighty suspicious that Glover's going so far to make folks turn against you. Even if Hank does plan to stay the night, it won't hurt to have both of us stand guard."

The strange thing was, when they reached Annabelle's ranch, there was no one there. No sign of Hank, no note, nothing. An uneasy tingle started up John's spine. "Look, I've got to go take care of my animals. You need to get in your house and lock up until I get back."

"I'm perfectly capable of defending myself," she said with those green eyes shooting sparks. "I've got stock to care for too, you know."

Rather than argue and waste valuable time, John helped Annabelle care for her animals. Then, while she cooked supper behind a locked door, he rode as fast as he could to his ranch, fed and watered his stock, milked Bossie, and ended up back at the Hollis place by dusk. They'd eaten a fine supper and now he lay on Annabelle's hard sofa, worried and unable to sleep.

There had been no sign of Hank anywhere. If he'd headed back to town, it stood to reason they'd have passed him somewhere along the way. It was only another peculiar thing, in too many odd happenings of the day.

Tomorrow, I have to go search for Ethan again.

At about midnight, gunshots jolted him out of a sound sleep. A second later bright, flickering flames lit up the sky outside the parlor window.

John jumped up, reaching for his rifle just as Annabelle screamed.

Chapter Twenty-Eight

"John!" Annabelle called, her voice high with terror.

The scream turned John's blood cold, fearing the worst, but a second later Annabelle ran into the room, a rifle clenched in her hands. Her long red hair flowed down across the shoulders of a white muslin gown and worn gray robe. "It's them! They're burning my ranch!"

Together, they ran to stare out the parlor window. The night had turned blacker than the inside of a well, no moon to light up the faces of the men on horseback, riding roughshod through Annabelle's barnyard.

As near as John could make out, there were six or seven men, whooping and hollering as they tossed burning torches into stacks of hay, the storage building and then the barn. A scent of kerosene overpowered the sweet night air, giving speed to the flames racing up the sides of her sturdy barn. Chickens ran around, clucking their distress. A couple of squealing piglets, released from their pen in the barn, darted around the house and down the road.

Two men tied ropes around the fence posts and yanked hard enough to drag them down. A dozen market cattle stormed through the fence, heading for the fields, bellowing and stomping through her kitchen garden.

With a cry of rage, Annabelle hurried to the door and fumbled with the latch hook. "I'll stop those men if it's the last thing I do."

"No!" John warned, grabbing her arm and pulling her away from the door. "We're safer inside. Unless they set the house on fire too."

Then we're probably dead.

199

He'd been in worse situations with Sam, but tonight the idea of not being able to protect Annabelle filled him with a terror he'd never experienced before. For the first time in years, he found himself hopeful there was an Almighty looking out for them. *Please God, can you save us one more time?*

More a man of action than prayer, John took a deep breath, busted out the glass in the parlor window and fired into a swarm of men on horseback. He'd heard it said the Lord helped those who helped themselves an' John Wilder wasn't going to let anyone get the best of him while he could keep fighting.

"I'm not going to stand here and let them burn up everything I've got!" Annabelle argued.

"No," John agreed, firing and knowing he hadn't hit anything. The men were too far away, stampeding the cattle, sending them further away from the burning buildings. "Just shoot and hope they don't set the house on fire. If they do..."

He could make out in the dim light from the fireplace how pale Annabelle's face became at the thought. But at least she took the idea of dying with courage.

"Why those lousy..." Annabelle let loose a curse John expected to hear in Patrick's saloon. She took aim and fired the rifle out the window in the direction of the men's shadows. It didn't seem to stop them. If anything, the return gunfire only added to their fury.

John got off a few shots but with the darkness of the night and the way the men kept moving, he knew he hadn't shot anyone. As he bent to reload his Colt, a stray bullet came through the window and grazed his arm. He dropped the Colt and grabbed at the stinging wound, blood oozing through his fingers.

"Are you shot?" Annabelle asked, reloading her rifle and aiming out the window.

200

John scrabbled for the Colt, blood running down the barrel. "It's nothing. Let's try to keep them from away from the house."

By now the outbuildings were big fireballs, lighting up the sky and showing dark shadows of men on horses. One man rode up and knocked over two rain barrels, spilling the water onto the ground. Another yanked on a clothesline and tugged it into the dirt. They rode around the house, taking potshots, busting out windows and raining bullets on the tin porch roof. But, thankfully, for whatever reason, they didn't set fire to the house.

They don't plan to kill us then.

It was almost like they'd been given a signal; the men stopped whooping and galloping as another horse came from the west, riding past the burning barn.

"What the…" John muttered as a man rode in view of the front porch of the house, dragging a man behind him. A length of rope tied to the saddle horn held the young man as he tripped and fell, struggling to keep his face from the ground.

"Hello in there!" The man's ragged voice called out. "Sheriff Wilder. I know you're in there."

That voice. He hadn't heard it in years, but John knew exactly who the voice belonged to. "Ransom Baxter! What do you think you're doing here?"

A sinking feeling came over John as he stared at the barely conscious man at the end of the rope. As Baxter's horse stopped, the boy tried to crawl upright, then toppled into the dust.

Ethan!

Enough of a glow came from the burning fires to see Ethan's bloody, bruised face, his dark hair matted to his cheeks. It looked like he might be near death.

"I just came by to speak to Mrs. Hollis, to show her what might happen if she doesn't sell the ranch. She either sells or else."

"Or else what?" Annabelle raged at the man, leveling her rifle to her shoulder. "I could kill you right now. You..." she ground out another curse.

Ransom chuckled, deep, evil shadows under his eyes in the half-glow of the flames. "You could, but it wouldn't stop anything. It would only mean this boy's death instantly. If you shoot me, my men will kill him now."

A growl of rage erupted from Annabelle's throat, but she lowered the rifle.

"Let him go!" John called out, knowing that's not what Ransom had in mind.

"I plan to let him go, Sheriff," Ransom agreed, "as soon as Mrs. Hollis sells her ranch. She sells the ranch to me, or the boy dies. Simple as that. And, to show I'm not a dispassionate man, I'll give you until sundown tomorrow."

Before Annabelle could say yes or no, Ransom gave a cruel laugh, wheeled his horse around and took off at a gallop. Ethan's poor, almost lifeless body dragging behind as he tried in vain to get to his feet. By the time Ransom rode past the burning barn, Ethan's body was like a ragdoll, jerked and dragged by a careless hand.

I'm sorry, Sam.

John didn't realize tears were coursing down his cheeks until he felt the taste of salt sting his chapped lips.

***

Is it worth trying to save anything?

Annabelle stared at the burnt-out shell of her barn, the smoldering ruins still sending out wispy gray smoke. Everything she and Thomas had worked for since coming from Missouri now lay in ashes and ember. All gone. Well, not the house, but all her outbuildings. Hank's relentless work over the past year to bring it all back into shape, eaten up in flames.

A stray tear slid down her sunburnt cheek, but she swiped it away with an angry flick of her hand. There probably wasn't any reason not to sell out to Glover or Ransom now. Not long ago she'd worried about her feed being ruined, the loss of profits. That was a minor problem now with her livestock scattered all over, and worse trouble ahead. A boy's life hung in the balance now, the price to pay for keeping her ranch.

If they could believe Ransom, she'd have to sell the ranch or risk losing Ethan Garrett's life. Even though Annabelle didn't know the boy, she'd listened to John as they walked around her ranch, seeing if there was anything to salvage.

The chickens had come back as dawn crested the hills. One of the pigs crawled out from under the porch and even a few of the market cattle had been found close by. The rest were gone or stolen. Who knew?

"We need to figure out a way to save Ethan," John said while they surveyed the ruins by the pale gray pink light of dawn. "If he's not already dead. The way Ransom dragged him out of here, I'm not sure."

Annabelle's stomach twisted at the memory. "I'll have to sell the ranch. There's no other choice. Ransom said he'd let Ethan go."

She remembered the way John snorted, the look he gave her like she was a child who wanted to pretend life could be roses and sunshine all the time. Now, as she stood alone, waiting for John to ride and see if his ranch was still standing, Annabelle wanted to break down and weep.

She'd never felt lower. Sighing, she picked up a stray milk bucket with just a dent in it and turned to walk back to the house. As she dragged her feet through the dust, walking around a broken water barrel, she heard the distant clopping of a horse's hooves.

Annabelle turned, lifted a hand to shade her eyes and saw a rider, coming closer in a cloud of dust. She reached for the Colt in the waist of her dark riding skirt, her hand tight on the grip. Before she could pull it out, she recognized the man sitting astride a familiar golden mare. *Hank!*

"Hank! I thought you either left or were captured by the gang," she said as he stopped the mare and dismounted near her.

"I'd never leave you, Annie, to fend for yourself. I..." A pained expression caught his face as he caught sight of the barn and outbuildings. "I been out trying to round us up some more help to go against that Red Hand Gang, but I see I'm not in time."

"I don't understand."

Hank took off his hat and wiped his wispy white hair back out of his eyes. "Well, after you went to town yesterday, I got to thinking on it. And I figured if that gang was after your land and you didn't want to sell, maybe there were others in the same fix. I rode near about fifty miles in a couple of directions, asking and well..." he gave her a shy grin, "we got help, to go against Glover and maybe the Red Hand Gang. Lots of folks been paid a visit by Glover's lawyer like you and pressured to sell."

"And they don't want to either?"

"Not by a long shot!" he snapped. "A couple had accidents like you've had—feed spoiled, missing cattle. They're tired of it but didn't know how to fight. We figure if we all band together, we can do something. Only, I'm sorry I left you alone to face this. What happened here, Annie?"

Annabelle explained about the attack the night before and Ransom's demand she sell or else. "I think it's the only way to save Ethan."

Hank, just like John, snorted. "Not likely. I wouldn't take the word of an outlaw like Ransom Baxter. But don't you worry none, now that we got help, we'll turn this around. You'll see."

For the first time since Thomas's death, Annabelle felt a thrill of hope through her veins. *We can fight.*

"I didn't expect to find this," Hank said, motioning to the smoldering ruins, "but some of the ranchers are meeting here this afternoon. They had to find someone to take care of their stock so they could come. I kinda hope you don't mind, but I told them you'd cook a meal, maybe have some peach pie."

She laughed at the boyish expression on Hank's face. "I think I can manage that."

Chapter Twenty-Nine

A sigh of contentment rose from Annabelle's lips as she sat on the rocking chair. John sat on the top step of the porch, staring off toward the hills. For the last hour, after he'd helped her wash the dishes, they'd been talking about everything except the outlaws and what might happen. The normal, calm peace of doing a household chore had soothed Annabelle in a way she couldn't imagine. Now, they were enjoying the evening as she and Thomas had so many times in the past.

Annabelle had told him about her childhood, about Mama becoming a schoolteacher. John shared stories of his life and some of the funnier moments of being a sheriff. It surprised her to find herself drawn to him in a way she never thought she ever would again. Almost like those first girlish yearnings she'd had for Thomas when he came calling so many years ago. Like a butterfly fluttered its fragile wings inside her heart.

Am I beginning to care for John Wilder? Could I learn to love another man again?

Evening shadows spread from the sagebrush tree and the chicken coop—the only outbuilding the outlaws hadn't burnt the night before. A heavy odor of smoke and charred wood still filled the air, but Annabelle could detect a faint scent of the peach pie she'd baked for her saviors earlier that evening.

Maybe to someone else, the rugged group of men in their sweat-soaked shirts and muddy boots might look like everyday ranchers or farmers, but Annabelle thought of them as her rescuers. The whole time they spooned in her beef stew and praised her peach pie, she'd listened to them plan how to save her ranch.

"Our ranches, too," a lean, hungry-looking man mumbled as she tried to thank him.

Not long ago, she'd fed ten men around her cramped table and parlor. Listened to them talk to John and Hank about how they would trap Ransom and the gang. The fear that Annabelle felt earlier had been replaced by a bubbling sense of hope and anticipation.

As soon as they'd come up with a plan, every man having a part to play in the final fight, they faded into the hills. Now she and John were sitting on the porch, waiting for sundown to see if Ransom had kept his word about Ethan.

Poor boy.

That was the only unsettling thing about the long afternoon, the uncertainty about Ethan's fate.

"Rider coming," John spoke quietly and stood up.

A fist of fear closed over Annabelle's heart, although she knew Hank was hidden inside the house and two of the other ranchers were nearby with weapons. She stood from the rocking chair and walked to stand by John's side. His strong hand reached out to catch hers in a firm grip.

A man Annabelle didn't recognize reined in a piebald mare at the edge of the steps. Ransom must have sent someone else to do his bidding. This man was younger, dark eyes and long brown hair covering his ears beneath the silly bowler hat. He wore a light-colored leather duster and kept one hand on the saddle horn. Beneath the duster, a worn holster spanned his waist with pearl-handled revolvers showing. Spurs gleamed on mud-spattered boots.

"Evening," John spoke up like it was a social call. "Who might you be?"

"Jack Jones. Got a message for you from Ransom."

The boy's dead.

Annabelle thought she might sink through the wooden steps of the porch.

Why did I try to save the ranch?

John nodded, although he must have been torn up inside too.

"First, I gotta know if the lady plans to sell."

"I'll sell," Annabelle lied, her voice quivering with emotion, "if Ethan is still alive. Ransom was supposed to have him here by sundown."

Jones gave them a wicked lopsided smirk. "As I recall, he told you he'd let you know by sundown. So, what's your answer?"

"I just said I'd sell," Annabelle snapped. "You have someone here tomorrow for me to sign over the papers. And that's only if the boy is still alive. So, help me…if he's dead, I'll put a bullet through your skull."

Jones snickered, flicked a two-fingered salute and pulled the reins to turn his horse around. "I believe you would at that, ma'am. We'll bring your friend when we come tomorrow to have the papers signed."

As she watched Jones ride away, the helpless feeling came back over Annabelle. Even with all the men who'd come to help, she clutched John's arm craving reassurance.

"Tell me we'll be able to save him, to save the ranch? I feel so helpless."

His arm felt solid and strong beneath her fingers as he looked down at her. Those blue eyes were wide open studying her face. Up close she saw the flecks of brown in those calm depths. The spiky way his eyelashes had grown back in after his barn caught fire and the crinkle lines around his mouth.

John's breath warmed her as he took a soft step toward her, his other arm coming around her waist. Annabelle found herself melting inside, filled with an assurance this man would keep her safe.

Before she could stop herself, she raised on tiptoe and tilted her head with the intention of planting a kiss on his cheek. To thank him for being there, for helping her. But as her lips formed for a kiss, Annabelle felt herself drawn like a moth to a flame, seeking out his firm, strong lips. She tightened her hold on his arms and raised forward until their lips touched.

Almost like a spark, she felt both shock and delight as his lips pressed down on hers. The kiss deepened as John responded to her, his breath still scented with peaches and cinnamon. Pressed against his chest, she felt the rapid thumping of his heart rushing forward to meet the wild jumping of her own.

Inside her mind, a guilty voice whispered. *What are you doing? What would Thomas think?*

Annabelle stilled the voices and pressed closer into John's embrace. She had never truly thought she'd feel this depth of emotion for another man again. But suddenly, it felt good and right.

Chapter Thirty

Near the Hollis Ranch

Next Evening

The sun dipped behind the rough, rocky hills in the west. Patches of golden sunlight and deep purple shadows lay over it all, brushed with dots of dark green sagebrush. John crouched behind a cluster of jagged rocks, rifle steady in his hands. Waiting. Praying.

Scattered through the hills, hidden in crevices, behind trees, were friends and neighbors, armed and ready to fight. Hank, Christopher, young Herbert Dawson, Patrick, and other ranchers who'd come to help. This evening, they all wanted justice. Tonight, they would end Ransom and Glover's stranglehold on the town of Pecos River. End it or die trying.

Their plan to trap Ransom and the gang had been simple. John expected Ransom's right-hand man, Jack Jones, to have told him Annabelle would sell her ranch. In exchange, they wanted Ethan back—alive. Hopefully, Jones had spread the false information, and things would come to a showdown that evening.

Earlier that morning, Patrick had ridden out to Annabelle's ranch with the word Ransom was bringing out papers for her to sign about sundown. It was then John had figured out they should be waiting in the hills. Ransom would expect an easy victory, to ride in, and grab the signed deed to the ranch. Whether or not he'd give the deed to Glover was anyone's guess. What he wouldn't expect would be a posse of determined men, ready to fight for justice.

"This time, Ransom, you'll be caught," John whispered to himself. "I swore I'd get you if it's the last thing I do."

A smile tipped John's lips as he clutched the rifle, hoping catching Ransom didn't end his life. Not after that kiss with Annabelle's last night. When this was all over, he wanted to tell her his feelings, to ask her...but no, that could wait.

"Riders coming," Christopher crawled up and told John. Of all the men waiting, he had the most to lose. Especially when his brother and Ransom found out he'd left the gang.

"So, they are." John gave the signal, a mockingbird's call. It was answered by other men in their hiding places. "Time to fight."

Every man pulled up a rifle or pistol, ready to fire at John's second signal.

Ransom Baxter and the Red Hand Gang rode in sitting tall and proud in their saddles. Ransom in his ill-fitting dark suit rode first, followed by Deke Parsons, the wild man who had helped Ransom escape from prison. Jack Jones, in his ridiculous bowler hat, came third, holding the rope of a fourth horse that held a battered and bloodied Ethan. They rode past a rocky hill toward Annabelle's.

"Leave the boy here," Ransom called back to Jones. "Let's make sure Miz Hollis is true to her word. I don't trust any of those sodbusters."

John watched while Jones tied Ethan's horse to a nearby tree. The boy's hands were bound in front of the saddle horn, and he looked half-dead, swaying like he might fall off any second. John gave Christopher a signal for the men to hold back. *I've got to rescue him now! He's been through so much.*

As soon as Ransom's men had passed out of sight, John hurried forward, grabbed Ethan's horse and led him back into hiding behind a nearby outcropping of rock.

"Herbert," he called to Hank's young son as he pulled a limp Ethan out of the saddle. "Stay with him until we get done here." Ethan was still breathing, but his face had taken a terrible beating. He was so bruised it was hard to tell where he'd been injured. He moaned, in pain or fear or both, John didn't know. But thankfully, Ethan was still alive if just barely.

"Yes, sir, Sheriff."

I'm not the...

John shrugged and hurried forward to follow Ransom and the gang. *Maybe I'm no longer the sheriff in town, but it's time someone took charge. Guess that someone is me.*

Even though he'd made Annabelle go into town and stay in hiding, he didn't trust the gang not to create more trouble at the ranch.

"Let's take them, men!" he hollered.

***

Trust Patrick to give a wild war whoop as the men scattered out of hiding and took off after Ransom and his gang. Although John didn't expect the Red Hand Gang to give up without a fight, he wasn't prepared for the way the outlaws fought, almost like cornered bobcats.

John's men surrounded them near Annabelle's barnyard. Deke and Jack took up positions behind the burned out barn. They managed to shoot and keep Patrick and Hank away for several minutes. Maybe they didn't expect Christopher to have turned on them, but he snuck up around his brother, Jack, jabbed him in the ribs with a Winchester rifle and said, "It's over, Jack. Throw down your weapons."

With a snarl of disgust, Jack threw down his Colt but then grabbed Christopher's rifle and tried to wrest it from his hands. In a few minutes, Patrick had entered the fight and between the two of them, they knocked Jack Jones to the ground, trampling his bowler hat.

Deke Parsons, cruel and vicious, was made of sterner stuff. He kept a couple of the ranchers busy firing at them, hitting one man in the shoulder and another in the leg. They exchanged shots as Deke rounded the ruins of the barn and headed for cover behind Annabelle's buggy. After the exchange of intense gunfire, Mr. Johansson, the blacksmith, got off a good shot and hit Deke in the shoulder. The outlaw dropped the weapon, cursing, and raised his other hand in surrender.

The gang had been captured, except for Ransom.

John had followed Ransom as they entered Annabelle's barnyard. The outlaw was wily and sneaky enough to outwit anyone, but John had dealt with him before. The old pain in his leg flared up as a reminder as he tiptoed carefully around the old chicken coop. There weren't many places left to hide on Annabelle's ranch, but John had seen Ransom drop out of the saddle and dart behind the house. For all he knew, the outlaw had gone inside, hoping to find Annabelle to use as a hostage.

"You might as well give it up, Baxter!" John hollered. "We got your men!"

From somewhere nearby, Patrick yelled, "Sheriff Crane is on the way! Herbert saw him riding out from town. Said Glover is with him."

Crane. Glover. Now?

John didn't figure the lawman could do much, but maybe he wanted to take some responsibility for the capture of the Red Hand Gang. As far as John knew there was a hefty reward for their capture. A reward that now belonged to the men who'd fought this evening. *I'll make darn sure they collect it too.*

"Crane can't catch me!" Ransom yelled, giving away his location. "Nobody can send me back to prison. Not even you, Sheriff Wilder! You doomed me once, but you won't take me alive again."

"That's your choice, Baxter!"

John eased around the porch of the house, trying to decide where the outlaw's voice had come from. "You might as well give yourself up, Baxter. You're surrounded; your men have given up."

"Then they're fools," he shouted back. A second later John ducked as Ransom sent a volley of shots toward his head. While none of the bullets hit him, John grimaced and stepped cautiously onto Annabelle's porch. As near as he could figure, Ransom had taken cover by her kitchen door where a small cedar grew.

"Either give yourself up or die, Baxter," John kept his voice calm and steady, easing himself around a corner of the house. The rifle in his hand felt cumbersome so he stood it against the chinked walls of the house. Pulling a Colt revolver from his holster, he checked the chamber, snapped it shut and held it upright. "It's your choice."

"Sure, it's my choice! If I give myself up, I'll swing from a noose this time. I'll die either way."

John couldn't deny the truth of that statement. Ransom Baxter was a wanted man—dead or alive. If he were captured alive, he'd head for a trial and the gallows.

Bang! A bullet whizzed past John's head as Ransom came from behind the house shooting, attempting to escape. His horse was nearby, the reins dangling, and Ransom made an effort to get there.

"Give yourself up," John tried again, coming out from behind the house and aiming at Ransom.

"Never." Ransom raised his gun, aimed straight at John's heart, and pressed the trigger.

John's gimpy leg gave out beneath him. He hit the ground on one knee, lifted the Colt, and fired back.

Ransom gave him a wicked smirk a second before John's bullet hit something vital inside. Blood oozed out the wrinkled white linen shirt, dripping into the dust. His hand dropped in a limp gesture and the gun fell from his hand. It landed with a puff of dirt on the ground.

"You got him," Patrick said as he came running up, rifle ready just in case. "You hit?"

"No," John groaned, "it's just this darned leg injury. Guess maybe I ought to be glad about it today. If I hadn't fallen, Baxter's bullet would have gone straight through my heart."

"As me old mammy would say," Patrick reached out a hand to help John get to his feet, "every cloud has a silver lining."

Sheriff Crane rode up, an annoyed expression on his face. "What's going on out here, Wilder? I should have been told the Red Hand Gang were going to be riding in, causing trouble. Why didn't you tell me?

"I tried to tell you," John said and kept it at that. He gave Glover a look of sheer malice. "Maybe your friend here can tell you more."

"Why would I know anything?" Glover asked. "You can't prove I had any dealings at all with these people. I gave Mrs. Hollis a generous offer to buy her land, that's all. Whatever Ransom Baxter did were his own crimes, not mine."

John glared back, knowing what Glover said was true. There was no way to prove he'd done anything truly wrong. Not when he had the Red Hand Gang doing his dirty work for him. "Someday Glover, you'll get what's coming to you."

"Is that a threat?"

"No," John said, "consider it a warning."

Sheriff Crane gave Glover an uneasy glance, then turned to glare down at John and Patrick. He nodded toward Ransom's dead and bleeding body. "If you expect to claim the reward, you'd best bring that body and those prisoners into town. Malone," he barked out an order to Patrick, "you're deputized to clean up this mess out here. I'll need a full report of what happened here when you get back into town."

Without waiting for Patrick's agreement or refusal, Sheriff Crane jerked the reins and turned his horse back to town. John was too angry to say anything.

Glover didn't try to speak. In seconds, he turned to follow the sheriff into town.

It's finally over. John knew he should be glad, but instead there was a let down feeling in his gut. Would Annabelle still want to see him if there wasn't a reason to defend her?

Chapter Thirty-One

Pecos River

A few weeks later

"Good morning, Annabelle," Clara Dawson greeted her as she opened the door and heard the pleasant jingling of the mercantile bell. "What brings you in today?"

Annabelle laughed, feeling as if the weight of the world had been lifted from her shoulders. It *was* a good morning, a fine morning now that Pecos River was calm and peaceful again.

It had only been a few weeks since Ransom Baxter's death and the end of the Red Hand Gang, but it felt like a year. "Good morning to you, Clara!"

The women looked at one another, smiling and happy. It felt good to smile, to feel relief from all the terror and bad days behind them. "What can I do for you on this beautiful day, Annabelle?"

"Hank sent me in to buy more nails and another hammer and well," she pulled the slip of paper out of the pocket of her dark blue dress. "Here is the list. John put a few things down too. Oh, and I suppose you'd best give me more flour for bread and the rest of these ingredients as well. Feeding those men is using up more supplies than I expected. Not that I mind."

Every day since the end of the Red Hand Gang, John and Hank had been working hard to rebuild Annabelle's barn and outbuildings, along with Christopher Jones's help. True to his word, he had gone against the gang and wanted to make something of himself. He'd attached himself to John, like a little brother, and followed him around.

"Christopher working out all right?" Clara asked as she glanced down at the list. "I sure was glad when that judge granted him immunity when those other men went to prison."

Annabelle shivered, remembering how frantic John had been when the circuit judge came to town for the trial. It had gone about as they expected. Deke Parsons and Jack Jones would hang for their crimes, including murdering the Montgomery family. As far as Annabelle was concerned, they were the worst examples of men she'd ever met. Still, in the end, both men had testified that Christopher had never done anything more than serve as a guard or kept watch over the other's horses.

"I was thankful when the judge said if John wanted to take charge of Christopher, he'd release him." Clara reached for a small sack of coffee beans. "Like I told Hank, there's often some good in the worst of us. That young man can turn over a new leaf and grow up to be a fine man."

"I agree. It's like he wants to make amends for all the wrong his brother, Jack, and Ransom did. He can't do enough. Do you know he even found my missing bull, Prince Oxford! That darned critter had got himself boxed into a grassy meadow. Christopher searched high and low and brought him home. I just about cried."

Annabelle didn't admit she had cried later, but not only about the bull. It was her friend's determination to rebuild her ranch into a fine place once again, like Thomas would have wanted it to be. Ever since Thomas's death, she'd felt alone except for the Dawsons. Now, she had any number of friends she could call to help.

Now that she didn't need to fear being alone, Annabelle found herself strangely lonely when the men left at the end of the day to go to their own homes. Often, she wondered what it would be like if someone lived with her. *Someone like...*

"How's young Ethan doing these days?" Clara interrupted Annabelle's thoughts as she bustled around the store, getting together the other supplies on the list. "Doc said he'd been out to John's last week and most of the infection is gone in his leg."

"He's doing fine," Annabelle was pleased to tell her. "Lily is doing an excellent job nursing him. John says he thinks soon Ethan will be able to do a full day's work again, hopefully by the end of summer."

"Hank told me John asked Sam's kids to stay on at his ranch where he can keep an eye on them."

Annabelle nodded, picking out a couple of spools of white thread and adding them to the wooden counter. "Yes, he did. Said it would give him company, and if he was late getting back from my ranch, Lily could milk Bossie and feed his livestock. He took his market cattle in and got a fair profit. It helps John feel he's taking care of Sam's children for him."

"Tea, flour, cornmeal," Clara muttered going from one shelf to another and putting the supplies in a wooden crate. "Let's see, the nails will be in the storeroom. I'll have to get Herbert for that..." as if she hadn't stopped in the middle of her conversation, Clara went back to the Garrett siblings. "Does John think Ethan and Lily will stay on once Ethan's recovered? Or will they go back to the place Sam had?"

She and John had talked that over on another night. "He's going to ask if they'll sell the old homestead and stay here. John has plans about taking Ethan and Christopher in as partners in a cattle-raising business. I'm not sure how it will all work out yet, but that's what they've been saying."

And when they all live happily over on John's ranch, when my ranch is rebuilt, where does that leave me? Alone again?

"I'm sure it will all work out." Clara gave her a cheerful smile and smoothed back the wispy strands of her dark hair coming out of an untidy bun. "Look at how life has changed in just the last few weeks. The Red Hand Gang is gone. Mr. Glover is no longer around to worry people about their land. Folks can live in peace, even if we do have Sheriff Crane at the jail."

The storekeeper's lips made a sour twist of displeasure. Everyone knew talk around town was that by the next election, Sheriff Crane would be out of a job. There had even been talk about having John come back as sheriff.

Not that John would say one way or another whether he liked the idea or not.

Annabelle shrugged. Whatever happened to the sheriff, he brought about himself, just like Isaac Glover. When the Texas Pacific Railroad heard how he'd tried to strongarm people into selling, using Ransom Baxter to do his bidding, they made it clear they'd buy nothing from him. One of the representatives had even tracked down relatives of the Montgomery family and repaid them for their family's stolen ranch.

Annabelle could not say everything had completely worked out.

Getting rid of Glover and the Red Hand Gang had cost them Thomas and Sam Garrett, and the lives of the Montgomery family. Ethan would always carry scars on his legs and arms where he had been dragged and beaten when Ransom captured him. Lily and all the other women would have wounds inside that would never fully heal, secret fears that might torment them on dark, sleepless nights. Still, the people of Pecos River could go back to the serene lives they had lived before Ransom escaped from prison.

Life is good for everyone again...almost.

"That all you need, Annabelle?" Clara interrupted her thoughts again. "I'll have Herbert get the hammer and nails and carry all this out to the buggy. As soon as we get a free day, you come to the house for dinner, you hear?"

"I will, Clara. I'll send in fresh-baked bread with Hank when he comes home tonight."

It didn't take long for Herbert to load the buggy or for Annabelle to drive back to the ranch. The sound of hammering met her ears, along with a loud bellowing from Prince Oxford. Christopher had built the bull a sturdy new pen near the barnyard.

A couple of new piglets darted past and ran toward the kitchen garden with Hank in pursuit. "Ya porkers...come back here!" he hollered as he ran along with a pitchfork in his hand. Seeing Annabelle, he called over one shoulder. "Wiggled under the barbed wire! I'm gonna have to shore up that section of the fence. Again."

Annabelle laughed, pulled on the brake, and climbed out of the buggy. Before she could reach for the crate of groceries, John was beside her lifting it up in his strong arms. "Here, let me get that for you."

She blushed, feeling the warmth in her face, glad she'd worn the dark blue dress today and not her usual riding skirt. Some days, a woman just liked to look more womanly, instead of a lady rancher. "Thank you."

As she followed him into the kitchen, Annabelle tried to still the wild leaping of her heart. She couldn't help it, but every time she was alone with John, she remembered the kiss they'd shared the night Jack Jones came calling.

It embarrassed her that John had not repeated the kiss. In fact, he seemed to regret it right after their lips parted. Hadn't he almost stumbled over his big feet leaving the porch and heading out to the makeshift lean-to he'd built for Cletus and his horse, Ranger? "I'd best stay outside with the horses," he had called over his shoulder.

Annabelle was left feeling shameful, a hussy, for forcing her kiss on him. But, truthfully, she didn't feel that way. Her feelings for John had never wavered since that night. Each day when he came to work on her ranch with Hank and Christopher, she watched him, loving him more each day. If only he felt the same way.

"You can set it down on the table, John," Annabelle said as she turned toward the black iron stove. Pulling on a white apron, she tied the string behind her back and stopped, surprised to find him still standing there. "Did you want something? I can make coffee. Or if the men are hungry now, I can fix dinner earlier."

John smiled and took a step closer. If he took another step, his boots would tread on her shoes. "I do want something, Annabelle, but it's not to eat. That's not what I'm hungry for. It's you I want."

For just a second, the words left her breathless with a wild soaring in her heart. "You... want...me?"

There was no denying his intention when John bent and kissed her, his lips pressed firmly on hers, tasting of coffee and slightly grainy from sugar. "I've fallen in love with you, Annie Hollis. And if you'll have me, I'd like to make you my wife."

"I love you too, John," she managed to say when she could pull her lips away from his. As his arms wove around her waist and he pulled her tighter to him, Annabelle whispered, "I love you more than I can say."

***

John struggled to swallow around a lump in his throat. He tugged at the black string tie around his throat, wondering why it felt so tight—like a noose.

"Ay, laddy," Patrick whispered, standing beside him, "every man feels a tightness in the throat on their wedding day. Don'tcha recall when you married Ada?"

Standing at the front of the church, waiting for Annabelle to join him at the altar, John tried to remember that long ago wedding day with his first wife. Truth be told, he couldn't recall a whole lot about that event.

"Reckon I was too young then to be afraid."

Patrick grinned with a wise look in his brown eyes. "You an' Annabelle were made for one another."

John hoped so. The night before he and Annie had sat down for a talk about Thomas and Ada. "You think they're looking down from heaven, wishing us well?" she asked.

While John hadn't known Thomas Hollis enough to say where he might have ended up on the other side, he couldn't say for certain Ada had gotten there. Mostly he remembered her constant nagging and bickering. He reckoned he'd loved her once, but those feelings were long gone and far away.

Standing at the altar, the small clapboard church fragrant with white lilacs and peonies, John wiggled his nose to keep from sneezing. At the wheezy organ, worse the wear for it's trip along the Oregon Trail back in the 60s, Miz Millie managed to play a couple of old hymns.

From his vantage point, John could look out over the wooden pews, filled with about the whole town. Everyone had come to celebrate, to wish them well. Clara and Herbert Dawson sat in the front pew. As usual, Mrs. Dawson's burgundy dress was wrinkled, and part of the sash had a damp spot where she'd spilled her morning coffee. Still, from her floppy bun of dark hair to her bright, shining smile, Clara was there to share their joy.

Sitting a few rows back, Ethan and Lily wore elegant, new clothes. Ethan looked like he'd rather be elsewhere, but Lily could have been a belle from the *Godey's Lady's Book*. Her chestnut brown curls framed a sweet, heart-shaped face with a faint pink flush as she smiled to the young man sitting beside her. Christopher Jones.

John frowned, distracted by the glow on Lily's face as she looked at Christopher. *I'll have to think on that union some. Wonder what Sam would have to say about it.*

Before he could worry anymore, Miz Millie began to plunk out the *Wedding March*. John glanced at the door of the church to Annabelle. She stood there, dressed in a cream-colored dress, her lovely auburn hair down and flowing over her shoulders. A pale peach hat sat on her head with a spray of ribbon roses. Annie held onto Hank, her arm draped through his. In her hands was a bouquet of white lilacs tied with peach ribbon.

"Here she comes," Patrick whispered as Annie and Hank began the slow walk toward the altar, "yer lovely bride-to-be."

John's breath caught in his throat and all he could see was her face, those green eyes sparkling as she looked into his.

My Annie. Now and for always.

Epilogue

A Year Later

Annie Wilder pulled a peach pie out of the oven and set it on the wide counter John had built especially for her baking. Face flushed, she lifted a white apron and fanned her cheeks.

"As soon as it cools, we can start to set the table, Lily," she said to the younger woman. "I'm so glad you could come today."

"I wouldn't miss yours and Uncle John's first anniversary! Can you believe you've been married a whole year already? Does it seem like forever?"

Annie shook her head, unable to believe she'd known such joy for an entire year. It seemed like just yesterday when her trembling legs took her down the aisle of the church to John Wilder. "Sometimes it feels like it happened yesterday. Other days like we've known one another our whole lives."

Lily gave her a smile from knowing brown eyes. "I hope someday, someone will look at me the way Uncle John looks at you."

"Someone who's name might be Christopher Jones?" Annie teased.

Lily blushed, busied herself stacking up the china plates that were Annabelle's pride and joy. No more eating meals on tin plates, not since John's cattle business had blossomed into real profits.

"Maybe, someday. Ethan says I have to be eighteen before Christopher can even ask for my hand. I don't think Pa would have been that stubborn."

"Ethan loves you and wants the best for you. Christopher did begin his life with an outlaw brother. I think your brother is trying to make sure he does a good job raising you."

"Maybe so," Lily answered, her stubborn streak coming out like it did every so often. "Still, I think Ethan could let me know my own mind once in a while."

"He will." Annabelle promised.

Just then John came through the kitchen door, carrying an armful of corn on the cob. "Look what I got for our supper. It's ripe just in time. And Ethan brought over more of Bossie's butter. That cow of mine always did give the best cream."

"Uncle John, you and that onery cow. I'm surprised you didn't bring her over here to live with you and Annabelle."

John dropped the corn on the table and went to hug Lily. He'd often told Annabelle he considered the girl his adopted daughter. "Well, now, and deprive you of living with another female as onery as you?"

"You!" Lily picked up some corn silk and draped it over his dark hair. "You're impossible, Uncle John. I don't know how Annabelle has coped with you for a whole year."

"Reckon she just loves me," he said, coming to kiss Annabelle with a passion that never ceased to surprise her. "But maybe not as much as I love her."

Lily picked up the plates. "I'm going to take these out to the table. I'll leave you two sweethearts in here."

As soon as Lily went out the front door of the house, Annabelle reached for her husband's face and pulled it down to shower more kisses across his tidy beard, the tip of his crooked nose and then to press her lips on his chapped ones. "Now, who loves who more?" she asked.

John chuckled, hugged her tight, and let her go. "You sure you want to share our good news with everyone today?"

Last night, Annabelle had told John her joyful news. They were expecting a little one in late winter. "If you don't mind. I want everyone to know at once."

"Whatever you want, Annie," he murmured and kissed her neck. "I want you to be happy."

There was no need to tell John he'd already made her happier than any woman alive.

The next few hours were filled with eating and reminiscing as their friends came to celebrate their first anniversary. Clara, Hank, and Herbert Dawson were the first to arrive with Clara's famous baked beans. Patrick arrived full of good cheer and Annabelle figured a keg of beer for the men to share later. Lily had been at the ranch most of the day helping Annabelle cook, but Ethan and Christopher arrived just in time to eat the meal.

"You get all the chores done at your ranch?" John quizzed the two young men, just like a father.

"Uncle John," Ethan moaned as he usually did. "You sound just like Pa. When you turned the ranch and the cattle business over to me and Christopher, you said you trusted us to run it."

John had the grace to look sheepish and flushed. "Well, now, I guess it's just habit. Took me a few years to build up the place and I want it to stand longer for you all."

"You're welcome to come over anytime you want, Mr. Wilder," Christopher said, scooping out a ladleful of stew. "You too, Mrs. Wilder. Lily can cook, but not as good as you."

Lily threw him a murderous frown, until she realized he was teasing.

The good-natured teasing went on as Annabelle sat beside Clara, gossiping about the women in Pecos River, the new dress styles, and how things were going at the mercantile.

Hank and Patrick got into a heated argument about who was a better horse shoe player. And as always, someone asked John the question uppermost in everyone's mind. "Sheriff Crane's leaving office the end of next month, John. You figure on running for sheriff again? There's probably not a soul in town who wouldn't vote for you."

"Been giving it some thought," John answered, reaching under the table to squeeze her hand, "but me an' Annie figure maybe it's time to let someone younger take over the job. Especially since I'm gonna be busy here on our ranch."

Everyone looked at him, knowing John and Annabelle had one of the finest ranches around. Thomas Hollis had known how to pick a good place and despite the ravages of the Red Hand Gang, they'd manage to rebuild and improve until it was one of the finest one-hundred-and forty acres around.

"Busy doing what, Uncle John?" Ethan asked.

All eyes turned to John, but he turned to her, picked up her hand and clasped it tight. "I'll let Annabelle tell you our good news."

"This winter..." Annabelle found herself flushing, lowering her eyes as she predicted the reactions. "John and I are going to have a baby."

Lily screeched out a glad yell. Clara didn't holler but jumped from her chair and embraced Annabelle in a fierce hug. "I'm so happy for you. So glad. I know how much you and Thomas..." Maybe Clara remembered Annabelle was now married to John, not Thomas. "I'm real glad for you too, John. I'd say you will be busy around here. A child is a wonderous investment in the future." Clara sent a fond smile at Herbert, eating his third piece of peach pie.

"I'll come help you out, Miz Hol... I mean, Miz Wilder," Herbert said. "If it's a boy I can teach him a lot of things."

"What if it's a girl?" Annabelle asked.

Herbert gave her a cheeky grin. "Maybe her ma will teach her how to make a peach pie like she does."

"Oh, you and your peach pie!" Clara tossed a napkin at her son with a fond smile.

"Aye, laddy," Patrick looked at John, "I'd say it's a fine thing you havin' a son or daughter of your own. Have you thought of any names yet?"

"Names?" John looked startled by the idea, but Annabelle put a firm hand on his shoulder.

"If it's a boy, he'll be Sam Garrett, of course," she stated, leaving no room for doubt. Although the tears that sprang to John's blue eyes showed her he approved the choice.

"What about a girl, Annabelle?" Lily asked. "What will you name her?"

"My ma's name was Margaret," Annabelle answered, "so I've always been partial to that."

Clara nodded. "It's a nice, old-fashioned name. Margaret Wilder has a lively ring to it."

Annabelle waited, thinking of the little one growing inside her, listening to the grownups planning a name.

"What's wrong with Annabelle, after her mother?" John wanted to know. "Prettiest name I know."

"It's awful!" Annabelle laughed. "I liked it better when Hank began to call me Annie. No, even though I like the name Margaret, there's one I like even more. When I was a little girl, there was another girl in Mama's class with pretty golden curls. I always thought one day I'd have a little girl and name her Aurelia Rose."

"That's right pretty," Clara said, and Lily nodded.

"What do you think, John?"

He looked at Annabelle, joy lighting his face, "Whatever she wants is fine with me. Although there are two names, I might take exception to."

"Oh?"

John snickered and said, "I refuse to call any child of mine Ada or Prince Oxford. A man's got to take a stand somewhere."

"You rascal!" Annabelle grabbed him around the neck and hugged him hard, joy bubbling up inside her. No matter whether this child turned out to be a boy or a girl, they'd love him or her. Maybe, God willing, there might be other babies down the road to share the ranch and their lives.

When Thomas had died, Annabelle never expected to be this happy again. Weeks, months, and years had gone by in grim, gray, weary sameness. Today, surrounded by her husband of a year, all her dear friends old and new, she had never felt such joy before.

Life was good and each day shining with promise.

"Herbert Dawson!" Clara snapped, "Save some pie for someone else!"

Annabelle laughed along with everyone else with a heart overflowing with joy.

THE END

Also by Zachary McCrae

Thank you for reading **"Wilder's Vendetta "**!

If you liked this book, you can also check out **my full Amazon Book Catalogue at:**

https://go.zacharymccrae.com/bc-authorpage

Thank you!

Printed in Dunstable, United Kingdom

70231119R00131

Printed in Great Britain
by Amazon

Dedication

I dedicate this book to all the brave "Angels" who are choosing to create alchemy in their own life and the lives of others.

Special thank you to my first coach, Robby Fullerton, my now coach, Brian Cyr, and Shirzad Chamine for creating the Positive Intelligence program. You all contributed to my alchemy.

To my husband, John Foxwell, who has encouraged my alchemy, and whom I love more every day.

Finally, to my first Positive Intelligence coaching group who so bravely wrote their Love Letters and jumped into their growth with such courage. Your transformation and bravery have touched me deeply,

Anel, Wynette, Nicola, Franca, Robi, Paul and Amanda.

The *Glass* Angel

*A guide to freedom,
peace, transformation
and growth*

Christina Foxwell

The *Glass* Angel

The Wild West

A Captivating Guide to the American Old West, Including Stories of Famous Outlaws and Lawmen Such as Billy the Kid, Pat Garrett, Wyatt Earp, Wild Bill Hickok, and More

Free Bonus from Captivating History
(Available for a Limited time)

Hi History Lovers!

Now you have a chance to join our exclusive history list so you can get your first history ebook for free as well as discounts and a potential to get more history books for free! Simply visit the link below to join.

Captivatinghistory.com/ebook

Also, make sure to follow us on Facebook, Twitter and Youtube by searching for Captivating History.

Contents

We are rough men and used to rough ways.

- Bob Younger, member of the James-Younger Gang, which conducted over twenty robberies during the wildest period of the American Old West.

Introduction

The story of the Old West is one that is as heartbreaking as it is exciting. It is a brilliantly colorful period in history, and its many icons have names that ring familiar even to modern ears: Billy the Kid, Lewis and Clark, Wild Bill Hickok, Wyatt Earp, Doc Holliday, and Buffalo Bill Cody. Yet, there is so much more to the tale of the Wild West than simply a pitched battle of outlaws versus lawmen.

In fact, the history of the Wild West extends far further into the past and encompasses so much more rich heritage than we might first expect. There is so much to learn, such as the Native Americans and what they were truly like and what they truly lost or how modern-day Texas and New Mexico were first explored and colonized by Spain. There were the mountain men who first explored the wilderness of the Northwest, gold rushes, buffalo hunters, and infamous outlaws who populated the American West 150 years ago.

It's a hard tale to hear at times and one that sometimes seems impossible to believe. There are times when the reality is even stranger than the tall tales. But the story of the Wild West holds vital importance for us today. We should not only enjoy the incredible and fascinating stories of the places and people that forged the United States into the country it is today but also relearn the hard lessons that

our ancestors forgot. Lessons about true justice, human rights, and what it really means to be free.

The Wild West was a place where wilderness and freedom clashed. And its story is a breathtaking one.

Chapter 1 – The Free West

Illustration 1: Plains people photographed in 1915

Long before cowboys wielded six-shooters, bandanna-masked outlaws roamed the prairie, or courageous homesteaders eked out a living in some of the most inhospitable wilderness America had to offer, the West was a rich cultural tapestry, one that was all but destroyed by the arrival of European settlers.

For thousands of years, Americans lived, farmed, worshiped, played games, fell in love, built societies, and survived in the vast region known as the West. Their cultures, languages, and religions differed tremendously. Pre-Colombian America and the pre-frontier West teemed with human life.

Over 562 separate American tribes thrived throughout North America in pre-Colombian times; they spoke over 2,000 different languages and numbered some 60 million individuals. More languages were spoken in modern-day California alone than in the whole of Europe. These people built beautiful societies, practiced medicine, and had cultures and beliefs as elaborate and sophisticated as those of the Old World.

But they didn't have ships. And they didn't have gunpowder. And so, the Native Americans would be swept away in the face of colonization, leaving only a decimated handful of survivors. Entire tribes were wiped out by disease, while others were crushed by enslavement and war. Whole cultures, languages, and religions were simply wiped from the face of the earth.

Before that day, though, the West was filled with societies that built cities, made war, and created art. A long, long time before the West was ever known as being wild, it was free. This history focuses on the late 19th century, which was when this area of the United States was known as "the Wild West." But the late 19th century was also the time during which the native peoples were massacred. It would be remiss not to include a glimpse of what was lost in that lawless time.

The Plains Culture

The vastness of the Great Plains, stretching from Canada to the Gulf of Mexico and from the Mississippi River to the Rockies, was almost unpopulated before the 18th century. In fact, the basis for the Native American stereotype that has been perpetuated in pop culture didn't even exist before European settlers came to North America. There were no feather-dressed braves galloping bareback on horses as they hunted buffalo on the wild prairie back then.

Instead, the tiny, scattered handful of people who made the Great Plains their home were farmers and hunters who lived in quiet, lonely settlements and villages. There were far more fertile areas to be farmed in the vastness of North America, so the Plains were generally avoided. It was only when Europeans started pushing eastern natives out of the homelands they had lived in for generations that they started to wander westward, eventually ending up in the Plains. In fact, some of the most famously western tribes we know today didn't originate in the West at all. Tribes like the Sioux, Cheyenne, and Crow originated in the East and were forced to move to the Great Plains by the constant influx of European settlers.

Once on the Great Plains, many tribes attempted to carry on with their way of life, living in their quiet villages and tilling this far less fertile land. Hunting was a part of survival for them. Everything they killed was thoroughly utilized; every bit of skin, bone, meat, and hair would be used for food, clothing, equipment, or shelter. Many Plains tribes celebrated an annual Sun Dance during the summer solstice—a merry festival that is still celebrated today.

In fact, these people didn't have horses at all before their first encounters with Spanish traders in the 18th century. Despite the fact that the wild horse has become a symbol of the West and the frontier, these animals are actually not wild at all. Even the mustangs, which have been roaming the prairies for centuries, originated from domestic horses that escaped or were abandoned, making them feral, not wild. The Native Americans didn't capture their first horses from the wild; rather, they traded with the Spanish for them. And almost instantly, their lives and cultures were changed.

The horse changed transport for the people of that era as swiftly and surely as the invention of flight would do centuries later. Suddenly, the Plains cultures found their horizons broadened. War and travel were revolutionized, and perhaps more than anything else, hunting changed completely. The Plains people had always venerated the buffalo as one of the most powerful and useful animals, but

bringing down one of these enormous, swift beasts was all but impossible for a man on foot. On horseback, though, hunters could keep up not only with individual animals but also with the herds that migrated across the expanse of the Plains.

Over time, the buffalo became central to the Plains people's diet, lifestyle, and even religion. A single buffalo provided so much more than just its meat. Every single part of the buffalo could be utilized in some way, from its hide to its bones, and the Plains hunters revered this animal for its strength and usefulness. In fact, it soon became evident that hunting buffalo was much easier and more useful than attempting to farm the often-dry and infertile Plains. As a result, more and more Plains tribes abandoned their homes and quiet farms and began to live as nomads instead, wandering wherever the buffalo herds led them. Once, they had lived in small, cozy homes. Now, they had to resort to a lighter and more portable shelter to live in, and so, the teepee was born. It was constructed, of course, from buffalo hides.

By the time the West became a place that the Europeans wanted to invade and tame for themselves, the Plains cultures were unrecognizable compared to what they had been before the arrival of Europeans in North America. These people had been uprooted from their homes in the East, and then they even abandoned their villages on the Plains. Many trekked across the expanse of wilderness, following wherever the buffalo led, and theirs was a life of total liberty. Tragically, it would not remain that way for long.

The Southwest Cultures

The people of the Southwest culture area lived mainly in an arid desert encompassing modern-day Arizona and New Mexico, but it also extended to Utah, Texas, Colorado, and even as far as Mexico itself. And despite the unforgiving desert sun, one of the Southwestern cultures became the very first farmers in America.

The Ancestral Puebloans, more correctly known as the Anasazi, were probably the first culture ever to attempt farming in the modern-day United States—and they were excellent at it. This tribe of former hunter-gatherers was the first culture to start growing corn, a crop that would become a staple all over the world in the centuries to come. In 2000 BCE, though, the Anasazi were the only people in North America growing anything at all, and corn became their staple diet for quite some time. In fact, this crop became so important to the Anasazi that it eventually featured in their creation myths. To them, corn was life.

It was also the only crop that would grow in the inhospitable conditions of the Southwest—that is, until another similar group of people developed one of the most sophisticated systems of pre-Colombian America. The Hohokam, too, farmed corn, but they had also grown used to the squash and beans that grew wild in some parts of the Southwest. However, these plants required far more water to grow than corn did. So, the Hohokam came up with a solution. They dug an incredibly intricate series of canals and formed an irrigation system that spanned thousands of miles, bringing life-giving water to the Southwest and creating fields where there had once been nothing but desert. This massive project, which reached its peak around 800 CE, must have been a huge undertaking. It would have required the cooperation of many different tribes, but the end result was breathtaking. Squash and beans brought some much-needed variety into the diet of the Hohokam, Anasazi, and Mogollon—collectively known as the Puebloans.

Soon, the Pueblo culture was built around farming. Instead of hunting, men tilled the fields. Whole villages would be involved in farming numerous fields, and soon, the villages began to grow. Since the Puebloans no longer needed to roam around the desert hunting and gathering, they began to dig in and build larger and larger towns. Using adobe and stone, they constructed the large buildings that would give them their name: "pueblo" is Spanish for "dwelling."

Eventually, Pueblo towns grew until they could hold thousands of occupants, and their buildings became large and intricate, with multiple stories and many different rooms. In fact, some Pueblo homes were as large as some modern-day apartment buildings. Each town would also have a central ceremonial building known as a kiva, which was a gathering place for rituals and other sacred festivals. The Puebloans evolved into different tribes, among them being the Hopi, Zuni, Yuma, and Yaqui.

These large towns traded extensively with one another, not only in basic necessities for survival but also in all kinds of trinkets and luxuries, like seashells or birds. A need arose for a trade center that could unify the tribes and make business easier. As a result, Chaco Canyon became a bustling hub for trade, with over four hundred miles of roads leading to the canyon from places as distant as California, Central America, and the Rocky Mountains.

However, around the early 12th century, disaster began to strike the Puebloans. This was an advanced and sophisticated people, but they had focused their attention on building towns, trade, and farms, not weapons. Even if they had weapons, the first disasters to befall them were natural. Drought shriveled their crops for decades in the 12th century, which was followed by a terrible flood that wiped away much of the Hohokams' life-giving irrigation system in the mid-14th century. Some canals survived—and can still be seen to this day—but it was the beginning of the end for the Puebloans.

As a result, when the Spanish arrived in the Southwest, most of the Anasazi and Hohokam had abandoned the area completely. The handful of Yaqui, Hopi, Yuma, and Zuni that remained could do little against the gun-wielding foreigners who decided that they were entitled to the land that the Puebloans had been farming for centuries, and they were overwhelmed and enslaved. Now, they discovered a very different type of farming. Entire communities once worked together to take care of the land, the crops, and one another. But the Spanish farmed on vast fields under the encomienda system. These enormous

tracts of lands were owned by men who might never put their hands to the soil. These men lived in the lap of luxury in their mansions instead, and the Puebloans were forced to work on the fields. No one lasted long.

By the time Anglo-Americans began to arrive in the Southwest, the Puebloans had been all but exterminated by the Spanish; in fact, only a handful of Pueblo people remain in New Mexico today. The remaining cultures were very different from the sophisticated Puebloans. These were wild, warlike, and nomadic peoples: the Navajo and Apache.

Where the Puebloans had been farming the Southwest for over a thousand years before the area was known as part of the "Wild West," the Navajo and Apache had only arrived around the 13th century. Unlike the Puebloans, they had little interest in agriculture and didn't build permanent dwellings. Instead, they roamed around the Southwest, looking for prey to hunt, food to gather, and crops to steal. These nomadic tribes became a thorn in the side of the Puebloans since they raided their towns and made off with their crops. The Navajo and Apache lived in mud and bark dwellings called hogans, which were always built to face toward the east and the rising sun. Perhaps because of their nomadic nature, they were able to escape the Spanish, and they still roamed warily around the Southwest by the time Americans arrived in the area in the 19th century.

The West Culture

The rest of the West was populated by a diverse array of tribes, particularly in the rich and fertile Great Basin. In fact, modern-day California alone contained over one hundred individual tribes. These tribes would be unified by their beliefs and lifestyles, but they were further divided into tribelets, which were small groups of people who lived in close proximity.

Unlike the Puebloans, most cultures of the West were primarily hunter-gatherers; thus, they lived on a far healthier diet than their agriculturally-minded counterparts. While the Puebloans lived almost exclusively on three staple foods, the people of the West enjoyed the wonderful variety of an entirely natural diet. They gathered all kinds of wild plants and hunted many different kinds of animals, from the mighty buffalo down to snakes, lizards, and rodents.

In fact, one of the cornerstones of their diet was salmon, and as a result, the western tribes' population was most dense around rivers. Using traps, spears, or harpoons, as well as fishing from canoes, these people caught fresh salmon every season. As the buffalo was to the people of the Plains, so was the salmon to the people of the West—an almost sacred creature, part of the very lifeblood of civilization. It is a recurring theme in the beliefs of these pre-Colombian peoples that they venerated and revered—even worshiped—the creatures that gave them sustenance, which was in sharp contrast to the attitude of the average European of that era toward a pig or a cow.

Another important part of their diet was acorns. While most of a raw acorn is toxic, the interior can be hollowed out and ground into a flour that can be made into flat cakes or bread. Acorns were also used as currency, along with seashells, in the bustling trade that took place among these diverse and distinct tribes.

While almost none of these tribes practiced agriculture, many lived in areas that were so fertile that they could live in permanent villages even though they hunted and gathered instead of farming. Others were nomadic, going wherever they could find enough resources, and they lived in portable homes made of wood, bark, and other light materials. These dwellings were called wikiups or wigwams.

Regardless of whether they roamed or stayed, many of these tribes had a very intricate society, which included a strict hierarchy. These societies were so strict, in fact, that they may have practiced slavery long before Europeans shipped Africans across the Atlantic. The Chinook tribe, in particular, is known to have practiced slavery. While

they didn't have fields to put their slaves to work in, they were adept hunters who would frequently bring down huge quarries such as the ubiquitous buffalo. Slaves were useful during buffalo season to process these enormous animals, so they were thoroughly utilized by the Chinook.

The Great Dying

Prior to the 16th century, the United States was populated by a dizzying variety of people. But colonization changed all that. Just a few centuries after the arrival of Christopher Columbus, fields would be turned into wastelands. Teepees, hogans, wikiups, and pueblos would be burned to the ground. Vibrant cultures and religions would be wiped from the earth. And where large towns of people had thrived, traded, and enjoyed their freedom, there would be nothing but silence.

It was known in that time as the Great Dying: the relentless and devastating epidemics brought on in waves by the introduction of European diseases into a world where there was no smallpox, plague, or even the flu. The European settlers flooding into the New World carried these illnesses without being sick, as they were immune to them. But the Native Americans' immune systems had no way of fighting these diseases, and the contagions spread at a horrifying pace among these people, wiping out entire villages and even whole tribes.

While war, slavery, and other cruelties committed by the colonists certainly contributed to the appalling rate at which Native Americans died as colonization began, disease was undoubtedly the main culprit. And the Great Dying was one of the most appalling events in human history. Ninety percent of the pre-Colombian population was wiped out by the middle of the 17th century. The figure is absolutely staggering, almost incomprehensible. The Great Dying killed 10 percent of the global population—a figure so vast that it actually caused global cooling at the beginning of the 17th century, sparking harsh winters and famines that would have staggering repercussions in Europe and Asia.

In fact, the only known event in human history that killed more people is World War II. Eight million people died during that dark time, compared with the fifty-six million Native Americans that died during early colonization.

By the time colonists began to arrive in what we know as the Wild West, the greatest tragedy of all had already taken place. The vibrant cultures, bustling trade routes, adobe towns, and ancestral beliefs of the people who originally lived in the West had been reduced to almost nothing. The fields lay empty. The towns lay abandoned. And the West was no longer free.

But soon, it would become wild. And the Wild West would be one of the most iconic chapters in all of American history.

Chapter 2 – Early Exploration and Spanish Settlement

As the Age of Exploration reached its peak, and the world became more and more connected, the West would ultimately become one of the last European frontiers. But before the East was even fully colonized, there were bands of intrepid—and occasionally greedy and opportunistic—explorers making their way into the beautiful wilderness of the West. One of the very first was Francisco Vázquez de Coronado.

The Seven Golden Cities of Cibola

Coronado had always been an opportunist.

It would seem, considering his early life, that he wouldn't have to be. He was born to a wealthy, noble Spanish family in 1510, and he grew up educated and well cared for. But Coronado had one stroke of bad luck: he wasn't the eldest son. As a result, none of the wealth and opulence that surrounded him growing up would ever belong to him, and so, Coronado had to find his own way in the world.

As for many other young European men of the time, the New World seemed to be the ideal place to seek a fortune. When Coronado's family connections led him to Antonio de Mendoza, who

had just been appointed as viceroy over New Spain, he jumped at the chance to travel with Mendoza as his assistant and take his chances in Central America.

Mendoza and Coronado traveled to New Spain—modern-day Mexico—in 1535, and Coronado wasted no time in building himself a life there. He married well in 1537, inheriting a considerable chunk of wealth from his new bride; that same year, he was involved in dealing with a number of slave rebellions by the hapless African and Native American people who had been subjugated into slavery by the Spanish. Coronado was successful in quelling these uprisings. This won him Mendoza's respect, and by 1538, Coronado could have been very comfortable with his life. He had been made the governor of Nueva Galicia. He was well-off and respected, and things were going just fine for him in the New World.

But Coronado still wasn't satisfied. He wanted more—more wealth and more fame. So, when explorers and Native Americans started to come to Nueva Galicia with stories of mind-boggling wealth, Coronado was listening.

The stories all centered around that most coveted of the New World's natural resources: gold. Ironically, it was the one resource that most Native American tribes couldn't care less about. They said that there were entire cities flowing with gold up north, cities of unimaginable riches, ripe for the taking. They were called the Seven Golden Cities of Cibola, and whoever discovered them would be rich beyond all imagination.

It didn't occur to Coronado or Mendoza that the Seven Golden Cities might rightfully belong to the people who lived in them. In their eyes, the New World's wealth was there for them to take. What was more, none of the myths suggested that the Golden Cities had been built by the native people who had been living there for so many centuries. Instead, they suggested that Spanish bishops fleeing Muslim invasions in the Middle Ages had somehow made their way to North America and built the Golden Cities. Even after the terrible fall of the

wealthy city of Tenochtitlan, the capital of the Aztec Empire, the Spanish still arrogantly believed that Native Americans were uneducated, uncultured, and incapable of building large cities or societies.

No matter how far-fetched the stories might have seemed, Coronado met with numerous people who seemed able to confirm the reports about the Golden Cities. Excited about the idea, he told Mendoza everything. This was an era when exploration was key to the future wealth of European nations. Mendoza was on board with launching an expedition to the north to look for the Seven Golden Cities, but he needed investors. Coronado was more than willing to chip in. He poured most of his wife's wealth into the expedition, and by February 1540, he was ready to go.

Coronado's expedition left Nueva Galicia with about 1,300 men; 300 of them were Spanish, while the rest were Native American—it is possible they were enslaved. Their guides led them northward into the desert of the modern-day Southwest. They traveled through the wilderness for days that turned into weeks that turned into months. But eventually, their guides told them that they were not far away. Soon, they would feast their eyes on cities composed of glimmering gold.

In June, four months after leaving home, the tired expedition had trekked over a thousand miles through the inhospitable desert. Their guides finally told them that they were approaching the first of the Golden Cities; its name was Hawikuh. Coronado and his men must have gained an extra spring in their step, a little hope now that they believed they were so close to their goal. Surely all the exhaustion, thirst, and suffering of the past four months would be worth it once they found the unimaginable wealth of a golden city.

But when Hawikuh finally came into view through the shimmering desert mirage, it was nothing like what Coronado had expected.

There was no gold in Hawikuh. The walls, instead, were made of adobe. There were no jewels; just laughter, food, and verdant farmland stretching in every direction. There was no silver, no diamonds, no rubies. This was no golden city—it was a Zuni city, home to a Pueblo tribe. The treasures held in the city of Hawikuh were very different than the gemstones and precious metals that Coronado desired. Hawikuh contained a close-knit community, thriving farms, a unique culture, and happy families. Perhaps one could argue that the city contained the treasures the city contained were beyond the value of mere metals or jewels.

But to Coronado, the sight of the tall adobe buildings towering against the desert sun was bitterly disappointing. He had spent his entire life chasing money, and Hawikuh held none.

Still, even if the streets of Hawikuh were not paved with gold, Coronado still wanted it for his own; he still wanted to have something to show for his efforts. Accordingly, he wasted no time in attacking the town. The Zunis were farmers, not warriors, and when Coronado's hundreds of men swept down upon the town with their firearms and bayonets, they put up only a brief fight. The Zuni had hardly any weapons to speak of; for a short while, they fought with what they had, throwing stones at the attacking colonists. One of these struck Coronado himself, wounding him, but the attack was far from dissuaded by this eventuality. The Zunis fled into the inhospitable desert, and the colonists claimed Hawikuh for their own, capturing and enslaving as many of the Zunis as they could.

Coronado never did find the fabled Golden Cities because they never existed. Instead, he spent the rest of the summer in Hawikuh recovering from his injuries, and his men explored parts of New Mexico and Colorado, going as far as the Grand Canyon itself. By winter, he decided that Hawikuh hadn't been worth it after all. His men lacked the knowledge to thrive here as the Zunis had done for generations. They moved to a new base on the Rio Grande for the

winter, did a little more exploring in modern-day Texas when the winter was over, and eventually returned to Nueva Galicia in 1542.

Mendoza was bitterly disappointed in Coronado's efforts. Coronado returned with no news of fabulous natural resources, riches, or fame. In fact, he would only hold his position as governor until 1544, when Mendoza removed him from the position.

Ultimately, Coronado's expedition was considered a dismal failure since it didn't bring in any money for the Spanish government. However, he was the first European to explore much of modern-day New Mexico, along with parts of Texas, Kansas, and Colorado. One of his men became the first European to ever lay eyes on the Grand Canyon itself. As far as we know, Coronado was the first European to explore the American West.

Francis Drake and San Francisco

If Coronado was a failure in regards to exploration, Francis Drake was a golden child.

His origins were improbable for a man who would become one of the most influential explorers in human history. Drake grew up as a commoner, the son of a farmer, preacher, and possibly petty criminal. His Protestant family was forced to move from his birthplace in Devon, possibly because of their religion or because of his father's nefarious ways. They ended up living in Kent in—of all things—an old, abandoned ship.

While there is little doubt that Drake's mother must have hated raising her twelve sons in the belly of an unseaworthy vessel, for young Francis, the ship was an utterly enchanting thing. He fell in love with everything about it, from bows to rigging to bowsprit to stern, and it wasn't long before he took an apprenticeship with a sailor. By the time he was twenty years old—sometime in the 1560s or early 1570s—Drake inherited a ship from his master. And so, his life on the open seas began.

Drake would eventually be hired by Queen Elizabeth I, a generally peaceable monarch who avoided conflict where possible, but she still wanted to cash in on the New World's treasures and make her mark in the Age of Exploration. While she had long been avoiding open war with the Spanish (the Anglo-Spanish War had been simmering between the two nations for decades), she was certainly not above plundering their ships for New World treasures. Accordingly, the queen hired Drake as a buccaneer, and he began to voyage the open seas and raid Spanish ships and trade ports at every possible opportunity.

In 1577, Drake was sent out with an entire fleet of ships: five, to be exact, including the most famous of them all, the *Golden Hind*. He headed for the Pacific side of South America, determined to plunder the wealthy Spaniards there. Two of his ships had to remain there, but Drake made his way north up the Strait of Magellan with the other three, raiding and pirating merrily as he went.

While it wasn't long before Drake's ships were filled with gold, silver, and other treasures, storms began to batter the *Golden Hind* and her companions. It wasn't long before one ship had no choice but to turn back, and it would eventually limp back across the sea to England, badly damaged. The other was not so lucky. In one of the chaotic storms, she was wrecked, and the ship, her treasures, and many of her crew were lost to the devastating force of the American seas.

Only the *Golden Hind* was left, but Drake was undaunted, butting his way beyond Spanish territories and into the waters along the western coast of North America. He was seeking the fabled Northeast Passage, the very same thing that Christopher Columbus had been looking for when he stumbled upon the New World nearly a century before. But there was none to be found. Drake didn't know yet the vastness of the continent that lay between him and Asia, but he did try to map much of it. Decades later, Drake's maps of this coastline would assist the Pilgrims in their search for Plymouth Harbor. In fact,

in 1580, Drake even explored Plymouth Harbor itself, nearly forty years before the *Mayflower* would ever anchor there.

Before finding Plymouth Harbor, though, Drake would explore many other lands, and one of those turned out to be the first western state to be claimed by an Englishman. He had sailed all the way around South America and headed up the western side of North America, becoming one of the first explorers ever to do so. In fact, Drake sailed all the way up to modern-day Washington State before he decided to turn around. On his way back, in 1579, the *Golden Hind* was desperate for some repairs. He sought a suitable bay to anchor in while he put his ship back together, eventually sailing into a little harbor that would eventually be part of modern-day California.

Together with his crew, which included an African woman who was most likely a slave, Drake became the first Englishman to set foot in the American West, and he was likely the first European ever to walk on the soil of modern-day California. The harbor was located near the spot where the city of San Francisco would eventually be founded. For now, it was a beautiful, pristine wilderness populated by a glorious abundance of Native American cultures.

Luckily for them, Drake didn't intend to conquer anything inland. He was bent on getting back to his ship, as he was forever called by the open sea. Instead, he merely staked England's claim on this part of the New World, naming it Nova Albion, and then sailed off again.

Drake's voyage would ultimately take him all the way around the Cape of Good Hope before he returned back to London, becoming the second person in history (after the Portuguese explorer Ferdinand Magellan) to circumnavigate the globe. The *Golden Hind* made her way into home waters in 1580, and the following year, Drake was knighted for his feats of navigation and exploration.

Nuevo México

While the English would focus their colonial efforts on what is now the eastern United States, pouring their effort and energy into settlements like Jamestown and Plymouth, the Spanish were the first to establish a European colony in what would become the Wild West. The growth and role of Hispanic culture in the Old West have been much neglected in favor of the stereotypical American cowboy, but in reality, the Spanish were subjugating the West long before the California Gold Rush.

After the doomed expedition of Francisco Coronado, a slow trickle of Spanish colonists nonetheless began to move northward from modern-day Mexico. The ever-expanding population was always seeking somewhere to go, and while kings and governments were focused on finding untold wealth and riches on the frontier, most of the people moving northward were just ordinary families looking for a bit of fertile land to farm. Following the Rio Grande's abundant banks, knots of settlers began to eke out a living for themselves wherever they could. They were encouraged to do so by the government, but they were not particularly supported in a military capacity.

Still, this was all just a disorganized trickle before the arrival of one of the Old West's first dreadful villains: Juan de Oñate.

Oñate had been born in Mexico, then known as New Spain, to noble Spanish parents, and accordingly, he was both wealthy and well-trained in warfare. This made him the ideal candidate to become the first governor of the territory that Coronado had explored. It was time for the Spanish to marshal their people's efforts to subdue the Native Americans and take over their lands, and the ruthless Oñate would lead these efforts.

With a large band of missionaries, soldiers, and settlers, Oñate left New Spain in 1598 for the territory that had been dubbed Nuevo México. If the native people of the land were worried by the sight of real soldiers with armor and weapons flooding toward them, they had

a right to be. Oñate would prove to be both greedy and cruel, even by the standards of colonial America.

After conquering the hapless Pueblo town of Ohkay Owingeh, Oñate established Nuevo México's first capital there and renamed it San Juan de los Caballeros. The Hispanic population there rapidly began to grow. People flooded into this new land, driven by hope for more natural resources and wealth, as well as by a hope to Christianize the Native Americans of the area. But as it turned out, Oñate's men would be far from peaceful missionaries spreading the word. Instead, Oñate actively encouraged his settlers to mistreat the Puebloans. He wanted them to oppress these native people and demand tribute from them, and it wasn't long before opportunistic settlers took full advantage of this.

Oñate's soldiers were particularly brutal. They physically mistreated and even killed Puebloans at will, with Oñate's encouragement always driving them on. Eventually, this resulted in the Acoma Massacre in the fall of 1598.

This was still early on in the development of Oñate's colony of Nuevo México, and there was no way that the Spanish could survive without the help of the Puebloans. Often, this meant simply enslaving them, but the Spanish also engaged in trade with some of the tribes. This trade was seldom ever a good thing, as was made abundantly clear to the Acoma Puebloans when a group of Oñate's men visited their town wanting to buy stored food for the winter. Adept farmers though the Acoma were, they had only stored enough food for their own people, so they declined to trade with the Spanish. When the Spanish grew angry and violent, the Acoma retaliated, capturing and killing twelve Spaniards, including Oñate's nephew.

Of course, Oñate did not take kindly to this act of violence. In January 1599, when the worst of the winter was over, he declared that the Acoma had been acting in rebellion and that the insurrection needed to be stopped immediately. He sent his soldiers to attack the Acoma, and the event that ensued was no battle. It was a slaughter.

The Acoma had been able to stand up to the small band of unsuspecting Spanish who had come to take their food, but this was more than any of them could stand against. Blood flowed, staining the desert sand, and when it was over, around one thousand Acoma were dead. It was the first massacre of Native Americans by colonists in the Old West, and horrifically, it would not be the last. The surviving Acoma were enslaved, and the adult men had their toes brutally amputated in an attempt to disgrace them and break their spirits.

Today, Acoma Puebloans still live in New Mexico, with their population now numbering around five thousand.

The Puebloans, however, were not the only people to suffer at Oñate's hands. He was cruel and oppressive to his colonists as well. When the harsh conditions of Nuevo México forced some colonists to abandon San Juan de los Caballeros and head back to New Spain instead, Oñate reacted violently. He sent his soldiers after these people, labeling them as deserters, and had them beheaded.

As a result, when King Philip II of Spain got wind of Oñate's butcher of the Puebloans and colonists alike in 1606, Oñate found himself on trial for his cruelty. While he would continue in his position as governor until 1610, his days were numbered.

During the twelve years of his rule in Nuevo México, Oñate established the Province of Santa Fé de Nuevo México, with its capital numbering around two hundred colonists by 1610. In the later years of his governorship, Oñate led a small expedition eastward in the hopes of discovering another fabled golden city. These explorers made it all the way to the Great Plains, exploring parts of modern-day Oklahoma, Texas, and Kansas, but they never did find any golden cities. Eventually, attacks by wary natives of the region forced them to turn back. In 1605, Oñate launched another expedition and followed the Colorado River all the way to the Gulf of California. This was land that had already been claimed by the British Crown, even though there were no colonists living there at that point.

Ultimately, Oñate's cruelties eventually caught up with him. His position as governor was taken away from him in 1610, and he was entirely exiled from Nuevo México. Although he was forced to return to New Spain, Oñate nonetheless still managed to gain positions of power back in the Old World.

That left Nuevo México without a governor. While Oñate had requested that the governorship be given to his son, the Spanish viceroy had had more than enough of Oñate and his troubles. He firmly informed Oñate that another replacement had already been found. This was a Spanish-born noble named Don Pedro de Peralta, and he was already on his way to San Juan de los Caballeros by the time Oñate was getting ready to leave.

Peralta was well aware that Oñate had caused chaos and division with his tyrannical ways in Nuevo México, and he would have his work cut out for him if he wanted to unify the colony and help it thrive. Accordingly, Peralta made an effort to be more diplomatic than his predecessor. He arrived in the capital with only twenty men accompanying him: twelve soldiers and eight Franciscan monks. Peralta desired prosperity for the Spanish colony, but he was willing to gain it peacefully.

As a result, Peralta proved far more successful than Oñate. His first decision was that the capital at San Juan de los Caballeros was situated in a terrible position. The soil was dry and infertile there, and colonists were struggling to scratch out an existence in the desert even though there was an expanse of beautiful, fertile land just thirty miles away, the perfect place to establish a new capital. Oñate had recognized this fact, too, and drew up plans for building another city in this better, more prosperous position.

While some colonists would remain at San Juan de los Caballeros, which today exists once again as Ohkay Owingeh, Peralta wasted no time in building a new capital. By the end of 1610, he had already made a good start on building a new city. The center of the city was a church, a sturdy adobe building named the San Miguel Church, which

still stands today more than four hundred years later as the oldest church in the United States, predating the King James Bible. Peralta had also started building his Palace of the Governors, which was completed in 1612; today, it remains the oldest US government building still in use.

The city itself was named La Villa Real de Santa Fé de San Francisco de Asís (the Royal Town of the Holy Faith of Saint Francis of Assisi), and it is known today as Santa Fe. It is the third oldest town in the entire United States of America, with only St. Augustine, Florida, and Jamestown, Virginia, predating it by a few years. Santa Fe is also the oldest state capital in the United States. Peralta made it the state capital of Nuevo México during his time as governor, and it is still the capital of New Mexico today.

Peralta himself would eventually be accused of cruelty to the Native Americans just as Oñate had been. He spent a year in prison because of this, but he was ultimately found to be innocent. He would spend many years governing Nuevo México, only resigning in 1654 when he was very old. His governorship ushered in a time of comparative peace in Nuevo México, where colonists thrived and violence toward the Puebloans was generally low. However, Puebloans were still stripped of their rights and had many of their possessions taken from them. A few decades after Peralta left Nuevo México for good, these tensions inevitably bubbled over into open revolt.

The Pueblo Revolt

Known as the "first American revolution," the Pueblo Revolt of 1680 started with Spanish conquistadors' determination to stamp out any vestige of the Puebloans' ancestral religion.

Po'Pay, a holy man and war captain from Ohkay Owingeh, was a victim of this religious persecution. He had always been determined to cling to the old ways and preserve the culture of his people, but the Spanish were bent on Christianization. Sometime in the late 1670s, Juan Francisco Treviño, the governor of Nuevo México at the time, ordered that all Pueblo holy men be captured and executed. Po'Pay

was one of them. While he was not killed, he was brutally beaten in front of all his people. They could only watch in horrified silence as one of their most respected community members was struck again and again with a whip.

The experience only fueled Po'Pay's rising resentment toward the Spanish, a resentment shared by other Puebloans for obvious reasons. Along with his tireless campaign to preserve the ancestral Pueblo beliefs, Po'Pay also started reaching out to like-minded people—people who might even remember a time before the Spanish culture began to take over the Puebloans' world. People who wanted things to go back to the way they used to be, before the conquistadors came. And Po'Pay was the leader who wanted to make that happen.

Setting up a base in Taos Pueblo near Santa Fe, Po'Pay started meeting with more and more people, even involving some leaders from the Apache and Navajo tribes who had been the Puebloans' enemies. While the Apache and Navajo did not see their towns captured and used by the Spanish as the Puebloans did, their way of life was being threatened too, and they did not take kindly to the Spanish presence. They were willing to unite with the Puebloans, no matter their differences if it meant they could get rid of the Spanish.

Po'Pay told his followers that if they succeeded in driving the Spanish and Christianity out of their homeland, it would bring an end to the drought that had been plaguing Nuevo México for several years by that point. The powers of the Pueblo religion, he told them, would reward them for returning to the old ways by sending rain on their lands again. This was a powerful factor that convinced many Puebloans to join the rebellion. The drought would have made life difficult enough, even without the oppressive Spanish regime, as the Puebloans were expected to produce food for the Spanish as well as for themselves, and they were often punished if they failed to meet the expectations of the Spanish.

After the long, dry summer of 1680, with a meager harvest on the horizon, Po'Pay started planning the final stages of the rebellion. Several men were selected to carry a secret message throughout Santa Fe and the surrounding settlements. Each carried a knotted cord in full view, and every day, one knot was undone. When there were no more knots in the cord, the rebellion would begin.

That day was August 11ᵗʰ, 1680. Santa Fe was running very low on food; the harvest had not yet begun. That was when the Puebloans struck. They laid siege to Santa Fe, determined to starve out the Spanish inside the city, and launched raids on the settlements outside the city, where they were aided by the experienced Apache and Navajo. Over four hundred Spaniards were killed that day, many of them innocent families and children, and Santa Fe was locked in the siege for nine long days. Food had been scarce enough even before the siege; now, people were actively starving to death.

After the Spanish executed a desperate attack on the Puebloans, breaking through their ranks just enough to open a way to flee, the entire Spanish population of Santa Fe—then numbering around two thousand—bolted south along the Rio Grande, heading back toward the safety of New Spain. To their surprise, the Puebloans did not pursue them. They only followed them until they had left northern Nuevo México behind. Po'Pay's objective was not to massacre the Spanish. He just wanted his people's towns and lands back.

And at first, it seemed as though Po'Pay had been successful. The Spanish of Santa Fe resettled in other parts of Nuevo México, and for twelve years, Puebloans once again enjoyed their city as free people. They burned down the churches, slaughtered all the European livestock, and even cut down the fruit trees that the Spanish had planted. Po'Pay was determined to return life to the way it had been before the Spanish had ever come to the land of the Puebloans.

Po'Pay himself, however, would not remain in command of the Puebloans for those full twelve years. One year after the rebellion, the people had grown discontent with him as their leader. The greatest

issue was that the rains Po'Pay had promised never did come. The sky remained shut up, as empty and hard as stone, and the continued drought increased the people's hunger. The Spanish were gone, but the Puebloans were still starving. Accordingly, the fickle Apache and Navajo, who had assisted in the rebellion, returned to their old ways of raiding and stealing from the Puebloans. Po'Pay was deposed, and the Puebloans tried to scrape together a life for themselves once again, despite the drought.

It was not to be. In 1692, when the Puebloans were struggling with hunger and enemies, the Spanish decided that the time was right to take back Santa Fe. Diego de Vargas rode into Santa Fe in September 1692, hoping to take back the city with minimal bloodshed. After lengthy negotiations, the Puebloans realized that they couldn't fight both the Spanish and the weather. They signed a peace treaty on September 14th, and Vargas retook control over Santa Fe. Spanish settlers streamed back inside, ready to rebuild their churches. San Miguel was one of the few that had more or less survived the onslaught.

By December 1693, the Puebloans were regretting their decision to let the Spanish return. They attempted another uprising, and this time, Vargas was not interested in a peaceful resolution. He suppressed it harshly, buying an uneasy peace that lasted only three years. In 1696, still frustrated by their lack of religious freedom and the exploitation of their land and people, the Puebloans attacked and murdered five innocent missionaries. This act appalled the Spanish; the missionaries had not been soldiers, so their deaths were incredibly shocking. Vargas reacted harshly. He started a bloodthirsty campaign to suppress the Puebloans once and for all, and he traveled from town to town in Nuevo México, shedding blood in every pueblo and cutting the entire tribe down to their knees. It was a devastating conquest, and the Puebloans would not rise again.

In one way, Po'Pay's rebellion had achieved its aim: it preserved Pueblo religion and culture for generations to come. While Christianization continued and the Pueblo culture did meld with the Spanish culture to some extent, their way of life and beliefs were not completely wiped out the way they might have been without Po'Pay's efforts. Today, around sixty thousand Puebloans still live in New Mexico, many of them along the Rio Grande, including in Taos Pueblo itself.

The Pueblo Revolt was the first major conflict between Native Americans and colonizers in the American West, but tragically, it would not be the last.

The Battle of the Twin Villages

By the mid-18th century, European forces were stretching farther and farther across the West. Despite Sir Francis Drake's arrival in California in the 1670s, the British had not yet made any substantial claims on the West at this time. The Spanish, however, continued to spread farther and farther across Nuevo México, which included modern-day New Mexico and also parts of other southwestern states. Small missions began to crop up across Nuevo México. Their first town in modern-day Texas was established around 1718 when the Misión San Antonio de Valero was founded. This would later become known as the Alamo Mission.

However, the Spanish were not the only European power colonizing the Southwest. France extensively explored Canada and parts of the northern United States. Most of their expeditions concentrated on the eastern part of the US, but some explorers made it as far as the Dakotas, claiming this area for France. From Louisiana, the French also made their way west across Arkansas and Alabama. In fact, parts of these states were included in "Lower Louisiana"; France's Louisiana Territory was considerably larger than modern-day Louisiana State.

29

As a rule, the French were peaceful in their interactions with Native Americans across most of their colonies. Arkansas, Alabama, and eventually Oklahoma were no exception to this rule. France was interested in trading with Native Americans, and most of their settlements were established as trading posts in or near Native American towns. In modern-day Oklahoma, the French traded and became allies with the Wichita and Comanche tribes to the point where they were welcomed into some of the strongest Wichita towns as friends and partners against the Wichitas' own enemies.

It would soon turn out that some of those enemies would be the Spanish. While the Wichita had no beef with the Spanish directly, they were actively at war with the Apache, which forced the luckless Apache deeper and deeper into Spanish Texas.

Unable to maintain a war with both the Wichita and the Spanish, the Apache agreed to peace with the Spanish by the 1750s. They submitted to Christianization and cooperated with the missions that were being built all over Texas, even living with the Spanish in small communities. Perhaps European culture was more attractive to the Apache because they had not established stable towns and agriculture like the Puebloans had; they had something to gain from learning skills from the Spanish, such as growing and producing their own food instead of having to raid it from the Puebloans.

The war with the Wichita, however, was going very badly. The Spanish refused to sell weapons to the Apache, particularly after the last Pueblo rebellion in 1696, which the Puebloans had conducted using weapons they'd bought from the Spaniards themselves. The Wichita and Comanche, on the other hand, had plenty of weapons from their French allies, which allowed them to slaughter the Apache in conflict after conflict.

It was inevitable that the Spanish would become collateral damage in this war between the two Native American tribes. That finally happened in late 1758 when a group of Wichita and Comanche attacked a small mission at San Sabá in modern-day Texas. Several

Apache were killed in the attack, and so were two innocent Spanish missionaries.

The Spanish were incensed by this attack, and they refused to become collateral damage in the Apaches' war. They considered the killing of missionaries to be an inexcusable act, and the Spanish had the full support of the Apache in this matter. They wanted revenge on the Wichita—no matter how much blood had to be shed to get it.

In 1759, that quest for revenge was led by Colonel Diego Ortiz Parilla, a Spanish officer who had seen plenty of combat against Native Americans in New Spain. With a mixed group of native and Spanish troops numbering around five hundred men, Ortiz Parilla headed for the ruins of San Sabá. Riding through the blackened buildings only fueled his anger. He headed out of Apache territory, beyond modern-day Texas, and into modern-day Oklahoma in search of a Wichita town he could attack.

After putting a small group of Yojuanes to flight, Ortiz Parilla reached what he had expected to be a little settlement of uneducated barbarians on the banks of the Red River. Instead, he came across a strong fortress with high walls—and French flags flying over the rooftops. This place was called the Twin Villages, and while the French had left in a bid to avoid war with the Spanish, there were still many Wichita warriors inside, possibly even thousands of them. They were well-armed as well, and they were ready to fight.

Outnumbered, Ortiz Parilla nonetheless prepared for battle. He tried to intimidate the Wichita with his two cannons, but this was a dismal failure. The Wichita laughed at him and mocked the Spaniards, then poured fire down from the walls upon them. The Spanish strove to fight back, and for hours, a bloody battle raged. But try as he might, Ortiz Parilla could not break down those walls.

When the Wichita started bursting out of the fortress on horseback at intervals, launching lightning-swift attacks on the flanks of Ortiz Parilla's troops and causing chaos among them, the hearts of the men began to fail. They started to desert, fleeing off into the wilderness in a

bid to escape what they presumed to be certain death. With his lines crumbling and his men dying, Ortiz Parrilla decided that he had no choice. He pulled back, fleeing from the Twin Villages. The Wichita did not pursue, but their haunting songs of victory followed Ortiz Parrilla as he fled in ignominy.

Spanish egos were badly wounded by this defeat, and about nineteen Spaniards died in the battle. The Spanish would later claim that the Wichita casualties numbered around one hundred. Either way, the Spanish never did subjugate this proud and powerful people. It was smallpox that brought them to their knees nearly twenty years later in an epidemic that claimed around one-third of the tribe. Eventually, after conflicts with American settlers in the 19th century, the Wichita were forced onto a reservation in Oklahoma.

Soon after the Battle of the Twin Villages, France lost its grip on the American West, giving its territory to the Spanish near the end of the French and Indian War in 1762. The Louisiana Territory would be returned to the French in the era of Napoleon Bonaparte, who ultimately sold it to the United States of America in 1803.

Another bloody Native American war would take place shortly after the Battle of the Twin Villages, and this time, the Native Americans would be on the losing side.

"Dangerous Man"

When Juan Bautista de Anza saw the chief riding toward him across the desert, he knew that the man he was about to face in battle considered himself to be immortal.

Taivbo Naritgant, whose name means "Dangerous Man" in the Comanche language, was better known to the Spanish as Cuerno Verde: "Greenhorn." It was easy for de Anza to see why. The chief's most striking feature was his headdress. Far from the elaborately feathered headdresses of the Plains Indians, Taivbo Naritgant wore bison horns that rose in two great curves from his forehead. They were tinted faintly green, and they were a sign of honor, of a pair of

shoulders strong enough to hold up the mighty horns of the bison. Only the boldest of Comanche warriors wore the green horns, and Taivo had inherited that honor from his father, a man who went by the same name.

The original Taivo Naritgant had been killed eleven years earlier, in 1768. For decades, the Comanche had been conducting regular raids on the Spanish in the area encompassing modern-day Colorado. As in Texas, Spanish missions had been popping up all over the region, and the Comanche were far from welcoming. They had been making war on the Apache for decades, and they were fearless of the Spanish and well-armed by the French. They weren't about to let their lands go without a fight.

The elder Taivo Naritgant had raided many Spanish people in his day, but he had been overly ambitious in attacking Ojo Caliente. This Spanish settlement, located near some hot springs in modern-day New Mexico, had been well guarded at the time, and Taivo Naritgant fell there in battle, killed by the Spanish. The warriors brought his headdress back to his firstborn son, who took the headdress and his father's name. He was determined to carry on his father's crusade against the Spanish.

As the raids increased, the viceroy of New Spain appointed a warlike governor to Nuevo México: Juan Bautista de Anza. De Anza had been born in New Spain and grew up on the frontier, which came with consequences suffered by many a Spanish boy at that time: he lost both his father and his grandfather to Apache raiders. Bitter and grieving, de Anza took revenge on the Apache by fighting against them numerous times in his decorated military career. He was chosen as governor of Nuevo México specifically to subdue the Native Americans in that area.

Now, it was 1779, and de Anza had been chasing Taivo Naritgant for months through the hostile landscape of untamed Colorado. The Comanche raids on Spanish settlements continued, and de Anza was determined to catch the man he knew as Greenhorn and kill him. In

his eyes, Tavibo Naritgant was just another murderer, just like the Apache who had killed his father. His accounts depict the Comanche chief as being unbearably cruel, a "scourge" in de Anza's own words.

Whether cruelty was part of Tavibo's psyche or not, it would appear that pride most certainly was. When de Anza and Tavibo Naritgant finally came face to face on September 3rd, 1779, the Comanche chief had a force of only about fifty men behind him. De Anza, by contrast, had around six hundred men with him.

Still, when Tavibo Naritgant rode toward the Spanish on his plunging, rearing horse, he was fearless. All his life, he'd been accompanied wherever he went by a Comanche holy man who had persuaded him that he was sacred somehow and could never die. What could de Anza do to him if the spiritual powers of his religion were on his side? Tavibo was a terrifying sight as he approached the Spanish. He wore his very long, black hair in two braids, with his scalp brightly painted and another single, slender braid hanging down his back with a feather at the end of it. He was the picture of a warlike Comanche chief. And the green horns only enhanced his frightening appearance.

But Tavibo Naritgant wasn't immortal. He was just a man, and when his fifty Comanche clashed with the six hundred Spanish, they were outnumbered more than ten to one. The battle was a devastating one. Tavibo Naritgant was slaughtered in the chaos, and his men were put to flight. They were allowed to flee by de Anza so that they could tell everyone that their great chief lay dead at the hands of a Spaniard.

Further British and Spanish Exploration

By the end of the 18th century, many parts of the American West were still completely unknown to the European world. The Spanish, however, had made a mighty effort to explore and colonize this vast area, and they had met with some success.

Apart from their growing colony in Nuevo México, the Spanish had also ventured northward by ship, reaching and settling the area that Sir Francis Drake had called "Nova Albion." The English had made no further attempt to claim this area for themselves, so the Spanish soon began to build missions along the coast. They gave this area the name it still bears today: Las Californias.

There are rumors that conquistador Hernán Cortés made it as far as California on his expeditions, but the first colonies built there would only come to life in the 18th century. At first, these were concentrated around the southernmost parts of modern California, with no one venturing farther than Baja California. But in 1763, when the brutal Seven Years' War in Europe had finally come to an end after millions of deaths and years of terrible suffering, the Old World powers were able to turn their attention once more to the New World. Spain started to push for heavier colonization, and California became an important focus of this effort.

Interestingly enough, while Nuevo México had largely been explored by military men in the late 16th century and early 17th centuries, it was men of the cloth, particularly Franciscan friars, who led most of the expeditions of the 18th century. This era of colonization, therefore, was significantly more peaceful than the brutal conquest of Nuevo México.

One such father, Junípero Serra, made the daring bid to venture toward northern California. Under Serra's leadership, an expedition pushed as far north as 170 miles from Baja California, then built a mission there for the local people. They called it San Diego. Shortly afterward, they continued more and more northward, building mission after mission, and these would eventually blossom into some of California's largest cities: Santa Barbara, San Francisco, and Monterey. Later, San José became the first secular settlement to be built in northern California. By the end of the century, there were over twenty Spanish missions in the area.

While most of these Spanish friars had peaceful relations with the native people of the region, they nonetheless caused the deaths of thousands upon thousands of Californians. There was peace in their hearts but death in their bodies. Old World diseases, to which these Spaniards were immune, devastated the Native Americans of the area. In a brief period, one-third of the Native American population of California was wiped out by disease. All of those verdant tribes and diverse languages were destroyed by the European scourge.

A few years later, now that there were established Spanish settlements in California, the people of Nuevo México began to hope that there might be a way for them to travel north and find their Californian counterparts overland. At the time, some scholars actually believed that California could be an island—there had been so little exploration in the West that no one really knew. Two more Franciscan friars decided that there was only one way to find out. In 1776, Atanasio Domínguez and Silvestre Vélez de Escalante set out from Santa Fe with a tiny group of men and livestock, hoping to find a road to Monterey, California. This was a distance of over one thousand miles, an almost unthinkable trek even for experienced explorers, let alone a little group of holy men with almost no weapons to speak of. Domínguez and Escalante took no soldiers and almost no weapons with them. They hoped that they would be able to make peace with any Native Americans they encountered and that the locals might even help them to find Monterey.

At first, the Franciscan fathers' hopes were realized. Having left Santa Fe in the summer of 1776, they traveled north and west through modern-day Colorado. Although they had taken a major risk by traveling in such a small and poorly armed group, they met with no resistance. Soon, they discovered a tribe that had had little contact with Europeans at this point: the Ute. The Ute were friendly and received the expedition with kindness, even sending two of their people along with the Spanish as guides. Their real names are lost to history, so we know them only by the Spanish names that Domínguez

and Escalante gave them: Silvestre, named after Escalante, and Joaquín. Joaquín was just a boy of twelve, but he was already well versed in the landscape that was his home.

With the help of these two guides, the Domínguez-Escalante expedition continued all the way through Colorado and into what is now Utah. Everywhere they went, the expedition was impressed by the fertility of the landscape and how suitable it would be for settlement. Their Ute guides appeared only too happy to cooperate and led them all the way into the Uinta Basin itself, making them the first Europeans ever to set foot there. Once in the basin, they met up with more friendly Ute. While their original guides opted to stay with their tribe members, another guide was provided for the expedition, who led them deeper into Utah Valley.

It was here that the expedition paused. They didn't know it yet, but though they had traveled almost six hundred miles, they were less than two hundred miles nearer to Monterey than they had been when they left Santa Fe. They had been heading too far to the north. Now, Domínguez and Escalante decided that a better course of action would be to build a mission and settle in Utah Valley.

However, it was not to be. They needed their guide to take them deeper into the valley, but when one of the native servants that the Spanish had in their retinue erred in some way, his Spanish master (it is unclear who exactly this was) punished him severely. The hapless servant was likely beaten, and their Ute guide was appalled by the sight. He melted into the landscape, returning to his home village, never to be seen by the Spanish again.

As a result, the Domínguez-Escalante expedition was forced to turn back and limp home to Santa Fe, struggling through parts of Utah, Arizona, and Colorado before they finally found their way back to Nuevo México. Even their return would have been impossible if not for the kindness and assistance of several Native American tribes they encountered along the way. And while this expedition, like that of Francisco Coronado, ultimately failed in its main objective,

Domínguez and Escalante did keep a meticulously detailed journal about their explorations. This information would be invaluable to the explorers who would later follow in their footsteps in exploring and colonizing the American West.

It was only in 1792 that any English explorers would reach the West again, more than a hundred years after Sir Francis Drake landed in California. This time, it was Captain George Vancouver, a decorated English explorer, who would map huge tracts of the Pacific from Canada to the United States to Hawaii. While he did very little inland exploration, he did visit parts of Spanish California and met with both colonists and natives there. He was also the first European to explore the coastlines of two western states: Oregon and Washington.

With the 19th century looming, the American West was already a very different place than it had been in the pristine days of the pre-Columbian era. Now, colonists were fighting natives and each other as they sought to take hold of more and more of the West. And the story of the Wild West that we know—the era of sheriffs and cowboys, outlaws and gunslingers—was only just beginning.

Chapter 3 – American Exploration and Settlement of the West

Illustration II: A map of the Lewis and Clark expedition

After the Louisiana Purchase of 1803, the newly minted United States of America first started to take an interest in the western part of the country. While much of what we know as the American West was still under Spanish control at the time, all that was soon about to change.

The first major American exploration of the West was the famous Lewis and Clark expedition, and it was an incredible feat that would pave the way for westward expansion in the years to come.

The Lewis and Clark Expedition

Perhaps one of the most daring and incredible feats of exploration in American history, the Lewis and Clark expedition was arranged shortly after the Louisiana Purchase. Although the American government had paid $15 million for this territory—over $350 billion in today's money—the majority of the land was unexplored.

While the Spanish, French, and English had been exploring the American West for centuries, the Americans themselves had hardly set foot in any part of it at this point in history. All that was about to change.

Like the Dominguez-Escalante expedition, the Lewis and Clark expedition was meant to find an overland route to the Pacific Ocean. The other objective of the expedition was to map the vast Louisiana Territory, over 800,000 square miles of largely untouched wilderness. President Thomas Jefferson considered Meriwether Lewis to be the perfect person for the job. Lewis had served as a captain in the US Army, and he now worked for Jefferson as a secretary. He was considered both tough and trustworthy.

Lewis himself was well aware that the undertaking that Jefferson had proposed was a tremendous one. He knew he would need a courageous and capable person to help him command the expedition, and for this role, he chose William Clark. Clark had been his superior in the army, and he trusted him deeply.

After almost a year spent training, equipping, and preparing their expedition, Lewis and Clark set off up the Missouri River on a keelboat on May 14th, 1804. Their expedition was not a particularly large one, numbering only forty-five men. With the exception of Clark's slave, York, this group was made up of well-trained hunters and soldiers that the commanders had handpicked. They were well-

armed, too, with blunderbusses and muskets, and they were ready to face whatever came their way. While their goal was to interact peacefully with whatever Native American tribes they met, these were no unarmed Franciscan friars but military men bent on achieving their aim.

While Lewis and Clark both treated their own men very harshly, punishing them by beating them for the smallest infraction, they were mostly diplomatic in their dealings with Native Americans. Jefferson had given them peace medals to hand out to Native American chiefs, and they had also brought along plenty of gifts, such as face paint, beads, mirrors, and colored ribbon. Some tribes met them, eager to trade; they had heard stories of the white men and the treasures they brought from their southern and northern neighbors. Others were hostile and tried to avoid Lewis and Clark as much as they could. But for the time being, there was no open conflict.

Peace was better than fighting, yet it's still clear that Lewis and Clark did not treat the Native Americans with any real respect. These people had been living on American soil for thousands of years, yet when the explorers reached them, they simply stated that the United States of America now owned the land on which the natives lived. The Native Americans had absolutely no part or say in the fact that their land was now suddenly the possession of an entirely foreign nation.

It was during this early phase of the expedition that Lewis and Clark suffered their first and only casualty. One of their soldiers contracted a gastrointestinal disease and died as they were sailing up the Missouri.

In an attempt to foster better relations with the Native Americans, Lewis and Clark held several large meetings with numerous tribes in August of 1804. By this time, they had reached Iowa and South Dakota, becoming the first Anglo-Americans to set foot there. Reaching North Dakota that fall, they were over one thousand miles away from their homes in St. Louis, Missouri. With winter looming, they would have to dig in and wait out the coldest months of the year.

They built Fort Mandan near modern-day Washburn, North Dakota, and settled there for five months.

This brought Lewis and Clark close to the border of Canada—then a British colony—and while in Fort Mandan, they encountered one of its citizens. Toussaint Charbonneau was Canadian-born and of French descent and had been trapping animals for the fur trade at that point, but he became an interpreter for the expedition.

However, Charbonneau would not prove to be essential to the success of the expedition. It was his wife, Sacagawea. She was a proud Shoshone, but she had been taken by a rival tribe when she was only a girl. Charbonneau had set her free from her captors - or possibly bought her against her will - and married her, and by the time they joined up with Lewis and Clark, Sacagawea was heavily pregnant. She had faced plenty of tribulation in her young life, and she was more than ready to embark on a dangerous expedition—one which would take them through the territory of her own people. She hoped she might be able to see her family and friends again.

It is almost incomprehensible that this girl of sixteen would undertake one of the longest expeditions in American history while breastfeeding a baby who was only two months old when the journey began. But Sacagawea was made of strong stuff, and she tackled the journey with vigor.

When summer came, the expedition headed west and north across what was then the Louisiana Purchase territory. They left North Dakota behind and headed into Montana, crossing the vast state and meeting with the Native American tribes there. Sacagawea was instrumental in forming good relations with these tribes. Soon, they reached her own people, the Shoshone. These were Plains people with herds of strong and tough horses, and Lewis and Clark needed horses more than anything to enable them to finish their long journey. For Sacagawea, however, meeting up with the Shoshone was deeply important for a far more personal reason. She was finally able to see her brother again for the first time since she had been kidnapped.

Perhaps it was tempting for Sacagawea to stay with her own people, but instead, with her baby son Jean Baptiste in her arms, she decided to continue on with the expedition. She facilitated the purchase of several horses from the Shoshone, and along with some guides, the expedition headed toward Idaho, following the brutal Lolo Trail. Here, cold, hunger, and disease plagued the expedition. It must have been intolerable for everyone, especially the young mother and baby. Without their horses and Shoshone guides, it is unlikely that the expedition would ever have made it down that trail. Ultimately, however, they did, and they did so without losing a single person.

The Lolo Trail brought the exhausted, starving, and sickly expedition into Idaho, where they met yet another Native American tribe, the Nez Perce. They welcomed the suffering travelers with open arms and nursed them back to health after the trials of the Lolo Trail. After spending some time with the Nez Perce, the expedition continued west, crossing through part of Washington before they reached Oregon. In November 1805, with fall slipping quickly past them, Lewis, Clark, Sacagawea, her little boy (who had been fondly nicknamed Pompey), and the rest of the expedition finally saw the glorious, glimmering expanse of the Pacific Ocean. On November 5th, 1805, they reached the sea.

The Lewis and Clark expedition still had a very long winter to spend by the wild sea, not to mention the equally long journey back to St. Louis, but they had achieved something that had never been done before: they had crossed North America. Their expedition remains one of the most ambitious successes ever recorded in exploration.

After wintering in Fort Clatsop, which they built near the ocean, the expedition would return home via Montana and North Dakota. It was on the journey home that the only Native American casualties were recorded when Lewis and his men fired on a group of Blackfeet who were attempting to steal their horses, which were vital to their survival. But on September 23rd, 1806, having left Sacagawea and her family in Mandan, they returned to St. Louis at last.

Further Exploration and Colonization

The United States of America was growing as a global power during the first decades of the 19th century, with the War of 1812 establishing it as a formidable military opponent. It was no longer considered a mere group of colonial rebels but a country in its own right. Accordingly, the US was working hard to establish its power on its frontier and to secure its borders with its neighbors.

Of course, Native Americans suffered as the US strove to claim their lands. The Osage Nation, which was part of the Southern Sioux, was one of the first Native American tribes of the West to fall to the US in open battle. The Osage were still no match for the US Army, and they were forced to sign the Treaty of Fort Clark in 1808, which left the US in possession of all of their lands in parts of modern-day Missouri and Arkansas.

New Spain won its independence from Spain after a bloody eleven-year struggle in 1821, becoming Mexico. Most of California became a territory of Mexico, but Russia had control over Alaska at the time, and Russian Americans built forts as far south as Fort Ross in modern-day California (then known as Russian America). California would only become an American territory in 1848, but Russia's claims to modern-day California were transferred to the United States by the Russo-American Treaty of 1824.

Russians weren't the only other Europeans to move to the modern United States either. A group of Scottish and Irish people was the first to build a permanent European fort in North Dakota.

In 1811, Fort Astoria in modern-day Oregon was built very near to where Lewis and Clark had reached the Pacific Ocean. Many more forts were built in the following decades in western states such as Arkansas (which became a territory in 1819), Nebraska, Oklahoma, Kansas, Wyoming, and Idaho. With forts cropping up all over the West and colonists trickling to them, the first western states were admitted. In 1812, Louisiana became the eighteenth state and the first

to have any western territory; Missouri would follow in 1821 and then Arkansas in 1836.

The US also solidified its boundaries in the West early in the 19th century, with numerous treaties confirming its borders with Canada and Mexico.

It was also at this time that two more important American expeditions took place. While Lewis and Clark were exploring the northern parts of the Louisiana Purchase, Lieutenant Zebulon Pike was conducting another expedition to explore the Southwest, leading to run-ins with Nuevo México. Later, in 1812, Robert Stuart would lead a desperate mission across the Continental Divide and into modern-day Wyoming, blazing a trail across the South Pass for hundreds of thousands of settlers later that century.

The expedition led by Stephen H. Long, which took place in 1820, was a very different type of exploration. Long had been involved with building the first fort in present-day Nebraska in 1819, but now, he sought not to subdue the landscape of the American West but to study it. Using a paddleboat steamer, he took a group of artists, naturalists, and scientists into the wild to document the breathtaking wilderness and its many species. They traveled along the Rocky Mountains up the Platte River, becoming the first scientists in the American West, and they scaled Pikes Peak as well as explored the Canadian and Arkansas Rivers. It was the first scientific documentation of the Great Plains, and Long would return to the East with awed depictions of the wilderness, beauty, and barrenness of that area.

The year 1820 also brought another change, one that had tremendous political importance. While the American Civil War would only begin in 1861, tensions were already building between slave and free states in the United States. There was a roughly equal number of slave and free states at the time, maintaining a tenuous balance in a country so thoroughly divided on the issue of slavery. That changed when Missouri tried to join the US as a slave state. This

would disrupt the balance, and tensions escalated violently. As westward expansion gained momentum, these divided states were particularly concerned over what would happen as more and more western states were admitted. Would the US become predominantly free, or would the western states, too, be filled with slaves?

The government's resolution to this conflict was the ill-conceived Missouri Compromise, which maintained a tenuous peace for a period of around forty years before the American Civil War began.

The Missouri Compromise admitted Missouri as a slave state, but it also made Maine, which had previously been part of Massachusetts, a new free state. It also decreed that the US would literally be divided along a latitude line—known as the Mason-Dixon line—which split the country into the free North and the Southern slave states.

As a result, of the western states, modern-day Alabama, Arkansas, and Missouri were made slave states. The great, vast territory of the northern Louisiana Purchase, which was still largely unexplored, was temporarily free. This included modern-day Nebraska, Idaho, Wyoming, and the Dakotas. The Oregon Country (including modern-day Oregon and Washington) would be free too.

The Missouri Compromise would ultimately have devastating repercussions in the East when the Civil War broke out, but it also affected the West. But that was all in the future. For now, settlers were heading west with renewed hope and vigor, ready to claim the land they believed to be their own.

Ashley's Hundred

Although many imagine the first Western settlers to have been quiet colonial families desperate to eke out a living in this hostile wilderness, the first few people to live permanently in the West were very different. They were the original mountain men, and they would become the stuff of legend.

Jedediah Smith was perhaps the most legendary mountain man of all. While he was born in modern-day Bainbridge, New York, in 1799, "Jed" Smith grew up dreaming of a wilder place. He loved venturing into the rich woods of the East and became an adept hunter and trapper in his youth. Trapping was a reliable stream of income at that time. This was before the fur trade had practically annihilated hundreds of American species and endangered others such as the beaver and otter. The fur of beavers and otters, as well as others, was coveted, particularly in Europe, to make hats, coats, and other fashionable items. Trapping and killing these animals to sell their pelts was a lucrative business for any enterprising young man.

However, it was more than just money that Smith sought. The wilderness called to him, and when he read the journals of the Lewis and Clark expedition as a boy, it poured fuel on the flame that was driving him to the frontier.

By 1822, Smith was a young man living in Ohio with his poverty-stricken family. He tried to support them as well as he could, but he needed a better opportunity, one that would bring in more money and allow him to fulfill his frontier dreams. That opportunity came in the form of a newspaper advertisement. Its first line immediately caught his eye: "To enterprising young men..."

As Smith read, he grew more and more excited about what he was seeing. The advertisement was asking for around a hundred men who would be willing to explore the Missouri River, with the goal being to find its source and tap into its natural resources. The contract would last up to three years, and Smith knew that the money would be good. He couldn't pass it up. He responded to the advertisement, packed up his meager possessions, and set off for St. Louis.

Once there, Smith met up with William Henry Ashley. An adventurer and businessman, Ashley had reached the rank of brigadier general during the brutal War of 1812, and now he was practically bankrupt and growing desperate. There was nothing left for him in the East, and he had no choice but to head west and claim the

riches to be found there. Together with Andrew Henry, he formed the Rocky Mountain Fur Company in 1822, and they decided to find one hundred capable young men who would travel up the Missouri River and trap animals for the insatiable European market.

That was how Smith ended up finding Ashley's advertisement in the paper, and in a few short months, he was traveling up the Missouri alongside ninety-nine other young men who were ready to seek their fortunes in the wilderness. They would become known as Ashley's Hundred, and they were some of the very first Anglo-Americans ever to live permanently in the American West. They were no homesteaders, though; there were no ranches, growing families, or little houses on the prairie. These were mountain men, and they were as rugged and fierce as the predators that roamed the wilds. They lived a life of utter loneliness and also absolute freedom.

Smith took to that life effortlessly. Ashley's Hundred started out by exploring around the Yellowstone and Missouri Rivers, eventually following the Cheyenne all the way to its mouth through modern-day Wyoming and South Dakota. Ultimately, however, Ashley decided to concentrate his efforts on the Rocky Mountains.

As a mountain man, Smith, like the other members of Ashley's Hundred, would spend many months all alone in the wilderness, hunting and trapping. There was absolutely no contact with the rest of the world; the mountain men had to rely on their wits and ability to read the landscape. They also had to survive almost entirely on whatever they could hunt or scavenge in the woods, relying on their survival skills for food, water, warmth, and protection from both the elements and predators. Smith himself would find out, painfully and brutally, just how dangerous those predators could be. During his time in the Rocky Mountains, he was attacked and mauled by one of America's most powerful predators—a grizzly bear. If he had been alone at the time, he likely wouldn't have survived. Luckily for Smith, he was with a small party of other mountain men, and he talked one of them into stitching his ripped scalp back together. He would be

scarred for the rest of his short life, and he wore his hair long to hide this fact until his dying day.

Most of the time, though, Smith and his counterparts were alone. They only had contact with the East during set times when they would rendezvous with Ashley and others to trade their furs and receive money and supplies. These gatherings would become enormous, attracting large numbers of friendly Native Americans who wanted to trade, as well as the growing number of mountain men in the region.

In a matter of a few years, there were hundreds of mountain men exploring the Rocky Mountains, and not all of them were hunters and trappers. Many were land surveyors or army scouts and men who had journeyed to the wilderness simply to explore and map the land. They would become known as the "generation after Lewis and Clark." The land that the famed expedition had once crossed would now be thoroughly mapped and explored by the mountain men.

By 1826, Smith had made enough money that he could not only assist his destitute family in Ohio but also—with two other mountain men—purchase the Rocky Mountain Fur Company from Ashley. By that point, Smith had been in the wilderness for four years. He had experienced some terrible trials, most notably the attack by the grizzly bear, as well as multiple attacks from hostile Native Americans such as the Arikara, Blackfeet, and Assiniboine. However, he was still bent on exploring the West. In fact, now that he owned the company and no longer had to spend all his time trapping, Smith could start to explore the West in earnest.

In just a few short years, Smith explored and recorded a truly amazing amount of the western landscape. Not only did he follow the Pacific Coast all the way along the Oregon Country and California, but he also found the South Pass that Robert Stuart had first discovered and then attempted to keep secret. Smith also crossed the Mojave Desert and explored enormous tracts of South Dakota and Wyoming.

Ultimately, however, even Smith grew tired of the rough and dangerous life of the mountain man. By the time he reached his early thirties, he had made a comfortable fortune off the profits of the company. In 1830, he sold the company, which allowed him to give his family enough money to buy a farm and a house, as well as two slaves.

He returned to St. Louis shortly after selling the company and started to seek what he might have considered to be a safer means of making a living. Smith couldn't put himself behind a desk, however. He decided on trading with Santa Fe, by then a major city in Mexico-controlled Texas, and set off along the Santa Fe Trail with a handful of men.

Smith had survived in the mountains on his own for so long, yet now, at the age of thirty-two, he would finally meet his match. Ever the wanderer, he left his party behind to scout ahead and never returned. He was most likely slain by a band of Comanche, as his belongings were later found in their possession. It was a tragic end to a wild explorer who was finally seeking a little peace, but at least Jed Smith died as he had lived—in freedom.

He would leave behind a lasting legacy for the colonists who would follow in his footsteps. While Lewis and Clark had established the existence of the American West, it was the mountain men who would make it feasible for colonization. Their maps made westward expansion possible, and not only were they the first Anglo-American residents of the West, but they also paved the way for the families that would follow.

The Old Three Hundred

Stephen F. Austin was a man with a vision, and that vision included carrying on his father's legacy.

Considering what Austin's early childhood was like, it is almost surprising that he would be so dedicated to a cause his father, Moses Austin, had first conceived. Born in modern-day Austinville, Virginia,

Stephen's family moved to Ste. Genevieve, Missouri, when he was a very small child. In 1804, he was sent away at the tender age of eleven to go to school all the way in Connecticut—more than one thousand miles away. Perhaps it would have been easy for young Austin to feel abandoned by his father, whom he would hardly see for years to come. It was only in 1810, having been well educated in the East, that he finally returned to Ste. Genevieve to join his father's business. Moses owned a lead mine and needed help managing the growing business, but even this involved sending young Stephen away at regular intervals to handle lead shipments. One of these landed Stephen in New Orleans, where he contracted malaria. He would remain sickly for the rest of his life, but it does not appear to have affected his vigor and determination.

Moses's fortunes in lead mining would ultimately turn, leading him to uproot his life and start traveling through Texas. At the time, Texas was under Spanish control, although their grip on their colonists was growing more and more tenuous. Neither the Spanish Crown nor its Mexican residents had any beef with the United States, however, and so, Moses was able to explore the wild and barren beauty of this western state. Spain had colonized parts of it, but much of it was rich, empty, untouched land. To the 19th-century American psyche, this made it ripe for the picking.

Moses conceived the thought of getting permits from the Spanish government to settle Anglo-American colonists on their soil, and with the help of a high-up friend, he managed to secure these permits in 1821. But Moses himself would never see colonists arrive in what would eventually become the Lone Star State. He died that same year, leaving all of his possessions to Stephen—including the permits and the dream of colonizing Texas.

Stephen F. Austin unhesitatingly decided to carry on his father's legacy, even though he was part of Missouri's territorial legislature at the time. Upon starting to live out his father's dream, he almost immediately ran into what would seem to be an insurmountable

obstacle. After a brutal war, which lasted more than a decade, Mexico finally succeeded in winning its independence from Spain. The Treaty of Córdoba was signed on August 24th, 1821, and "New Spain" became Mexico. "Nuevo México" became a Mexican territory, which included Texas.

Luckily for Austin, however, the Mexicans had no quarrel with the Americans, and he was able to renegotiate his permits and gain permission to settle three hundred families in Texas.

Austin quickly began to advertise his offer in the United States. It was an attractive one in many ways. Settlers would be given an allotment of land that they would legally own. For farmers, it was just under 200 acres; for ranchers, it was just under 4,500 acres. This was good land around the Brazos, Colorado, and San Bernard Rivers, with fertile soil and plenty of water. With the eastern US getting more and more crowded as the population boomed, there was a constant hunger for farming and ranching land, and this opportunity to colonize a whole new area was a good one.

However, there were disadvantages. Chief among them was the fact that this land that Austin and the Mexican government were happily giving away as "untouched" had actually been populated for thousands of years. Tribes like the Comanche were not welcoming of colonists who suddenly believed they owned the land that these people had been living on for generations.

Another caveat was that these new landowners couldn't sit on their hands once they were given the land. Within two years, they had to have settled there and also "improved" the land by utilizing it for some form of agriculture. There wasn't time to mess around, so Austin was looking for hard workers.

Still, there was no shortage of people willing to take this opportunity. By 1824, Austin had issued 307 permits to new settlers. Some of these settlers had taken two permits per family, and as a result, there were 297 families moving to Texas that year. They are known as the "Old Three Hundred": the first farmers and ranchers of

the American Old West. Despite the presence of Native Americans, they were quick to put down roots and build a small town, and only 7 of the 297 families failed to improve the land within two short years.

These "families" didn't always consist of a conventional set of parents and children, however. When young, single men wanted to apply for this opportunity, they were simply grouped together in twos and threes to form legal families.

On the surface, the story of the Old Three Hundred is a familiar one with a tagline we know all too well. Courageous and enterprising Anglo-American settlers set out to tame a hostile wilderness and succeed by their sheer grit and gumption. However, there is a dark side to their story, one that is little told. The Old Three Hundred families were far from desperate Easterners, stricken by poverty, who had to struggle to scratch out a living in this hostile territory. In fact, most of these people were literate, upper class, and already fairly wealthy before they moved to Texas. While they nominated themselves as livestock ranchers in a bid to get the larger allotments of land, most of them were more interested in farming crops.

And of the 297 families, 69 were slave owners.

As a result, the Old Three Hundred would eventually develop vast slave-holding plantations, which would ultimately contribute to the chaos of the American Civil War. These were Texas's first settlers, to be sure, but they would also become the first plantations in the American West.

What was more, the presence of the Old Three Hundred and their almost immediate success would soon encourage more colonists to stream to Texas. While many of these gained legal permits from Austin, who continued to act as an agent for Mexico in selling them, some were squatters who simply moved onto open land and started farming it. As a result, the Anglo-American population of Texas boomed. By 1835, it numbered as many as twenty thousand, and this was just eleven years after the Old Three Hundred had moved there.

As for Stephen F. Austin, his contribution to history was far from over. Tensions were brewing between Mexico and its Texan territory. And those tensions would eventually erupt into a little-known period when Texas was part of neither the United States nor Mexico.

Texas was about to become a country all its own.

Chapter 4 – Anglo-Americans Go to War for the West

AGE 82   ELIZABETH (BROWN) STEPHENS   TAKEN 1903

Illustration III: Elizabeth Brown, a survivor of the Trail of Tears

By the early 1830s, many parts of the American West had been explored. While much of those lands were still wild and free and would remain so for decades, the explorers and mountain men had mapped most of them. Early settlements, often beginning as forts or small trading posts, were popping up all over the West. Native Americans everywhere were starting to realize that Anglo-American encroachment was not far away, and the Mexican government of Texas was beginning to feel threatened by the insatiable Anglo-American thirst for western land. Westward expansion had begun in earnest.

Much of this expansion was driven by the idea of manifest destiny. While the term would be used for the first time as late as 1845, manifest destiny was an idea as old as America itself—something akin to the thought process that had driven the Pilgrims to Plymouth in the 17th century. The majority of Anglo-Americans held the firm belief that they were divinely destined to control and colonize the whole of North America. They considered this to be inevitable. This drove much of their confidence as they swept aside entire nations in their unstoppable expansion toward the Pacific.

As a result, the United States was more than willing to make war on anyone who would dare to stand in its way. Its conflicts with the Native Americans are fairly well known, and rightfully so; this was a cruel and bloody chapter of American history, one that caused deep and lasting pain. However, the native tribes were not the only people who would go to war with the United States for their land. Mexico was another combatant, as well as Texas as an independent republic.

First, however, President Andrew Jackson would sign the Indian Removal Act, causing terrible suffering to tens of thousands of people.

The Indian Removal Act

Conflicts with Native Americans were starting to flare up all over the Old West by 1830. While the first open war by Anglo-Americans on Native Americans in the West would only begin in 1838, skirmishes, small conflicts, and the raiding and plundering of entire

towns were common by this time. The buzzword of the day was the "Indian problem." To much of the United States, Native Americans were an inconvenience. They were in the way.

President George Washington had even come up with ways to deal with the "Indian problem" during his time as the first president. His idea was slightly more peaceful; he considered it a necessity to "civilize" Native Americans, practically forcing them to give up their cultures and start behaving like Anglo-Americans. Of course, they would never be considered equal, but Washington hoped to assimilate them into the greater Anglo-American culture by having them Christianized, giving them English names, and educating them in English. Many eastern tribes realized that their options were civilization or death, so they chose civilization, most notably the Chickasaw, Cherokee, Choctaw, Seminole, and Creek. All five of these tribes—known as the Five Civilized Tribes—had had conflicts with the United States before and knew that if they failed to comply, they would be massacred.

But try as they might to give up their cultures and blend in, these Native American tribes just couldn't seem to please the Anglo-Americans. President Andrew Jackson was the driving force behind the thought that civilization would never work when it came to Native Americans. He had fought against the Creek during his time in the US Army as a major general, and by the time he became president, the country was rapidly expanding into areas like Alabama, Mississippi, Missouri, Oregon, and beyond. He was tired of fighting the Native Americans, and he simply wanted them gone—all 125,000 of them living in the Southeastern states at the time.

His solution was the Indian Removal Act. Under this act, Native Americans could be moved off their land and onto the "Indian Territory," which was originally a large tract of disorganized territory in the West, encompassing states like Wyoming and the Dakotas. The act stipulated that Native Americans had to move voluntarily and could not be forced and that the US government was obliged to

provide them with food, supplies, money, and transport for the journey. What was more, it also guaranteed to Native Americans that the "Indian Territory" would be their undisputed possession for all time. None of these stipulations were met. The act was passed on May 28th, 1830.

The first tribe to sign over their ancestral land in Alabama and Mississippi was the Choctaw. Once they signed over their land, they voluntarily began the long migration to modern-day Oklahoma in 1831. Their journey took them over five thousand miles across nine states, and it would take them months to complete. What was more, the financial assistance promised by the United States was not forthcoming. Some of them were even bound and chained on the journey by the US Army and forced to march. Women, children, young men, the sick and elderly—they all had to go. They left behind a heartbreaking document by one of their leaders, dutifully named George W. Harkins in accordance with "civilization," titled "Farewell Letter to the American People." It included the line "we as Choctaws rather choose to suffer and be free." Suffering was a terrible reality for them; freedom never would be. Over the four years after the signing of the Indian Removal Act, 12,500 Choctaw would leave their homes and journey west. Only around 8,500 would reach their destination. The rest were dead and buried along the trail, which quickly earned its name as the Trail of Tears.

The Trail of Tears

The Creek were the next to be removed. Leaving in 1836, 15,000 Creek took on the deadly trail, losing 3,500 of their people along the way.

Having seen what had happened to their Creek and Choctaw counterparts, the Cherokee were far less willing to make the long journey west. Many were adamant that it would be better and safer to stay and fight, even though they had seen an unrecorded number of their Seminole neighbors killed during the First Seminole War. It didn't matter whether they fought or fled; people were going to die

either way. Some of the Cherokee reasoned it was better to die fighting.

However, a small number of Cherokee believed that it would be far less risky to take on the Trail of Tears and move. Maybe they would find peace and freedom in the Indian Territory, after all, even though there were Native American tribes already living there that might not be so welcoming of their new neighbors. A small group of people in this camp decided to represent their entire tribe by negotiating the Treaty of New Echota in 1835. Their actual chief, John Ross, was not involved in the negotiation of this treaty—a fact that Jackson conveniently ignored.

It would appear that the majority of Cherokee were deeply reluctant to take on the Trail of Tears. While two thousand Cherokee moved voluntarily in 1838—a well-planned journey that took less than a month and resulted in under twenty-five casualties—John Ross instead wrote a petition that protested the fact that the majority of Cherokee were not represented or involved in the signing of the treaty. Sixteen thousand Cherokee signed his petition. It was thoroughly ignored. The treaty was ratified, and the Cherokees' land was officially no longer their property.

Meanwhile, in northeast Texas, other Cherokee tribelets had decided to go to war with the Anglo-American settlers of the area. The war would continue until 1839, killing hundreds of Cherokee and members of other tribes and ultimately resulting in their removal. Many Anglo-American and Spanish soldiers also died during this time, as well as an untold number of settlers who were murdered during Native American raids. The Cherokee would journey north to join what was left of the Choctaw after they themselves had traversed the Trail of Tears. Known as the Cherokee War, this was only a tiny part of an enormous conflict collectively known as the Texas-Indian wars, which would continue throughout the 19th century—just as war with Native Americans continued all over the Wild West.

Back in the East, John Ross and the other Cherokee were running out of time. When they had still refused to move by the summer of 1838, President Martin van Buren—Jackson's successor—decided that it was time to deal with them violently. Seven thousand US Army soldiers were sent to get rid of the Cherokee, whether they liked it or not.

The Cherokee had been living in their homeland, which encompassed parts of Alabama, North Carolina, Tennessee, and Georgia, for thousands of years. They spoke an Iroquoian language and had inhabited the Appalachians since around 1000 BCE. As a Woodland culture, they were a sedentary people, living in organized towns and villages and practicing agriculture. In their religion, every daily experience was spiritual, from the growing of the crops that sustained them—corn, squash, and beans—to cooking, cleaning, hunting, dancing, singing, and maintaining the fire in the central council house of each town.

It had been a long time since the Cherokee had been allowed to live the way their ancestors had done for hundreds of years before the Anglo-Americans came, and now, they were hardly being allowed to live at all.

The scene that unfolded throughout the Cherokees' homeland was a horrifying one for everyone who had to survive it. One moment, a young man might be outside in his fields, tending squash, beans, or corn the way his people had been doing for over two thousand years. The next, a contingent of well-armed soldiers would be charging down upon him, trampling his crops with the hooves of their horses. With guns and bayonets aimed at him, our hypothetical young man would have no choice but to stumble back toward his town. He would be informed that he was under arrest and that he would be removed from his land.

Once the young Cherokee reached his town, he would come upon a scene of absolute terror. The shrieks of frightened people being chased with bayonets into stockades, like cattle, would echo through

the air. Soldiers were everywhere, and they were not only harassing the people but also freely looting their homes, taking everything that they owned. The Cherokee had been told that they would be given money in exchange for their land and that they would be supported on their journey to the Indian Territory. Instead, they were literally robbed, and they were powerless to stop the soldiers.

The Cherokee would spend several nights imprisoned in the stockades. Their comfortable homes were hollowed out and empty, and they were allowed none of their possessions. They slept on the ground, with families huddling together under the open sky, regardless of the weather.

With guns trained upon them, the Cherokee were then forced to start walking. No matter how old or young or sick or lame they were, they had to walk to the nearest river with soldiers surrounding them as if they were driving "hogs," in the words of Reverend Daniel Buttick. Buttick was a missionary who had been living and working among the Cherokee for decades; they were his congregation, and he was heartbroken to see what was being done to them. He joined them on their journey, as did 1,500 Africans, some as slaves and some as freemen.

The camps were appalling. With no shelter or sanitation, disease was absolutely rife, and hundreds of Cherokees were killed in the first two weeks. Dysentery, whooping cough, and measles were the main culprits; the camps echoed with the moans of the dying. The US Army made no effort to help tend to the sick, hurrying the living along instead. Many were left to die or hastily buried in shallow graves.

Eventually, the Cherokee would reach the nearest river and find themselves shoved onto cramped, airless, and crowded boats. More disease would spread as they continued their journey on the water, with the stifling heat and filth making the holds reek of sweat and excrement. If our hypothetical young man was still alive by this point, he would be weakened and sick and have witnessed the deaths of his people—of people he knew.

In the fall, the Cherokee would continue their journey overland. There was still eight hundred miles to go before they reached the Indian Territory, but they were able to ask the commanding officer if they would be allowed to oversee the journey themselves from this point onward. The US Army was well aware that their main objective had been achieved: they had removed the Cherokee from their homes. The officer agreed, and the Cherokee would suffer less harassment for the rest of their journey, although the army still accompanied them to prevent any revolts.

Conditions barely improved. The Cherokee were still largely starving and had to rely on rations of flour and salt pork—a plain and tasteless diet that also left them intensely malnourished. Disease continued to spread, and at the pace they were moving, they were unable to reach the Indian Territory before the winter. Instead, the winter was unusually cruel, and the Cherokee had to break the ice on streams or pools in order to get water for themselves and the horses.

Perhaps our hypothetical young man was one of the lucky ones who was still able to walk. He would be burdened with supplies and plodding through great drifts of snow; there were no roads to the Indian Territory back then. Or if he was sick or hurt, he might be able to hitch a ride in one of the wagons. However, twenty people would be crammed into a single wagon, and they sat shoulder to shoulder with the sick and dying as they bumped along the trail.

The scene was so appalling that, in later years, a soldier who had witnessed both the Trail of Tears and the brutal American Civil War would claim that the Trail of Tears was by far the worst.

Some of the Cherokee groups took as many as four months to reach the Indian Territory. One unlucky group covered only sixty-five miles in three months, having to stop continually to bury the dead and rest the sick. It was only in March 1839 that all the Cherokee finally reached their new homes. However, they would only be able to stay there for about twenty years before more settlers would push them farther and farther west until all that remained of the once-vast Indian

Territory was a tiny piece of Oklahoma. By 1907, there was no Indian Territory anymore. Today, most Cherokee live on a reservation in Oklahoma—a far cry from the vast, free lands that they were promised.

The story of the Cherokee is by no means a unique one. All over the West, Native American tribes were forced from their lands. Conflicts with Native Americans would continue to rage throughout the history of the Old West until most tribes had been forced onto small, infertile reservations. The Trail of Tears remains a particularly tragic chapter of the long, heartbreaking story of the Native Americans.

However, the Native Americans weren't the only people against whom the Anglo-Americans went to war. Another nation had control over vast tracts of the American West, and that nation was the newly minted independent Mexico.

The Birth of the Texas Rangers

One of the most enduring symbols of the Wild West remains the Texas Rangers. And while this group of men would serve in many different capacities in their effort to keep Texans safe, the roots of the Texas Rangers are tightly intertwined with the Texas Revolution and the Mexican-American War.

Stephen F. Austin's attempt to settle American families into Texas had been a resounding success. However, those families faced significant trouble in the form of Native American tribes who wanted them off their land. What was more, Anglo-American and Mexican thieves had teamed up with the Native Americans in conducting raids on the growing farms and homesteads. Mexico, whose government was in total chaos directly after the revolution, was not particularly interested in protecting some immigrant families in one of its more far-flung territories. What was more, the people living in Texas were true settlers, not mountain men who could defend themselves against these threats.

Austin's solution was to form a group of Texan men who wanted to protect their fellow settlers. He would have to pay for this himself, so he could only afford ten. But he wanted ten of the very best, men who could hunt, track, ride, shoot, and fight. The original force of ten proved so effective that Austin ultimately would hire many more, and volunteers would join the force too. They came from a variety of different backgrounds; many were Anglo-Americans, but there were some Mexicans and Native Americans who had befriended the Anglo-American settlers and wanted to help protect them or get back at the thieves who had stolen from them.

Lack of protection wasn't the only problem that Austin and the settlers had with the Mexican government either. Mexico was being governed by a line of power-grabbing despots at the time, as corrupt men took advantage of the post-revolution chaos. Chief among them was Antonio López de Santa Anna. His tyranny drove many powerful people out of Mexico itself and into Texas, which became a hotbed for Santa Anna's enemies.

Santa Anna's corruption affected even the far-flung settlers of Texas. They faced the pressure of tremendous taxation, particularly very high customs on goods being imported and exported from the United States. Smuggling grew rife, and the Mexican government's crackdown on smugglers was far more organized than any attempt to protect the settlers from thieves or raiders. As a result, the settlers grew deeply dissatisfied. They complained to Austin, who resolved to travel to Mexico City and speak to Santa Anna himself.

By the time Austin made his trip in 1833, tensions were high between Texas and Mexico. The Mexican residents of Texas were dissatisfied too, and skirmishes between government forces and smugglers were growing more and more common. The Crises of Anahuac, culminating in the Battle of Velasco, had already seen Mexicans and Texans fighting bloody battles against one another. While Mexico had tried to solve the problem by dismissing the Mexican commander whose ire had sparked the conflict, things were

far from peaceful in Texas. In fact, many residents had been talking with Austin—a well-respected leader—throughout Texas—about seceding from Mexico and perhaps becoming a part of the United States instead.

Austin was on his way to Mexico City when Santa Anna got wind of these discussions. When Austin arrived, Santa Anna promptly had him thrown into prison for eighteen long months. Austin was never given a trial or even told what he had done to earn his imprisonment, but he was left to languish there anyway. And a Mexican prison in the 19th century was a miserable experience.

Austin's imprisonment was the straw that broke the camel's back for the people of Texas, particularly the Anglo-Americans. There were more Anglos in eastern Texas than Mexicans by that point, and many of them were powerful people. Chief among these was a man who would become nothing less than a legend: David Crockett.

Davy Crockett, King of the Wild Frontier

Born in Tennessee in the summer of 1786, Davy Crockett had an inauspicious start for a man who would ultimately sit in Congress. His father sent him off to work as a hired hand when he was only twelve. His task was to drive a herd of cattle on horseback, and he became a cowboy long before that term had officially been coined. When his new employer tried to kidnap him after his contract was over, young Davy simply ran away, covering seven miles in two hours through snowdrifts. This was just the beginning of his career as an outdoorsman, one which would even outshine his prowess as a politician.

Crockett's family, like thousands of others in America at the time, was quick to take advantage of the opportunities presented by western expansion. They constantly moved west, always seeking the next great opportunity. Crockett avoided school passionately and even disappeared for long periods of time, making his own way in the world, but he ultimately managed to get a little education.

The War of 1812 and the Creek War of 1813 gave him his first taste of blood, and after that, Crockett felt ready for anything. He was willing to go to war, but he preferred exploring and hunting. He gained a reputation for being an adept shooter.

His status as a legend truly began in 1827 when he was campaigning to be elected to Congress. Newspapers started to publish tall tales and yarns about him, singing his praises as an outdoorsman. The yarns were wildly popular, some of them enduring to this day. These fun, outrageous stories only served to grow his reputation. Some of them told how Davy Crockett was born weighing two hundred pounds and dancing. A particularly entertaining version tells of how Davy Crockett and his mythical wife, Sally Ann Thunder Ann Whirlwind, were being kept up by the sound of alligators dancing on the roof of their cabin. Both Davy and Sally Ann climbed onto the roof of the cabin, seized the alligators by their tails, swung them over their heads lasso-style, and launched them all the way across Tennessee and into the Mississippi.

The yarns were always told in the drawn-out style of the old frontier, and they gave birth to the tall tale that would characterize so much of American mythology.

While this makes it difficult to separate fact from fiction when it comes to Crockett's real life, it is very clear that he earned the title "King of the Wild Frontier." And the yarns made him hugely popular. He was elected to Congress for the state of Tennessee that year and enjoyed a brief but successful career in politics.

Originally, Crockett supported President Andrew Jackson. However, when Jackson turned fickle and favored Crockett's opponent in another election to Congress, Crockett quickly became anti-Jackson and won his seat back in 1833. Jackson's political opponents, the Whigs (this was long before the Republicans), were even grooming him for president, but Crockett lost his seat for the last time in 1835.

Tired of politics and ready for a new adventure, Crockett moved back to the one place that had always been home: the frontier. This time, he chose Texas, just as tensions were boiling over. He arrived there while Austin was still in jail and while trouble was brewing all over the state. Ready to go back to war, Crockett quickly became an important figure to the Texan militia that was gathering to attack Mexico.

The Texas Revolution

It was in 1835, shortly after Crockett had arrived, that the revolution truly began. Releasing Stephen F. Austin from prison did little to appease the Texans, especially when Austin returned to Texas feeling thoroughly anti-Mexican.

Aware that the Texans were growing out of control, a Mexican force approached Gonzales, Texas, to seize the cannon stationed there, which was under Texan control. A battle broke out, commanded by members of the Old Three Hundred, and the Texans fought a hard victory. The Texas Revolution was under way.

Shortly after this, Texans declared their independence, forming the Republic of Texas, and chose Samuel Houston to become their general. Open war between Texas and Mexico had begun, and it would be a hard and bitter fight.

One of the most brutal battles of the Texas Revolution was the Battle of the Alamo. It had been over a hundred years since the Alamo Mission had been established by the Spanish, and it now acted as an important fort near San Antonio. Capturing it was an important early foothold for the Texans. General Houston, however, decided it should be abandoned, and he promptly did so. The volunteers inside the Alamo ignored him. John Bowie and Davy Crockett were among those who decided they would defend it to their last breath.

It was an ill-conceived plan at the start, and this became obvious when thousands of Mexicans attacked. If this had been one of Davy Crockett's yarns, he would have conquered them single-handedly with

nothing more than a bit of rope and a toothpick. But this was no yarn. It was reality, and when the battle began on February 23rd, 1836, the odds were weighed heavily against the Texans.

Somehow, though, for thirteen long days, the Texans held out, all the while pleading for reinforcements. Houston never responded. There was only one group of people who came, courageous figures who would later become the stuff of legend: the Texas Rangers. They were mostly volunteers at that time, and they rode boldly to assist the Alamo despite the ridiculous odds.

Yet this tall tale had a tragic end. Ultimately, despite the unrelenting courage of the two hundred men inside the Alamo, the Mexicans prevailed. The Texan casualties were devastating, with Davy Crockett himself dying in the fight. He lived as the King of the Wild Frontier, and he died defending it.

His death was only fuel for the Texas Revolution. Davy Crockett had been one of the most adored folk heroes of his time, and his death outraged his fellow Texans.

The Mexican Army felt unstoppable after defeating the Alamo, and they swept east toward the US border, terrifying the colonists who lived there. Houston was forced to withdraw his forces all the way to the San Jacinto River. Here, again, the Texas Rangers played an integral role. They fully conformed to their original mission—to protect the colonists—and helped thousands of families to safely escape the Mexicans by protecting them and harrying Mexican troops to slow them down so that Texans could flee.

Eventually, having pursued the Texans hard for miles and fighting a brief victory against them near the San Jacinto River, the Mexicans came to a halt on April 20th, 1836. The Texas Rangers, who had been acting as scouts and spying on the Mexican Army since the start of the revolution, were quick to bring Houston the information that Mexico had set up camp and that their guard was down. Thanks to their intelligence, Houston was able to strike, and he struck both fast and hard. While it had taken the Mexicans 13 days to overwhelm 200

men inside the Alamo, Houston's Texan army, which numbered 910 men, defeated the 1,360 strong Mexicans in only 18 minutes. The Mexicans were annihilated; the entire army was killed or captured by the end of those fateful few minutes.

The **Battle of San Jacinto** brought the **Texas Revolution** to an end, ushering in the nine years during which Texas would be a country of its own. Ultimately, however, Texas negotiated its annexation by the United States of America and became a state in 1845. The US was forced to defend its right to Texas in the **Mexican-American War** of 1846–1848, but this was a decisive victory for the US and fought almost entirely on Mexican soil. By the time it was all over, the American West had grown considerably. Mexico ceded many territories to the United States, including modern-day Utah, New Mexico, Texas, California, Nevada, and Arizona.

During the Mexican-American War, the Texas Rangers truly began to make their mark in history. They were actually known as the "Texas Devils" during the war. Ultimately, they would be known for bringing together the best of all the different places that had influenced Texan history, shooting Spanish pistols and Tennessee rifles as they rode Mexican ponies and wielded **Bowie knives**. They became a symbol of Texas's proud freedom and tough tenacity, and they continue to serve as Texas's state investigative bureau to this day.

Another symbol of the Wild West that had its roots in the Mexican-American War was the Colt revolver—the six-shooter championed by outlaws and lawmen alike later in the history of the West. Samuel Colt patented his revolving gun, the first handgun to be able to fire multiple shots between reloads, in 1836; however, it was during the war that the Colt revolver was popularized. Later, the Colt revolver's successor, the Colt Single Action Army revolver, would be widely used in wars with Native Americans in the West. It became known as the "gun that won the West."

The Texas Rangers, of course, were quick to adopt the six-shooters, and so, the Texas Ranger adored by legend was born.

With that, the American West as we know it belonged to the United States of America. And the US was quick to tap into its riches, particularly its mineral wealth. This would lead to one of the greatest migrations westward in history: the California Gold Rush.

Chapter 5 – A Different Kind of Wildness

Illustration IV: A photograph of Belle Starr, the Bandit Queen

With the Western frontier now thoroughly explored and mostly conquered, colonists were streaming into the West. At first, many of them were simply seeking land they could ranch or farm; after all, the richest natural resource of all was space. Soon, however, Easterners would realize that the West held more than just land. There was

mineral wealth there—great untapped lodes of precious metals—and if there was anything a colonist valued more than land, it was gold.

The California Gold Rush

By the time California became a United States territory in 1848, it was still largely untouched by colonists. Only about 6,500 Hispanic people were living there, mostly missionaries and farmers. The Native American population still controlled most of the land. Only around seven hundred European Americans had made California their home.

One of them was John Sutter, and he wasn't even looking for gold on a cool winter's day early in 1848. He just wanted to have a waterwheel built. Sutter, a Swiss immigrant, had come to California from the Old World looking to start a new settlement. He named it Nueva Helvetia, and his first idea was to make money out of the vast forests that stretched throughout California. These giant forests were breathtaking, as they were filled with pine trees and species that have since all but vanished. All that changed with the arrival of the Europeans, and Sutter was chief among them; he even enslaved hundreds of Native Americans to work his lands. But the greatest change of all was still to come, and it wouldn't be caused by lumber.

Sutter wanted to have a sawmill built to process timber for Nueva Helvetia, and he enlisted the help of one of his colonists, a carpenter named James Wilson Marshall, who hailed from the East. Marshall was meant to build a waterwheel that would be powered by the steady flow of the American River.

Marshall was splashing around in the river, preparing to build the mill, when something glittering caught his eye. When he bent down, he saw them: little flakes of brilliance peppering the pebbly bottom of the river, sparkling like bits of sunshine made solid. According to Marshall himself, his breath instantly caught in his chest, his heart pounding as he bent down to lift one of those tiny flakes from the river. It sparkled on his fingers, and he immediately knew what it was. It was gold.

When Marshall took the discovery to Sutter, the two men immediately agreed that they should keep their discovery as quiet as possible. They wanted to keep the gold to themselves. And as they explored more of the American River and its tributary, Sutter's Creek, they realized that both waterways were flowing with millions of dollars in gold. Quietly, they began to pan for gold, extracting it cheaply and easily and then taking it to the nearest town to sell. That town happened to be San Francisco, which was about ninety miles away.

But despite Marshall's and Sutter's best efforts, it was inevitable that people would begin to talk. After all, someone had to be receiving, refining, and reselling that gold. Word got out, and it rapidly spread around San Francisco. In the age of tall tales, the story was largely ignored at first; after all, just months ago, these people had been reading about how Davy Crockett fell into a crack in the earth and subsequently became best friends with a bear named Death Hug.

Their incredulity changed a few weeks after the discovery of the gold. By then, the United States had signed the Treaty of Guadalupe Hidalgo, which ended the Mexican-American War, and California had become a US territory. San Francisco was still a quiet little port town, but it certainly woke up when a shopkeeper paraded down the streets, holding something in his hand that glittered like a fallen sun. It was a vial of pure gold from Sutter's Creek—its value unimaginable to the people of the sleepy settlement—and he was saying that there was more. In fact, the American River was flowing with gold at Nueva Helvetia, and it was ripe for the picking.

The response was immediate. Men started to flow toward Nueva Helvetia, and with every lucky miner who panned gold from Sutter's Creek, its fame grew out of control. That summer, San Francisco was practically abandoned. Who would want to run a trade port or a shop when they could be picking gold right out of the river? There were four thousand miners in Nueva Helvetia by the end of that summer, and that was only the beginning.

Sutter's Creek wasn't the only place where gold was to be found. As more and more people were attracted to California, arriving via steamboat at San Francisco or overland from the East, surveyors were finding gold everywhere. People started to flow to various spots throughout the territory, and not all of them were from the eastern United States. News of the gold at Sutter's Creek spread all over the world; soon, people were arriving from as far away as Chile and China.

The Gold Rush really gathered momentum, however, after President James K. Polk mentioned the discovery of gold in an address in December 1848. When he confirmed the rumors that had been spreading across the globe, it set the eastern United States alight. Polk had had the matter investigated by one of his military officers, and the man had come back with reports of an almost fantastical amount of gold. Best of all, the gold was easily found; no expensive mining tools were required. Sometimes, men could just dig chunks of gold right out of the rocks with their pocket knives. At worst, all they needed was a pick and shovel. They would dig up handfuls of gold-rich gravel and take it down to the nearest running water to pan it, letting the water wash away the larger fragments of soil or rocks and leave behind nuggets and flakes of gold.

"Gold fever" ripped through the US, igniting thousands of men to rush west in search of their fortune. In many men, the thought of finding gold and making a fortune in the West inspired in them a kind of frenzy. Even early on in the Gold Rush, there were reports of entire towns being left abandoned, crops left to rot in the fields, and livestock wandering all over the landscape on their own. In the East, men would sell or mortgage everything they owned for passage to California, either overland or by steamboat. These became known as the forty-niners: men who uprooted their entire lives to go searching for gold in 1849.

The Gold Rush itself would last for three more years, and at its peak, it drew around 125,000 people to California. The territory's European population was eighteen times larger by the end of the Gold Rush. This was terrible news for the Native Americans living there, of course, as they were driven off the land. Gold was something they had never had any real use for, yet Europeans were violently driving them away or even, at times, enslaving them to get their hands on it. The increasing population and concentration of people in California also meant an increased opportunity for the spread of disease. What was more, gold-fevered men sometimes thought nothing of it to murder their Native American counterparts. Famine, too, spread rapidly among these people, as their crop-growing lands were ripped to shreds in the insatiable search for inedible gold. The death toll of the Gold Rush was practically equal to the number of people it drew to California: 120,000 Native Americans perished during this time. They were not the only ones to suffer, though. Chinese miners faced constant hatred, from dreadful mass lynchings to a Foreign Miners' Tax that cost Chinese citizens a high price each month. Hispanics suffered as well, and Anglo-Americans, of course, were not exempt from the terrible trials of the Gold Rush either. Casualties were high regardless of ethnicity.

For the rest of California, it meant that mining towns were appearing all over its landscape. These towns were chaotic jumbles of huts, tents, and ramshackle buildings slapped together to accommodate the rough and wild men who went to live there.

Despite the news of gold, hundreds of thousands of men who poured into California would often find themselves disappointed. While some men were lucky enough to strike it rich and make their fortunes, countless more would have ruined their families and finances to discover that not every square inch of soil was rich with gold. In the unhygienic, crowded conditions of the mining camps, disease spread swiftly. Even the lucky ones, the ones who found gold at all, would spend their time in California suffering in poor shelters

with limited access to supplies or services. The unlucky ones would die there, alone and poor with nothing to show for it.

The relentless greed of gold fever ultimately led to the destruction of much of California's landscape. Forests were felled to build mining equipment and towns, while fields were torn up. Eventually, the surface gold ran out. The Gold Rush went from being an opportunity for any lucky individual to strike it rich to becoming another battle between titans, as mining companies sought to dig mines and turn a profit. Many of the desperate and disillusioned miners who had flooded to California in a bid to bring home buckets of gold now had no choice but to turn to these companies and go to work in the mines for them, digging chunks of gold from dark mineshafts in exchange for pitiful wages and poor living conditions.

It was the mining companies who made the most money. The Gold Rush peaked in 1852 when the deeper mines were flourishing. A staggering $81 million worth of gold was extracted from this territory in a single year, which equates to almost $3 trillion in today's money. After that, the gold began to run out. Mines would still operate there for centuries, but the Gold Rush itself was over.

It left California deeply changed. Its native population had been decimated, the landscape was torn open, and forests had been hacked down. California was now dotted with mining towns. San Francisco had gone from a little port to a bustling city. Los Angeles was incorporated, and Nueva Helvetia became the city of Sacramento. One of the world's largest and most enduring companies, Levi's, had its roots in the Gold Rush when Levi Strauss opened his first store in San Francisco. It catered to miners and produced all sorts of supplies at first; his blue jeans would be patented by 1873, just in time for the cowboys of the Old West to popularize them.

California's population reached 380,000 by 1860. Most of these people, especially during the Gold Rush itself, were fortune-seeking men living in ramshackle mining towns.

These mining towns would be the beginning of the most well-known era of the Old West: the time we know best from Western films and American legend. For it was during the Gold Rush that the first towns filled with disreputable characters would be born. The mining towns were built around a population of young, lonely men, and it showed. Saloons and brothels were more common than churches or general stores; prostitution, drunkenness, and gambling were the most common forms of entertainment for tired forty-niners after a long day of mining. As people grew more and more desperate, crime became rampant. Law enforcement was practically nonexistent, though. Westward expansion was happening so quickly that the government simply couldn't keep up. In fact, it was during the Gold Rush that the phrase "Go West, young man" was coined by a journalist, and young men were responding to that call in droves.

This ushered in a whole new era for the West, a time when lawlessness was absolutely rife all across the area. The California Gold Rush was not the only one of its kind either; more gold and silver rushes would take place all over the West, rapidly populating it with desperate men who would turn to stealing as easily as to mining.

The West was once known as the "Wild" West because of its true wilderness, its vast landscapes of empty space, its teeming wildlife, its free tribes, and its untamed beauty. After the arrival of Anglo-Americans, the West would still be wild but in a very different way.

An era of outlaws and lawmen was about to be ushered in, one as violent as it was iconic. While many of the names to follow will ring with familiarity, the story to follow has often been lost to history. And despite being one of the most unbelievable tales history has to offer, it is entirely true.

Two Colt Revolvers and a Bowie Knife

Captain Jonathan R. Davis had had enough of violence, and that was before he killed eleven men in a matter of minutes.

Davis had served in the Mexican-American War, and while he had earned the rank of captain, he was quick to get out of the army as soon as the war was over. That had been five years earlier. Leaving behind the army life, Davis remained in California once the Gold Rush began, and he was one of the thousands who joined the stream to the Sierra Nevada Mountains looking for gold.

It was on a cold winter's day in December 1854 that Davis would be confronted with the worst odds of his life, and he wasn't even looking for a fight at the time. Instead, he was simply climbing a trail through the mountains, hoping to find some gold and make a fortune, just like the thousands of other young men in California at that time. He was accompanied by two friends, Dr. Bolivar Sparks and James McDonald, and they were just prospecting for gold and minding their own business.

They were doing this with a wary eye on the landscape, however. Reports had reached them that the Sydney Ducks, a gang of bloodthirsty Australian outlaws, had gone on a devastating killing spree earlier that week. Ten prospectors had already been murdered, and hundreds of dollars in money and gold had been stolen. No one in those days wandered the West unarmed; Davis himself had taken the added precaution of carrying two of the Wild West's most iconic weapons, the Colt revolver. He also had a Bowie knife at his hip, a twelve-inch-long blade with a razor-sharp point designed for self-defense and responsible for hundreds—if not thousands—of deaths by this point. Having been trained in fencing at university, Davis knew how to use it too.

And in just moments, he would need to use it more skillfully than ever before.

The three men were advancing innocently up the trail, their hearts full of thoughts of gold, when suddenly the landscape around them exploded with gunfire. In a matter of seconds, McDonald and Sparks had both dropped to the ground, their blood pooling into the snow around them. Davis's revolvers were in his hands as the shots rang

out, zipping through his clothes, the zing of tearing cotton in his ears as they broke through his hat and slashed two flesh wounds into his body. His war-trained eyes picked out the flashes of movement in the heavy brush, and without hesitation, Davis fired back. His revolvers whirred and cracked. Twelve shots rang out in rapid succession, and when the guns were both empty, seven men lay dead.

But there were seven more. Out of ammunition, they stalked from the bushes, armed with short swords and Bowie knives of their own. McDonald lay dead, and Sparks was barely breathing. Davis was alone, and the seven outlaws believed that finishing him would be easy now that his revolvers were both empty.

Davis wasn't done yet. Perhaps he could have fled, but Sparks was still alive, and he wouldn't abandon him. Drawing his Bowie knife, Davis turned to face all seven attackers at once. They came at him, and with quick, flashing strokes of the knife, he killed four more men in a matter of seconds.

With his enemies dying at his feet, Davis faced the remaining three outlaws. Three against one: the best odds he'd had all day. These outlaws, however, were well aware that facing this man was like facing a thousand. They turned and fled, and Davis dropped to the ground, ripping off his shirt and slicing it into shreds to form bandages and tourniquets for Sparks.

There was a clatter of feet while Davis was tending to Sparks's wounds, and Davis lunged to snatch McDonald's weapon where it still lay in his holster—he hadn't even had time to draw it. But the three men who ran up the trail were fellow prospectors; they had seen the lone gunman facing the fourteen outlaws, and they'd come to help.

Their help, however, was not needed. All they did was to help Davis bandage up Sparks and rifle through the pockets of the outlaws, where they discovered over $500 in stolen cash, watches, and gold— over $16,000 worth in today's money. Then Davis lifted Sparks onto his back and carried the wounded man back to the nearest town.

where Sparks would sadly die a week later. Davis donated all of his bounty to Sparks's family.

While much of the Wild West as we know it today is composed of tales as tall as Davy Crockett's, the story of Jonathan R. Davis and the fourteen outlaws is true. It was contested in its day, and Davis and three witnesses described the event in court, proving its truth. Why this incredible fight is often unknown is a mystery; however, in recent years, it has been commemorated with a sculpture by Michael Trcic. The sculpture was fittingly entitled with a phrase that summarizes this event: "One Man With Courage is a Majority."

In these early years of the Wild West, stories of heroes of law and order are few and far between. Instead, we hear many tales of wild outlaws, and one of the earliest was Jim Reynolds.

The Civil War in the West

The story of the American Civil War in the West is often untold, but the American West suffered under the burden of this bloody conflict just as the East did. And it all started with the Gold Rush itself.

By 1850, California's population was so large that it applied to be admitted as a state. This caused immediate trouble, adding fuel to the already fiery situation in American politics at the time. In 1845, after being annexed by the US, Texas became the twenty-eighth state, and it was admitted as a slave state. This tipped the balance of power toward the slave states of the South, upsetting the free North despite the Missouri Compromise. The South was quite comfortable with this state of affairs until California petitioned to become a free state.

Once again, America's leaders were left to scramble for a solution to prevent the all-out war that had been brewing for decades. Senator Henry Clay came up with the Compromise of 1850. It would admit California as a free state, define a border between Texas and New Mexico, establish the Fugitive Slave Act, which allowed slave-catchers to drag escaped slaves back to their masters even if they made it to a

free state, and abolish the slave trade in Washington, DC. All of this was an attempt to appease both sides slightly, but it brought only a stay of execution.

The uneasy peace was ready to fracture once again in 1854 when Kansas (which encompassed modern-day Colorado) and Nebraska were attempting to become US territories. The United States was very motivated to admit these two territories, as it would allow the government to distribute land to homesteaders and continue the all-important westward expansion, but both of these lay north of the Mason Dixon Line, which would make them free states. The balance of power would be even more skewed toward the North, and balance of power was key to peace in this period of United States history.

As a result, the Kansas-Nebraska Act would be passed. This was yet another attempt at compromise, but this time, it would fail. The act repealed the Missouri Compromise and allowed the Territory of Kansas (now Kansas and Colorado) and the Nebraska Territory (modern-day Nebraska, Montana, and the Dakotas) to vote on the issue of whether they would be slave or free states.

The North was immediately incensed by this development. As for Kansas and Nebraska, absolute chaos broke out in these states. Intense violence took place between pro-slavery and anti-slavery groups, particularly in the Territory of Kansas, leading to multiple massacres, shootouts, fires, and riots in a spate of violence known as Bleeding Kansas, which claimed fifty-five lives.

Trouble brewed all over America, and by 1861, peace was no longer an option. The American Civil War began, and bloody battles were fought all over the country, including the Old West. The bloodiest of all would be the Battle of Westport in 1864, which was fought near Kansas City. It was known as the Gettysburg of the West, and it was a resounding Union victory. The battle brought an end to Confederate power in Kansas, at least for the most part. The Battle of Palmito Ranch, which took place in Texas in 1865, is thought to be the last Civil War battle.

In the midst of all this, however, the story of the Old West outlaw was just beginning. One of the first and most legendary men to be labeled an outlaw in the West would turn out not to be an outlaw at all but a Confederate soldier whose illegal execution would change the way history has viewed him for centuries.

The Treasure and Tragedy of the Reynolds Gang

Jim Reynolds would go down in history as one of the West's worst outlaws, but newer evidence suggests that he was no criminal but a soldier.

In 1861, James "Jim" Reynolds and his brother, John, were captured in New Mexico and brought to Denver—the modern-day capital of Colorado but then a city in the Territory of Kansas. They were Confederate soldiers who had been captured by Union forces during the Battle of Mace's Hole, and they were brought there to be kept as prisoners of war. Yet little did their captors know that the jailer was himself a secret Confederate. In the night, he smuggled the men out of prison and set them free into the Wild West.

The Reynolds brothers had to lay low for some time, but over the next three years, they drummed up support in Kansas for the Confederate cause. There was no shortage of pro-slavery elements in Kansas at the time, as had become abundantly obvious during Bleeding Kansas. Soon the Reynolds brothers had put together a force of over twenty men. This group would become known as the Reynolds Gang; it would go down in history as a group of raping, pillaging outlaws. In reality, though, it was an official Confederate force; they were members of Company A of Wells's Battalion, Third Texas Cavalry.

The men began to make their way along the Santa Fe Trail through the West, hoping to stay behind Union lines and cause as much chaos as they could. There was plenty of trouble to be found there; in fact, they were forced to fight Apache more often than Union soldiers.

It's unclear exactly when the Reynolds Gang started robbing and raiding in Union territory, but by 1864, they had a solid purpose. With orders from their Confederate leaders to disrupt stagecoaches and ranches as much as possible, they would rustle cattle, burn ranch houses, and rob stagecoaches. Even though railroad surveyors had been looking for a way to build the first transcontinental railroad since the 1850s, it would only become a reality in 1869, and the stagecoach remained the fastest and most reliable way to transport goods and people from the East to the West.

One such stagecoach traveled through Buckskin Joe—modern-day Laurette, Colorado—and stopped at a vast cattle ranch known as the McLaughlin Ranch. It was here that Jim Reynolds first encountered the man who would later murder him: Abner Williamson. Williamson was a Union cavalryman who had been appointed to escort the stagecoach, and when the Reynolds Gang ambushed the coach at McLaughlin Ranch, he was utterly unprepared to fight them. The highwaymen quickly overpowered him and ordered the passengers out of the coach in a classic stick-up. Reynolds broke open the coach's safe, stole about $4,000 in gold dust, robbed the passengers, and then took an ax to the coach, utterly destroying it before making his escape.

There's little doubt that Williamson faced derision and perhaps even punishment for allowing the Reynolds Gang to take the coach, and his bitterness brewed with every new report of violence wrought by the gang. Ranches and towns were being pillaged, and panic quickly spread among the people of the area. It seemed as though the gang was everywhere. Reports of their violence grew out of proportion and probably beyond what was actually true. People were hearing that the Reynolds brothers were rapists and murderers, that they would butcher everyone in their path and worked only as wanton criminals who were more interested in their own wealth than in supporting the Confederate cause. This last thought may actually be true; by the

summer of 1864, the Reynolds Gang had amassed around $40,000, and they seemed pretty comfortable with the idea of keeping it.

Still, the people of Colorado were unwilling to allow the Reynolds Gang to pillage their lands. Groups of soldiers and citizens started to gather to defend their homes. By July 1864, the Reynolds brothers were wanted men, and Union forces were tracking them down.

Aware that they were being hunted, John and Jim decided that steps had to be taken to protect their vast treasure, which would be worth around $70,000 today. They gave each of their gang members (which had dwindled to about fifteen men) some of it, and Jim hid the rest somewhere in South Park.

They were finally cornered near modern-day Grant, Colorado, on July 31st, 1864. The resultant shootout killed one of the gang members—Owen Singletary—and scattered the rest. Most of them would be captured in the following days, including Jim Reynolds. John and one of his men, Jack Stowe, were the only ones to escape. In triumph, the Colorado men who had killed Owen Singletary preserved his head in a jar of alcohol and paraded it around local towns as a token of victory.

After Jim and the others were tried by the Union court in Denver, things grew ugly. The court failed to find them guilty of either rape or murder, but the robbery charges stuck, and they were sent to Fort Lyon for sentencing. One of the guards in charge of bringing them safely to Fort Lyon was Abner Williamson. His heart still burned with anger over the stagecoach they had stolen and destroyed right out from under him, and he was about to take bloody revenge. He may have been part of convincing his commanding officer, Sergeant Alston Shaw, to enact the terrible scene that unfolded next.

Only a few miles outside of Denver, Shaw ordered the prisoners to be blindfolded. They were bound to one another and to a solid tree, and then Shaw ordered his men to execute them—judge and jury notwithstanding. Most of his men flatly refused. Despite what the papers had been publishing about the "Reynolds Gang," these were

Union soldiers, and they recognized Jim and the others for what they were: Confederate soldiers and prisoners of war. Shaw insisted, however, so Williamson drew his weapon and killed them all, one by one. Together, Shaw and Williamson cooked up a story about how the devious Reynolds Gang had tried to escape and how the Union soldiers had been forced to kill them in the chaos. The press at the time, of course, ate it all up. And before Shaw's death, he had all his records destroyed. His version of the story was popularized for centuries, making Jim Reynolds one of the most terrible villains of the West in popular culture.

John Reynolds would have a similarly sad ending. He was killed in a shootout in 1871 but not before drawing a map to where his brother's treasure lay. To this day, the fate of that treasure—and even its existence—remains completely unknown.

Jim Reynolds might be one of the Old West's most notorious outlaws, yet it turns out that he might have been nothing more than a soldier on the wrong side of history. However, one man whose status as a true Wild West bad guy remains undisputed; that man is Robert "Clay" Allison.

The "Shootist"

Robert Clay Allison was riding down the street of Hemphill wearing nothing but what he considered to be absolutely essential: a gun belt, with his two revolvers—either Colt or, by that time, Smith & Wesson—in their holsters. And this was far from the weirdest or even most anti-social thing he had ever done.

Women panicked. The sheriff was called, and he tried to get Allison to get down from his horse and put on a pair of Levi's or anything, for that matter. Allison was having none of it. He drew his gun on the sheriff and marched the helpless lawman into the nearest saloon, where he instructed him to drink until he fell over.

This is just one of many colorful anecdotes surrounding the chaotic life of Robert Andrew "Clay" Allison, a Tennessee-born Civil War veteran who would become a cowboy, outlaw, vigilante, and rancher rolled into one. Born in 1840 on a plantation in Tennessee, Allison fought on the Confederate side during the Civil War from the age of twenty-one, but he was given a medical discharge in 1862 thanks to the fact that he tried to kill his commander's for refusing to let him pursue Union troops in retreat. The reason for his medical discharge was given as mania related to a head injury as a child, which might explain some of his greatly erratic behavior, which would only worsen as he grew older and ventured into the West.

His wild violence made him a valued member of the Ku Klux Klan (a hate group that targets minorities) in the area, but even the KKK couldn't get along with him. By 1866, Allison was heading west to make his fortune there. He journeyed toward New Mexico, causing chaos as he went. When a hapless ferryman had the audacity to overcharge him, Allison beat him to a pulp and left him for dead.

Once in New Mexico, Allison found that he was considered far less disreputable here than he had been back in civilized Tennessee. New Mexico was still very much a frontier at the time, although numerous advances in cattle ranching had changed its barren landscape into mile after mile of enormous ranches. Barbed wire had been invented in 1867, allowing for vast areas of the prairie to be enclosed for tough beef cattle to roam; a single ranch could manage a herd thousands strong. That meant that the ranchers needed men who could wrangle the cattle from horseback. They would have to be tough, skilled riders who could rope, brand, and herd with the best of them. The true era of the cowboy had begun. New Mexico was filled with Levi's-wearing, Colt-toting, lariat-wielding men who worked and rode long hours.

It was as a cowboy that Allison first found employment with a New Mexican rancher, and he would partake in yet another truly classic chapter of Wild West history: cattle drives. Before the

transcontinental railroad made it possible for cattle to be moved long distances via train, ranchers from the West, which had become the nation's main beef producer, had to drive their cattle vast distances over the open prairie. Cowboys had to do more than just drive the cattle; cattle rustling had become one of the most lucrative crimes in the West, popularized by villainous outlaws like "Hurricane Bill" Martin. Allison's first task was to help on one of these drives. He rode a horse for mile upon mile alongside a vast herd of cattle, dust rising into the air and the thunder of hooves a constant accompaniment. He was instantly smitten with the West. The openness, the wilderness—it was all he wanted.

At the end of his cowboy career, Allison was rewarded with three hundred head of cattle and enough money that he was able to start his own ranch near modern-day Springer, New Mexico. This turned out to be a highly profitable venture, and Allison chose to spend his money on binge-drinking at the local saloons. The drunker he became, the angrier he got, and Allison soon gained a reputation as a fighter who wouldn't think twice about drawing a gun and killing a man in one of his rages.

It was during his time ranching in New Mexico that some of Allison's most famous escapades took place. One involved the brother of the ferryman he had beaten senseless on his journey to the West. Chunk Colbert had earned himself something of a reputation as a gunslinger, and he swaggered into Cimarron—Allison's hometown—looking for nothing but trouble. He certainly found it. Inviting Allison to dinner at a nearby inn, Colbert tried to shoot his rival from under the table. The shot ricocheted, missing Allison by far. But when Allison drew his own revolver and shot Colbert point-blank in the head, he didn't miss.

He was also drinking and gambling at a Cimarron saloon when the panicking wife of a Ute man, who had been murdering people and hiding their bodies in his cabin for months (possibly even holding his poor wife hostage; she was covered in blood), came running in.

Allison tracked down her husband, tortured him to death, and then dragged his body over some rocks for good measure. His eccentricity was balanced only by his absolute brutality, and the humorous side of his stories turns chilling at the thought of how much he appeared to take pleasure in pain and violence.

One of the few times that Allison was on the right side of history was during the Colfax County War. During the lawless era of the Wild West, bloody feuds were common. Sometimes these would take place between families if one encroached on the ranching land of the other or perhaps killed a member in one of the fatal brawls that were all too common in Old West saloons. The Colfax County War, however, was the common man's stand against bureaucracy. Ranchers and other business owners in Colfax County found their land sold right out from under them to a group of investors associated with the Santa Fe Ring; a crime ring composed as much of corrupt lawmen as of outlaws. Allison founded and led the Colfax County Ring, which opposed the Santa Fe Ring, and attacked his enemies with his trademark ferocity. His fierceness only intensified after the Santa Fe Ring shot a friend of his, Pastor Franklin Toby, in the back, killing him.

Despite Allison's strenuous efforts, however, the Santa Fe Ring ultimately prevailed. He was forced off his land and moved briefly to Texas, where he rode through the streets naked in the above anecdote, only to return to New Mexico in 1883. Marriage and the birth of his first daughter, Pattie, seemed to mellow Allison somewhat; he didn't kill anyone for some time, even though he did yank a few molars out of a dentist whose services he found unsatisfactory.

It would almost be expected that Allison would eventually die in violence, but in the end, it was a freak accident that killed him. In 1887, he was moving some supplies by wagon when the wheels hit a rock and jolted, panicking the horses and throwing him right into the path of the wheels. The wheel ran right over his head and neck, killing

him almost instantly, and Allison would live on only as an emblem of the wildest days of the West.

Jesse James, The First American Bank Robber

In 2019, almost 2,500 bank robberies took place in the US. And while robbery has grown less dramatic since the chaotic time of the Wild West, it remains an enduring problem in the United States, and it is one that has its roots in an Old West outlaw whose name has become legendary.

Considering that Jesse James would become one of the most infamous outlaws of the Wild West, his upbringing was surprisingly calm and stable. Born in 1847 to a Baptist minister and his wife who owned a farm in Missouri, James and his brother Frank grew up with a stable family and a solid education. The Civil War changed all that, of course. When James was only sixteen years old, Union troops invaded Tennessee and began to burn and pillage everything in their path, especially slave owners' farms and fields. The fields burned to the ground, and James could do nothing but watch. The experience was devastatingly traumatic. James would never forget it.

He wasted no time in enlisting directly after this attack and was sent to the West to fight in the gruesome guerrilla war that was ongoing there. His commanding officer, Captain William Anderson, was none other than "Bloody Bill": the man responsible for dozens of terrifying atrocities during Bleeding Kansas and the Civil War itself, including the Lawrence massacre, which resulted in the death of nearly two hundred people. Bloody Bill was a vicious enemy, but he was well-loved by his loyal men, who were known as Quantrill's Raiders. Jesse, Frank, and the rest of the Raiders were bushwhackers—guerrilla fighters who became adept horsemen and soldiers during the chaos of the Civil War in the West.

James looked up to Bloody Bill, and their relationship became one of trust and respect between a commanding officer who believed passionately—if brutally—in his cause and a subordinate who was willing to die for what he believed in. Perhaps, having left his family at

such a young age, James looked to Bloody Bill as a kind of father figure.

This made it all the more traumatic for young James when, at the age of seventeen, he witnessed the violent end of a violent man. Quantrill's Raiders were cornered by Union troops in Missouri, and in the battle that followed, Bloody Bill received a bullet to the brain. He died as he had lived, in violence, and the two James brothers were left feeling lost and bitter without their beloved captain. The name of the lieutenant colonel who had led the Union assault on Bloody Bill, Samuel Cox, was emblazoned deep on James's heart. Revenge brewed within him, and his bloodthirst slowly grew.

When the Civil War was over, James, like so many other unsatisfied Confederates, found himself having to find a way to survive in a Union-ruled South. James had been raised to believe that slavery was the divine order of things and that the Union had it all wrong. The paradigm shift to abolition was one that James was unable to make. After all, he had been ready to die for the Confederate cause; he had even seen Bloody Bill killed for that cause. He couldn't let it go, and as a result, he started to draw nearer and nearer to his bushwhacker brothers.

Missouri's Reconstruction proved too much for James and his peers. They believed that the Union should be stopped, that somehow the Confederacy could still rally, and so, they decided to launch attacks on Union institutions in some desperate, crazy bid to weaken the Union. Somewhere during the planning, however, James and his gang lost sight of their original objective to fight against the Union. They left the war behind and strayed instead to simple lawlessness, deciding that they wouldn't attack their target—they would simply rob it.

On the day before Valentine's Day of 1866, Jesse and Frank James, along with the four Younger brothers who had joined their gang (Bob, Cole, John, and Jim), strolled into the Clay County Savings Association with drawn weapons. It was broad daylight. The cashiers

had no idea what to do when the gang aimed their guns at them and told them to open the safes and unlock the doors. They didn't know how a stick-up worked because there had never before been a bank robbery in the history of the United States. Ultimately, they complied, and the James-Younger Gang helped themselves to the bounty inside the bank. This was so much more lucrative than robbing a stagecoach; they made off with around $60,000 or around $1 million today. As they rushed out of the bank with their new wealth, some courageous or foolish soul tried to fire on them. The gang returned fire, claiming their first murder victim: a bystander who was only seventeen years old.

This was the start of one of the most famous and lucrative criminal careers of the entire Wild West. Jesse James and the rest of the gang would rob as many as twelve banks during the course of their career, and it quickly became obvious that while upholding the Confederacy might have been his outspoken cause, Jesse was mostly interested in making tons and tons of money. In this goal, he succeeded outright. During the next decade or so, the James-Younger Gang would steal around $200,000—about $3.5 million in today's money. Bank robberies, once unprecedented, became commonplace throughout the Wild West as other outlaws started to emulate trailblazer Jesse James.

For three years, James and his gang would continue to rob banks at will, sometimes murdering people in the process, sometimes not. In 1869, James committed his first murder in cold blood, and with that, the gang became notorious throughout the Old West. James and his gang were robbing a bank in Gallatin, Missouri, when he looked over the counter into the eyes of a cashier who seemed familiar. With adrenaline flowing through his veins, James suddenly and firmly believed that this cashier was none other than Samuel Cox, the man who had killed Bloody Bill. Without a second thought, he drew his weapon and shot the cashier in the chest. The bullet obliterated his

heart, killing him instantly, and James finished robbing the bank and left.

Newspapers all over the West blew up with wild accounts of this brutal act, and as a result, James and his crew became wanted men. And there was a pretty price on their heads too.

Banks weren't the only victims that James and his gang chose either. Just a few months after the James-Younger Gang robbed their first bank, two brothers named Simeon and John Reno made history by becoming the first train robbers of the Wild West. Things had been stolen from trains before this, of course. Transcontinental trains were simply too tempting to leave alone. All that gold and silver from places like California and South Dakota had to reach the East somehow, and much of it crossed the Old West by train, meaning that while most trains carried some passengers, many were absolutely laden with spectacular riches. Stealing from a train at the station was risky, though, as there were guards and soldiers everywhere.

The Reno brothers realized that a train in motion was largely unguarded and that if it could be stopped in an isolated area—like any of the many, many uninhabited miles of the Old West in those days— it was easy pickings for an enterprising outlaw. The Reno brothers looted around $13,000, a small fortune at the time.

By 1873, the James-Younger Gang turned to train robberies too. Jesse James has become a well-loved figure in popular culture: the gun-toting, bandanna-wearing cowboy with a cocky attitude and a rebellious nature, fighting against the government and the institution. What we often forget today is that the institution he was rebelling against was abolition. James and his gang wore KKK masks on their train robberies to draw the attention of the engineer and distract him from his task. On their first robbery, this worked so well that they were able to pull part of the track aside and derail the train, killing the engineer instantly and stealing thousands of dollars.

Jesse James would never be caught by the law. He came very close during a bank robbery in Minnesota during the fall of 1876, however.

While the gang was inside holding up the cashier, townsfolk attacked from outside, scattering the James-Younger Gang and defeating them for the first time since they had started robbing banks ten years before. Two of James's gang members were killed. The James and Younger brothers themselves narrowly escaped, but the Youngers would soon be caught and sentenced. All but Bob would die in prison.

James wasn't sure what to do. Frank seemed content to give up the outlaw life, settling down with a wife, a family, and his vast stolen fortune. Jesse, while he was married with children and appeared to have been very fond of his kids, was unable to give up his wild ways. He formed a second gang, the James Gang, in 1879 and started robbing anything that he could. This time, however, James wasn't surrounded by his Confederate brethren who had fought alongside him in the brutality of the Civil War. His new gang members were out to make money, and when a $10,000 bounty was placed on James's head, their loyalties were quick to change. One of them, Bob Ford, shot James in the head during a quiet afternoon at home in 1882. The outlaw died immediately at the age of thirty-five.

Frank James was far luckier. While he was arrested and tried, there was never enough evidence to convict him, and he would live out the rest of his years in the peace that Jesse never got to experience after the horrors he had witnessed during the Civil War.

Belle Starr, The Bandit Queen

Jesse James may have been one of the Wild West's most legendary outlaws, but he was easily equaled by a woman who obliterated societal constructs and headbutted her way through life with fearlessness and brutality: Belle Starr.

Born Myra Maybelle Shirley in Carthage, Missouri, Belle grew up as exactly that—a Southern belle. She was educated in one of the lady's academies of the day, as the men in her life considered her brain too delicate for mathematics or science and had her learn music and languages instead. While Belle loved playing piano and became an

adept musician, what her teachers at the academy didn't know was that their pet student had a wild side. Belle had four brothers and no sisters, and she particularly adored her oldest brother, Bud. Bud never seemed to see her as a sister; he treated her just the same as he treated his other younger siblings even though they were male. He taught her how to ride a horse and shoot a gun with the best of them. Belle took to shooting and riding—sitting sidesaddle and slinging any weapon you care to name—with as much ease as she made elegant conversation and delicate music.

Belle's life fell apart, however, in 1864. She had been born during the Mexican-American War of 1848-1849, and she was only a teenager when her best friend, Bud, was torn away from her. He joined Quantrill's Raiders during Bleeding Kansas, becoming a scarred veteran by the time the James and Younger brothers joined during the Civil War itself.

Bud's absence was not the only disaster to befall the Shirley family by this time. Belle's father ran a livery stable, and in the chaos of the war, the business fell apart. When Bud was killed in 1864, it was the last straw. The Shirley family had to get out of Missouri with all its hard memories and the heat they were feeling as sworn Confederates. They headed west instead, settling in Texas and hoping for a little peace and quiet. The grieving Belle's education ended, and for a few years, she was at a loose end.

Her first encounter with lawlessness would come in 1866. Right after committing their first bank robbery, the James-Younger Gang was roaming the West, seeking refuge. They knew the Shirleys because they had fought alongside Bud, and when the Youngers heard that the Shirleys were in Texas, they headed there for shelter. The Shirleys hid them without question. Belle, then eighteen, was immediately struck with the romantic and lawless idea of the outlaw, particularly the very handsome Cole Younger. He may have been her first conquest—and she had many.

If Belle had a relationship with Cole, it didn't last long. Later that same year, Belle married another Quantrill's Raider named Jim Reed, who was then just an ordinary farmer and homesteader. In 1869, however, he would be convicted of murder. Fleeing Missouri, Jim took Belle and their two children—Rosie Lee "Pearl" and James Edwin—to hide out in California.

It was during this time in California that Belle's own life of crime started. Now that he was a wanted man, Jim abandoned his efforts to be a normal member of society and started robbing and pillaging wherever he went. Unlike most outlaws' wives, Belle was not content to wait at home for his return. Instead, she rode right alongside him, effortlessly keeping pace and proving to be a useful ally in a gunfight. In one particularly brutal instance, she and Jim attacked an aging member of the Creek tribe who was rumored to know the location of thousands of dollars' worth of treasure. They savagely forced him to tell them where it was, then rode over and stole it.

Despite the ethnicity of this hapless victim, it appears that Belle was not particularly racist. When Jim's own posse picked a gunfight with Jim and killed him, Belle quickly moved on and began seeing a Cherokee outlaw known only as Blue Duck. Her first remarriage, however, was to another Cherokee named Sam Starr. In an age of glorious aliases like Hurricane Bill or Butch Cassidy, the romantically ringing "Belle Starr" was actually this outlaw's real name.

Belle and Sam put together an outlaw posse of their own, but this time, Belle was no sidekick. Instead, she was the leader of the gang, even though Sam might have argued with this assertion. She masterminded countless crimes such as horse theft, cattle rustling, and bootlegging whiskey. And despite numerous arrests, she was only ever convicted once. She would spend six months in jail for her crimes in 1882/83. The rest of the times that Belle and other members of the posse were arrested, she would charm their freedom out of the local lawmen, adding seduction to her long list of skills.

Even during her life, Belle became a legend and an icon. There was something irresistibly Wild Western about her, even though she was one of a kind. She wore a long dress and a feathered hat and rode sidesaddle like any proper Southern lady. Yet instead of choosing a quiet old hack, her horse was a fleet-footed red mare named Venus, which was as fiery and headstrong as the woman who rode her. She had left her children with her mother when her life of crime truly began, and her "baby" was her .45 Colt, which was always at her hip. Belle was deadly, unstoppable, and—to the stifled women of the Victorian world—perhaps an object of both horror and envy.

Ultimately, as with most outlaws of the Wild West era, Belle would succumb to her own wild ways. Sam was shot and killed in 1886, and Belle remarried badly. Her young new husband, Jim July, was nothing but trouble. There were many fights between them, and less than a year after they were married, Belle was ambushed and shot dead at the age of forty-one. To this day, no one knows who killed her, but Jim July is a prime suspect.

Belle's beloved daughter, Pearl, had a headstone erected over her mother's grave that featured a sculpture of her swift, treasured Venus at the top. The poem engraved upon it closed with the lines, "'Tis but the casket that lies here/The gem that fills it sparkles yet." And, indeed, Belle Starr would be immortalized as one of the most romantic and colorful figures in the entire Wild West.

The age of the Old West outlaw is one that lends itself well to stories, but ultimately, it was a time of difficulty and terror for the many law-abiding citizens of the Old West who were simply trying to make an honest living. The wanton violence that burned down entire towns or embroiled whole counties in crazy blood feuds would ultimately have to come to an end if the ever-growing society was to survive in the American West. And as the frontier slowly disappeared and as the West officially joined the United States, something would have to be done about the outlaws.

The era of the outlaws would soon be ended by a group of history's most questionable heroes: the lawmen of the Wild West.

Chapter 6 – The Men Who Tamed the West

Illustration V: The steely-eyed stare that made Seth Bullock a legend

The lawmen of the Old West were often barely any different to the outlaws themselves. Old West sheriffs and deputies often had criminal records of their own and sometimes abused their positions of power. Nonetheless, the West was ultimately tamed, and the bank and train robbers who had controlled the landscape for years would eventually lose their power.

Some of the earliest Old West lawmen would have their roots in a particularly gruesome chapter of Wild West history: the great buffalo hunts.

From 60 Million to 300 in 50 Years

During the time that the Plains Indians could enjoy their freedom, their lifestyles and even religions often revolved around one of North America's largest land animals: the American buffalo. These tremendous beasts numbered in the tens of millions by 1850, roaming across the plains in herds so vast that they made the ground tremble. While they served as food for the Plains people for centuries, there was a natural balance between the human population and the healthy buffalo herds. What was more, the Plains people practically worshiped these animals. They were something sacred, and to take one of their lives was considered a blessing and a necessity for survival. To waste any part of the buffalo's body would be considered heartless disrespect for the life of that great animal, and so, the buffalo herds remained huge and strong despite centuries or even millennia of hunting by Native Americans.

Even when Anglo-American trappers decimated the beaver and otter populations and turned to hunting buffalo for their pelts, there just weren't enough trappers in the West to make a dent in the vast numbers of these creatures. However, this state of affairs would not last long. These trappers-turned-hunters had already all but destroyed several other species. And the American buffalo would become yet another conquest.

When the transcontinental railroad was completed in 1869, it sounded a death knell for the buffalo herds. The American Indian Wars were drawing to a close: the Civil War was over. Violent men with a penchant for killing found themselves with nothing to do, so they turned to hunting for sport. This had long been a favorite hobby with rich and idle folk from all over the world throughout all human civilization, and the buffalo would simply become another target for wanton killing.

Soon, dignitaries from all over the globe were coming to America to hunt buffalo for sport, and out-of-work soldiers were only too happy to be employed as guides and hunters themselves. The result was an absolutely abhorrent scene that most likely fills the modern-day reader with appalled horror. As eastern hunters swept across the newly conquered Great Plains, they left a trail of dead buffalo in their wake and in unimaginable numbers. Entire herds could be destroyed in a single day, and hunters left the landscape littered with naked carcasses that were stripped of their hides and left to rot in the baking sun. One hunter killed six thousand of these creatures all on his own. Often, the transcontinental trains would slow down if a buffalo herd was spotted and allow passengers to open fire on these creatures from the safety of their cars. To the Native Americans, who were already rapidly losing their land, it was a horrifying sight akin to the burning of a church. To kill so many and to leave their valuable meat to decompose and fill with flies and maggots was more than just horrible. It was desecration and blasphemy in their eyes.

In fact, the killing of the buffalo herds sped up the final conquest of the Native Americans. Without the buffalo, many tribes were stripped of their lifeblood. They were left to move onto small reservations within the vast territories that had once been all their own.

By the end of the century, only three hundred buffalo were still alive on the Plains. In fact, the species was perilously near to being entirely extinct. It was only thanks to the efforts of early

being the vast herds of the early 19th century.

Buffalo Bill Cody

One of the most iconic people of the Old West earned his fame during the great and terrible buffalo hunts. In fact, the buffalo lent him the moniker by which we know him best today: Buffalo Bill.

Born in 1846, William Cody wasted no time in getting to the West. By the age of twelve, he was in Wyoming, helping out with a wagon train that was taking settlers to the ever-shrinking frontier. When gold was found in Colorado, Cody was there, chasing down those elusive nuggets of wealth. He was an adventurer to the core, a nomad, and a free spirit who always seemed ready for another great escapade.

During the American Indian Wars, Cody served as a scout, doing so with the kind of courage that earned him a Medal of Honor. Later in life, he would earn a reputation as an advocate for "fair" treatment of Native Americans.

Back in the 1870s, Cody was on the Great Plains, hunting buffalo. His time as a US Army scout had made him adept at reading the landscape and tracking both people and animals, and he was often employed by Asian or European royalty to take them to the buffalo. He became so good at this and was such an excellent shot that he was soon known as Buffalo Bill, a moniker that he defended during a legendary rivalry with yet another of the Old West's almost mythical "Bills": Medicine Bill Comstock. These two great buffalo hunters squared off in an eight-hour contest to see who could kill the most buffalo in that period. Buffalo Bill defended his title and won the match, but he found Medicine Bill to be a worthy opponent. Medicine Bill, himself an intriguing and colorful character, would become almost forgotten in the face of Cody's fame.

conservationists like Theodore Roosevelt and the first national parks, such as Yellowstone, that the buffalo survived at all. Today, their numbers are recovering, but at 200,000, they are still a long way from

However, it was Buffalo Bill's Wild West Show that truly made Cody famous. While he did a little acting in his earlier years, in 1883, Cody would start his own show. Buffalo Bill's Wild West was a kind of traveling circus of the West, showing off feats of horsemanship and shooting, as well as reenacting battle scenes from the American Indian Wars.

Buffalo Bill's Wild West Show proved wildly popular. Buffalo Bill became an icon of the West and one of its most well-known figures, and while his show was all fake, Cody himself truly was a frontiersman. He was as fearsome and controversial as the era he embodied.

Cody also brought fame and fortune to some of the Wild West's other icons, such as Wild Bill Hickok and another of the strong and fascinating women that became legends of the West: Phoebe Ann Moses, better known by her stage name of Annie Oakley.

Annie Oakley

Born in the summer of 1860 in the backwoods of Ohio, Phoebe Ann Moses was immediately plunged into a difficult childhood—one that would shape one of the West's most well-known heroines.

Phoebe Ann, who went by "Annie" from an early age, lost her father when she was only six years old. Despite being one of the youngest girls, Annie scorned the gentler playthings her sisters enjoyed and quickly began to take on responsibility for the household. Her mother remarried and bore a baby to her new husband, but Annie's stepfather passed away when she was still very young. Annie decided that if there was no man of the house, she would take charge.

She shot a rifle for the first time when her family had grown hungry and desperate. After spotting a fat squirrel sitting on the fence in the front yard, Annie loaded her father's old rifle. She thrusted the ammunition into the front of the muzzle—the weapon was practically an antique even then—and fired off a single shot. It struck the squirrel's head, killing it instantly. For the next seven years, although

she was often shipped off to live with other families in a desperate bid to have fewer mouths to feed, Annie would continue to hunt game at every opportunity. She sold it to a local grocer, eventually paying off the mortgage on her mother's house as a result. Her hunting perhaps served as an escape at times. One couple with whom Annie lived was extremely abusive to the point of putting her outside barefoot in the snow as a punishment. She would never reveal their real names, calling them only "the wolves." She ran away from them when she turned twelve.

By the time Annie was fifteen, she had become something of a local legend. So much so, in fact, that when competitive sharpshooter Frank Butler came to town, the locals encouraged her to compete against him. Annie was more than willing to oblige. Butler was, at first, amused by the idea of competing against a fifteen-year-old girl. The challenge was to hit twenty-five targets, and when Butler hit twenty-four of them, he was smugly satisfied. That was until Annie hit all twenty-five. He was awed by her. Just a few months later, the two were married.

This launched Annie into a whole new life. Butler made a good living as a sharpshooter, and he traveled all over the country, taking Annie out of Ohio for the very first time. She even became a part of his shows. But despite her obviously superior shooting prowess, Butler made her his assistant at first. In 1882, when Annie was twenty-two years old, his partner suddenly took ill. Butler was desperate for a replacement. Annie filled in and became an enormous hit. At this point, she took a stage name: Annie Oakley, supposedly after the town the two lived in after getting married.

Three years later, Buffalo Bill Cody had an opening for a sharpshooting act in his Wild West Show. He decided to hire the sensational couple. Butler quickly faded into obscurity, as the crowd absolutely loved Annie Oakley.

For sixteen years, Annie lived a life she could never have imagined as an impoverished child desperately hunting in Ohio's woods to pay off her mother's mortgage. They not only traveled all over the Wild West and the rest of the United States but also all the way to Europe and beyond. Annie was a sensation.

Annie met many fascinating figures during this time, but perhaps the most iconic was Lakota Chief Sitting Bull, the warrior chief who had put General George Custer to shame at the Battle of the Little Bighorn. Sitting Bull had a brief stint with the Wild West Show himself, many years after being forced onto the reservation, and he was so taken with Annie that he adopted her as his daughter. She was named "Little Sure Shot," and she would think of Sitting Bull as a close friend for the rest of his life.

She would perform in Buffalo Bill's show for sixteen years, only retiring in 1901 after a back injury sustained during a train accident.

Retirement was by no means the end of Annie Oakley's tale. When the First World War broke out in 1917, Annie wrote to President Woodrow Wilson with two offers that were considered absolutely preposterous at the time. Firstly, she was happy to put together a whole regiment of self-funded woman sharpshooters to go to the war. And secondly, she offered her services as a shooting instructor for male soldiers. Appallingly, despite her obvious prowess, both offers were turned down.

Five years later, Annie toured again but only for a short time. By 1925, the legend was ailing. She died in 1926, and Frank Butler, who had remained stoutly by her side, passed away less than a month later after half a century of marriage.

Pat Garrett and Billy the Kid

Another Old West icon who found his origins in the buffalo hunts of the 1870s was Pat Garrett. Alabama-born and Louisiana-raised, Garrett ventured west shortly after the transcontinental railroad was laid. He worked as a cowboy in Texas for some time, getting to know

the range and the wild men who worked it. Frontier life suited him, and he became desensitized to the violence of the era. He grew used to fending off cattle rustlers and drunken confrontations in chaotic saloons.

When buffalo hunting opened up a whole new economic opportunity, Garrett was quick to capitalize on it. In the 1870s, he joined the droves of men who headed to the Great Plains not to hunt for sport but for hides. Buffalo robes were all the rage back East and in Europe and Asia, and there was plenty of money to be made on them. The buffalo herds became yet another natural resource plundered by greed.

It was greed that motivated Garrett to kill his first man in 1878. As a group of hunters was skinning the fallen buffalo, leaving their bleeding carcasses on the dusty prairie, Garrett and another hunter started to argue over the ownership of some of the hides. The argument grew heated, and a reckless rage came over Garrett. He drew a gun, believing that he was in the right, and killed the other hunter. This made him a murderer, but he would still become a respected lawman in the years to come.

Perhaps because of this altercation, Garrett tired of buffalo hunting; not to mention, the industry was beginning to cause its own demise by that time. He moved to New Mexico and opened a saloon of his own, where he was well-liked by the locals and earned the nickname of "Big John" for his tall, slender height. While he was managing his saloon, he first ran into one of the unluckiest and yet most-loved outlaws of the Wild West: Henry McCarty, who was then operating under the alias of William H. Bonney. But readers perhaps best know him as Billy the Kid.

"The Kid" was a fitting suffix for this outlaw. He was only around seventeen or eighteen when he first met Garrett, but he had already killed his first man and would kill eight more. Although he would never attain the notoriety of a man like Jesse James, Billy the Kid had started young, driven to a life of crime by the sheer brutality of his

childhood. He'd grown up in the Irish slums of New York, lost his father and mother at a young age, and was so abused by his stepfather that he ultimately ran away. He'd quickly fallen into petty theft, then killed a man who had been belligerent and threatening toward him during his time working at an army post in New Mexico.

By the time Billy the Kid found himself in Garrett's saloon, he was already a notable outlaw. However, Garrett had no qualms about serving him booze. Of course, in those days, there was no national minimum drinking age. Thus, the Kid could knock back as much booze as he wanted, and Garrett was all too willing to sell to whoever was buying. Back then, Billy was a well-liked youngster with an affable demeanor offset only by his willingness to kill.

Two years later, however, everything changed between Garrett and Billy. Garrett had been active in local politics, and when the Lincoln County War prompted the local sheriff to resign, he was elected to become the new Lincoln County sheriff.

Garrett became the sheriff after one of the most violent chapters in Lincoln County's history. Rival posses had been clashing over the cold-blooded killing of John Tunstall, one of Billy the Kid's closest friends and one of the few men who had ever been a stable figure in his life. On one side was the Lincoln County Regulators, led by Dick Brewer and whose members included Billy the Kid, who was fighting against a monopoly on dry goods and cattle in the area held by a general store named The House. The House had local law enforcement in their pockets; the Regulators were a group of hired guns who had grown loyal to Tunstall and sought to avenge his death. Blood was inevitable.

The war would bring about years of brutal conflict that threatened to tear small towns apart. In fact, the Battle of Lincoln had done exactly that back in 1878. Multiple buildings in the small town of Lincoln were burned down, and seven people died, including the non-violent Alexander McSween—another friend of Billy's.

Billy the Kid had murdered several people during the Lincoln County War, some of them in cold blood, and he was a wanted man for his involvement in the war when Garrett became the sheriff. Billy had been jailed for a brief period of time; in fact, he was promised a pardon if he testified against his opponents in the Lincoln County War. However, he escaped when the pardon never materialized. Now, he was on the run, and it was Garrett's mission to bring him to justice. There was a $500 bounty for his capture, after all—a tidy sum in those days.

In the winter of 1880, Garrett finally tracked down Billy the Kid and two of his best friends, Charlie Bowdre and Tom O'Follard. In a desperate firefight, Garrett shot and killed both Charlie and Tom, and Billy narrowly escaped with his life. Garrett captured the young outlaw and took him back to the nearest jailhouse to be held for trial. But Billy the Kid had had quite enough of the local justice system. He escaped just months later, murdering one of the guards in the process, which only made Garrett angrier.

That summer, Garrett searched relentlessly for the young murderer, who had just turned twenty-one. Eventually, he tracked Billy down at Pedro Maxwell's house in Fort Sumner. Maxwell was a friend of Billy's, but he couldn't resist Garrett's insistence that he be allowed into the house. It was very dark, and Billy the Kid was asleep when Garrett entered and hid in the kitchen. Sure enough, deep in the night, Billy the Kid came down into the kitchen looking for a snack. Garrett would later swear that the young outlaw was armed, but no weapon was ever found with his body. In Spanish, Billy the Kid asked, "Who is it?" In response, Garrett shot him dead. Billy the Kid was given no chance to surrender.

Pat Garrett hoped that killing Billy the Kid would earn him a reputation as an excellent lawman. To an extent, it did, at least for a brief period of time; he was appointed as a lawman a few times after this. However, when word got out of exactly how Billy the Kid died, Garrett became a pariah. Despite a brief friendship with President

Theodore Roosevelt, who had himself been a lawman who had captured outlaws—a friendship that ended when Garrett directly embarrassed the president through his association with a well-known good-for-nothing gambler—Garrett never did find favor in the public eye again. He had a book ghostwritten in which he greatly exaggerated Billy the Kid's cruelty and gave his own version of how the young outlaw had died, but it never took off.

In the end, Garrett began to drink and gamble, spending all his money on these pursuits instead of paying his taxes. He ultimately had to hire out some of his lands in an effort to pay these taxes. On February 28th, 1908, when he got into a violent argument with the lessor and allegedly reached for his shotgun during the fight, he was shot and killed.

The Gunfight at O.K. Corral

The same year that Billy the Kid was killed, one of the most notorious gunfights in Wild West history took place hundreds of miles away in Tombstone, Arizona.

The years leading up to those thirty seconds of violence had shaped the stone-cold killers who would be the combatants of that brief but brutal fight. Their names ring with familiarity; Doc Holliday and the Earp brothers have been immortalized time and time again in popular culture as heroes upholding the letter of the law. In reality, though, like so many lawmen of the Old West, they were little different from the men they fought.

The most famous among these was Wyatt Earp; he was one of four brothers who were all acting as law enforcement in Tombstone at the time. The Earps had grown up in the Midwest, moving west during the American Civil War, where they worked together at various different occupations in California, Missouri, Texas, and eventually Arizona. Despite being known today as a great lawman, Wyatt was definitely the wild child. Even as a kid, he'd tried to run away from home and join the Union Army, only to be dragged back home by his annoyed father—who was a justice of the peace as well as a bootlegger.

Virgil was the one with a cooler head on his shoulders. Five years Wyatt's senior, he had fought in the American Civil War and lost everything when he was reported dead and returned home only to find that his wife had grieved him and then remarried. With his family torn away from him, Virgil decided to go west with Wyatt and his other two brothers, Morgan and James.

Things seemed to be stabilizing for Wyatt by 1870 when he became a local constable in Lamar, Missouri. Virgil was also working as a sawmill manager and earning a steady living. But Wyatt quickly shot himself in the foot; he mishandled public funds and got himself fired in 1871, at which point he headed for greener pastures by becoming a horse thief in Oklahoma for some time. He also hunted buffalo, like most young men, during the 1870s.

By 1874, when Virgil had become a deputy marshal in Tucson, Arizona, Wyatt seemed to have come to his senses again. It was not difficult to escape any kind of criminal charge in those days—one simply had to get away from whichever town held their warrant. Despite his earlier accusations, Wyatt was able to become a lawman in Wichita, Kansas, but he just kept on causing trouble for himself. He beat some luckless fool to a near pulp in a bare-handed fight during his time as a lawman there and fled under scrutiny from local authorities.

That led him to Dodge City, Kansas, in 1875. At the time, Dodge City was known as the "wickedest little city in the West." Dodge City was a boomtown teeming with cattle ranchers and everyone else involved in that industry, and it was growing too quickly for authorities to maintain control over it. Due to that fact, it had become a den of violence and vice. It was here that Wyatt was appointed as assistant marshal, and he appears to have conducted his duties well enough. None of them prevented him from moonlighting as a professional gambler, however. And it was here that he met one of his closest friends and a man who would stick with the Earps throughout their lives: John Henry Holliday, "Doc" to his friends.

Holliday had a difficult childhood, but not for the same reasons as many of the outlaws and lawmen featured in this book. In fact, Holliday's mother had been relentlessly loving and determined to give her boy a good life, despite the fact that Holliday had been born with a cleft palate. She spent endless hours working through his speech impediment with him. To his dying day, Holliday had a gentle mannerism about him that he had learned from her. Tragically, his mother died from tuberculosis in 1866, but her love still drove him on, and he graduated as a trained dentist in 1872. Intending to practice in his hometown in Georgia, Holliday's plans were harshly derailed when his own physician broke some very bad news to him: he had tuberculosis too. And if he didn't move away from the wet climate of the South, he would likely meet the same ending as his mother had.

Panicking, Holliday fled to Dallas, Texas, where he tried to set up a practice. But without his mother to keep him on the straight and narrow, he soon fell into drinking and gambling in the Wild West. Drinking led to fighting, and fighting led to a murder charge. Holliday fled Dallas as a wanted man in 1878.

The only place he could think to go was Dodge City, where he could lay low around other outlaws. However, when he met the lawman Wyatt Earp while gambling there, Holliday found that he had nothing to fear from the local law enforcement. The two men hit it off immediately, and the lonely Holliday practically clung to Wyatt.

Wyatt was still doing well for himself in Arizona, so Wyatt decided to move there around 1880, with Holliday loyally following him. At this point, Virgil had been made the city marshal of Tombstone, Arizona, and he had his hands full. Not only was he facing off with a group of cowboys, known as the Clanton-McLaury Gang, who supplemented their income by rustling cattle and stealing horses, but he was also struggling with the local sheriff, John Behan. Behan was well aware that Virgil wanted nothing more than to be elected sheriff

in Behan's stead, so the sheriff was failing to back him up against the Clanton-McLaury Gang.

As a result, Virgil turned to four men whom he knew would have his back in any kind of fight: his three brothers and their best friend, Doc Holliday. They were made deputy marshals of Tombstone, where violence with the Clanton-McLaury Gang was about to get ugly.

Behan knew that the younger Earps and Holliday were trouble the moment he saw them. He arrested Holliday for the suspected murder of a stagecoach driver. The charges never stuck, though, and Holliday would go free.

Still, although evidence suggests that Holliday really was innocent, Behan wasn't wrong that these men were out to cause trouble. Tensions escalated in Tombstone throughout 1881, and by the fall, they were ready to boil over.

On an October day in 1881, Ike Clanton and Tom McLaury were looking for trouble. They sauntered into town and stopped by the local saloon, where Doc Holliday was drinking. Fired up, Holliday demanded that Ike draw his weapon and have it out with him, there and then. But Ike incensed him by walking away, prompting Holliday to run to Virgil with his complaint. Virgil arrested Ike and Tom for carrying weapons inside the city, which was illegal at the time. Still, there wasn't much he could do to them. He just disarmed them and sent them on their way.

Irate, Ike and Frank knew that Virgil and Holliday were both looking for trouble. The next day—October 26th, 1881—they met up with some of their cohorts at the edge of town, including Billy Clanton and Frank McLaury. Soon, a group of Clanton-McLaury members was gathering just outside the back gate of the O.K. Corral, a livery stable on Fremont Street. These were all outlaws, and their intentions were unmistakable.

Once again, Sheriff Behan saw trouble coming. He rode over and begged the outlaws to get out of town or hand their weapons over to him. The gang responded by demanding he disarm the Earps and Holliday instead of them. Behan rode back only to find that the four Earps and Holliday were already on their way to the O.K. Corral, and when he tried to stop them, they had none of it. They wanted a fight. And in seconds, they would have one.

When the Earps and Holliday reached the Clanton-McLaury Gang, Virgil didn't mince any words. "I want your guns," he said.

It's uncertain how exactly the fight began. Some reports say that Billy Clanton fired on Virgil Earp; others say that Virgil simply shot Billy right in the chest. Either way, Doc Holliday responded by emptying a shotgun into Tom McLaury, who died instantly. Wyatt, too, was shooting his gun, sending a bullet into Frank McLaury's stomach; the outlaw fired as he died, drawing blood. Thirty shots went off in total—thirty shots in thirty seconds. By the end of those breathless few seconds, Billy Clanton and the McLaurys were dead. Ike and his companions had fled into the hills, and Virgil, Morgan, and Holliday were wounded.

Incensed by the way the Earps ignored his demands, Sheriff Behan had them arrested for murder. However, they would all be pardoned by the local judge, and Virgil would be reinstated as town marshal. After an attempt on his life by the remaining Clantons, Virgil once again made Wyatt his deputy, and the bloody feud would continue with the Clantons that led to the death of Morgan in 1882.

Ultimately, the Earp brothers regained control of Tombstone after some brutal murders of local cowboys, but they would never quite recover from the death of Morgan. Their reputation in tatters, they left Arizona for California, where Virgil opened a gambling hall, and Wyatt trained racehorses and refereed boxing fights. Doc Holliday left the Earps after the killings in Arizona. He moved to Colorado, where tuberculosis caught up with him just a few short years later, in

1887. Virgil, Wyatt, and Holliday would be some of the few early lawmen of the West to die peacefully.

Wild Bill Hickok

One of the most famous cowboys and lawmen of the American West would also precipitate the career of a less famous sheriff who was nonetheless one of the rare true heroes of the Wild West.

He didn't know it, though, and he never would. On the last day of his life—August 2nd, 1877—Wild Bill Hickok was sitting quietly in Nuttal & Mann's, a saloon in Deadwood, South Dakota. His back was to the door; he was partially blind by then, even though he was just forty years old. Still, he could vaguely see the cards in his hands. Two black aces, two black eights. Soon, it would be known as the dead man's hand. But right now, Wild Bill just wanted to get a drink, play some cards, and forget his hardships.

He had had many hardships in his life. James Butler Hickok was born in Illinois in 1837. Even as a boy, he worked hard to become an excellent shooter. The allure of the West was irresistible, and as soon as he turned eighteen, he headed for Kansas—right as Bleeding Kansas was erupting into chaos. While he'd gone to Kansas to farm the rich land, Hickok joined one of the forces that were fighting for abolition during Bleeding Kansas, and he would serve it well. Just a few years later, he had earned enough respect to be appointed as the constable of Monticello Township.

In 1861, he earned the nickname of "Wild Bill" when he shot and killed three men in self-defense despite being wounded himself. The incident would be called the McCanles massacre, and it was just the start of his reputation as one of the West's finest gunslingers.

Even the American Civil War seemed to go so well for Hickok. He served as a teamster, scout, provost marshal, and, according to some accounts, as a spy for the Union Army. By the end of the war, Wild Bill was cocksure and absolutely confident in his capabilities as a gunman. This was on full display in 1865 when one of the most

legendary gunfights of the Old West took place: the duel between Wild Bill Hickok and his once-friend Davis Tutt.

Hickok and Tutt had been friends once, but rivalries had driven them apart. By the time they met again in Springfield, Missouri, they were solid enemies. Gambling and drinking only sparked old fights between them, and finally, they challenged one another to an old-fashioned duel. They would face one another across the town square of Springfield, and whoever survived would be the winner.

The two men stood shoulder to shoulder, seventy-five yards apart across the town square. After a few moments of tense, steely-eyed staring, Tutt lunged for his weapon. But Hickok was quicker. Before Tutt could draw his gun, Hickok had shot him stone dead.

The duel became legend, and the story of Wild Bill spread all over the West, with people singing his praises as a legendary gunman. When he returned to Kansas shortly after the duel in Springfield, Wild Bill was quickly elected sheriff of Hays City, Kansas. The town was absolutely chaotic when he arrived, but between his reputation and his brutality, Hickok restored order to the town in just a few short years. He did the same in Abilene, Kansas. The city was the center of chaos, gambling, prostitution, drunkenness, and robbery, but Hickok whipped the residents into shape. His methods were questionable, but there was no doubting that the man was effective.

However, his trigger-happy ways and willingness to dole out barbaric frontier justice would eventually catch up to him. In 1871, while engaged in a shootout with a saloon owner, Hickok spotted movement and whirled around, firing straight at it. He had thought that another enemy was approaching him. Instead, he shot and killed his own deputy, Mike Williams, without even meaning to. Hickok had killed plenty of men by that time, but the death of Mike Williams shook him to the very core. When an inquest into the matter exposed Hickok's brutal frontier justice and got him fired, he was a broken man. He never aimed a gun at another human being again.

Instead, Hickok joined Buffalo Bill's Wild West Show, where he entertained scores of crowds with his feats of marksmanship. For a few years, it seemed as though Hickok had found his place in the world once more, even if he would never again be a lawman. Even after he suffered from glaucoma and started to lose his sight, Wild Bill fell in love with a circus owner named Agnes Thatcher and married her. He wasn't a young man anymore, but it seemed as though he was ready for a new start.

That was what had brought him to Deadwood in the first place. Two years before, gold had been discovered in the Black Hills of South Dakota, leading to a gold rush that saw mining towns cropping up all over the territory. Deadwood was one of them, and it was a lawless place, filled with brothels and saloons and packed with desperate miners. Many of them, including Wild Bill, failed to find any fortune at all. They turned to gambling instead, just as Wild Bill was doing on that afternoon in August 1876. He was just hoping to win a little money and get back to his lovely wife. But he would never rise from his chair.

The day before, Wild Bill had been playing poker with a prospector named Jack McCall. McCall had had terrible luck and lost a significant amount of money; Hickok had taken pity on him and given him a little cash for food. This seemed to be a gesture of kindness, but to McCall, it was disgusting slight.

McCall, drunk, swaggered into the saloon on that fateful afternoon and immediately spotted Hickok sitting with his back to the door. McCall gave no warning. He simply drew his gun and shot Hickok in the back, killing him instantly.

McCall would flee and escape from any kind of justice for months. Even though he was captured by a group of miners and dragged back to Deadwood, there was no official court to try him, and he was eventually released. While the law eventually caught up with him—he was tried and hanged in March 1877—Hickok's murder was a shocking wake-up call to the authorities of the time. If Jack McCall

could kill an ex-lawman and a beloved public figure so blatantly, then Deadwood truly was out of control.

Seth Bullock Tames the West

Luckily for the local government, the solution to their problems had come riding into town just one day before Hickok was murdered. His name was Seth Bullock, and he was the one lawman who truly held himself to the highest moral standards.

This American legend was Canadian-born, but after a troubled childhood, during which Bullock practically had to raise his siblings himself, he had come to Helena, Montana, at the age of eighteen in 1867. He had a passion for the wilderness, and while the likes of Wyatt Earp and Pat Garret were hunting buffalo to extinction, Seth Bullock was working hard at establishing Yellowstone National Park, which would ultimately be a huge part of saving the species. Bullock's father had also had a brief and very corrupt career in politics, and so, when Bullock was elected to the Territorial Legislature in 1871, he took his duties seriously. For two years, he was an exemplary leader.

As a result, Bullock had no trouble being elected as the sheriff of Lewis and Clark County in 1873. Unlike other lawmen of his era, Bullock had zero interest in frontier justice. He believed in the criminal justice system of the time, firmly refusing to shoot and kill outlaws.

Still, during his time as sheriff in Montana, he killed his first and only victim. Clell Watson, a horse thief, was fool enough to fire on Seth Bullock while he was busy stealing a horse. The two men traded bullets, and Bullock suffered a mild injury before taking Watson down—without killing him. He was sentenced to execution for shooting at the sheriff, but when Watson was to be hanged, an angry mob surrounded the platform, demanding that he be pardoned. The executioner fled, but Bullock put a shotgun on his shoulder and kept the crowd at bay while he pulled the lever. He would never kill another man in his life.

By the time Bullock's term as sheriff ended, he had gone into business with a close Jewish friend, Solomon "Sol" Star. The two men were trying to open a hardware store in Montana, but after the gold rush in South Dakota, they relocated their operation there. It was on August 1st, 1876—the day Jack McCall was losing money to Wild Bill Hickok—that Bullock and Star arrived. And after Hickok's death, the territorial government was quick to search for a sheriff who could tame Deadwood. They needed someone upright and honest, someone with a cool head and integrity. Seth Bullock was the obvious choice.

While Bullock only served as sheriff of Deadwood for a few months, he was unquestionably the single most important factor in turning the town around, and he never had to kill anyone to do it. "He could stare down a mad cobra," his son would later say of him, and his steely-eyed gaze seemed to be enough to marshal even the rowdiest elements of Deadwood into order. In fact, just a few short years after Bullock's arrival—he continued to serve as Deputy US Marshal long after his time as sheriff had ended—he felt that Deadwood was so safe that he could bring his wife and children there to live with him.

Bullock was more than a lawman, but unlike the Earps and Pat Garrett, he made his living as honestly as possible. Together with Sol Star, he built a huge cattle ranch, founded the town of Belle Fourche, and built the Bullock Hotel, one of the most luxurious establishments of the entire Old West. In fact, it is still in operation today. He was also a good friend of Theodore Roosevelt, and unlike Garrett, he never fell out of favor with the president. In fact, Theodore Roosevelt called him "the finest type of frontiersman." History is inclined to agree.

Seth Bullock would be one of the Wild West's last legends. By 1890, just a few years after the era of the O.K. Corral, Billy the Kid, and the chaos of Deadwood, the American frontier had officially

come to an end. Bullock himself would pass away in 1919, dying peacefully of cancer.

The Wild West era we know and love—the time of cowboys and outlaws—only lasted a few decades. Yet it remains one of the most iconic eras of them all, with its gray areas of morality, its fascinating stories, and its characters that loomed so much larger than life.

Conclusion

The end of the Western frontier was by no means the end of crime in the American West. Crime legends like Butch Cassidy, the Sundance Kid, the Dalton Gang, and Pearl Hart were still to come. Nor did the American Civil War or the Treaty of Fort Laramie, which ushered in the modern-day reservation system, bring an end to racial violence in the West. The American Indian Wars continued to be fought all over this area for decades more. Massacres were commonplace, with Native American tribes murdering and scalping whole families of colonists and with US troops butchering whole tribes of Native Americans. The cycle of violence would continue for many decades to come.

The days of the wild frontier, however, ended in 1890. Westward migration had finally slowed to a trickle as the population began to spread itself more evenly around the United States of America. By that time, almost all of the western states we know had been admitted to the Union. Utah, Oklahoma, New Mexico, and Arizona would all be admitted by 1912, and that was the end of the wild territories of the West. In fact, it would be forty years before the last two states—Alaska and Hawaii—would be admitted.

The story of the Wild West is one we all know very well. Yet our romanticized ideas about gunslinger cowboys who "tamed" the wilderness are far amiss. In reality, the West was more lost than won. Most lawmen of the era were as corrupt as the outlaws they pursued. And the natural resources of the West would be horrendously depleted by the turn of the century.

Still, the Wild West holds more than just entertaining stories for us. It holds hard lessons about the way we treat one another and the environment all around us. With every step we take into the future, we can be better. And perhaps the true heroes of the Old West—people like Seth Bullock—have blazed that trail for us, just like Lewis and Clark blazed the trail all the way from Missouri to the glittering waters of the Pacific Ocean itself.

Here's another book by Captivating History that you might like

THE HISTORY OF THE UNITED STATES

A CAPTIVATING GUIDE TO AMERICAN HISTORY, INCLUDING EVENTS SUCH AS THE AMERICAN REVOLUTION, FRENCH AND INDIAN WAR, BOSTON TEA PARTY, PEARL HARBOR AND THE GULF WAR

CAPTIVATING HISTORY

Free Bonus from Captivating History
(Available for a Limited time)

Hi History Lovers!

Now you have a chance to join our exclusive history list so you can get your first history ebook for free as well as discounts and a potential to get more history books for free! Simply visit the link below to join.

Captivatinghistory.com/ebook

Also, make sure to follow us on Facebook, Twitter and Youtube by searching for Captivating History.

Sources

Zimmerman, B. 2016, "Native American culture of the West," Khan Academy, viewed September 2021, <https://www.khanacademy.org/humanities/us-history/precontact-and-early-colonial-era/before-contact/a/native-american-culture-of-the-west>

History.com Editors 2020, "Native American Cultures," A&E Television Networks, viewed September 2021, <https://www.history.com/topics/native-american-history/native-american-cultures#section_5>

Koch, A. 2019, "European colonization of the Americas killed 10 percent of world population and caused global cooling," The World, viewed September 2021, <https://www.pri.org/stories/2019-01-31/european-colonization-americas-killed-10-percent-world-population-and-caused>

History.com Editors 2019, "Francisco Vázquez de Coronado," A&E Television Networks, viewed September 2021, <https://www.history.com/topics/exploration/francisco-vazquez-de-coronado>

Anonymous, "Francisco Coronado," The Mariners' Museum and Park, viewed September 2021,

<https://exploration.marinersmuseum.org/subject/francisco-coronado/>

Associated Press 2012, "Sir Francis Drake 'first set foot on US soil in San Francisco Bay area,'" The Guardian, viewed September 2021, <https://www.theguardian.com/world/2012/oct/21/sir-francis-drake-san-francisco-bay>

History.com Editors 2021, "Sir Francis Drake claims California for England," A&E Television Networks, viewed September 2021, <https://www.history.com/this-day-in-history/drake-claims-california-for-england>

Lawler, A. 2019, "Did Francis Drake Really Land in California?" Smithsonian Magazine, viewed September 2021, <https://www.smithsonianmag.com/history/did-francis-drake-really-land-california-180973219/>

Johnson, B. "Sir Francis Drake," Historic UK, viewed September 2021, <https://www.historic-uk.com/HistoryUK/HistoryofEngland/Sir-Francis-Drake/>

Burnett, J. 2020, "Statues of Conquistador Juan de Onate Come Down as New Mexico Wrestles With History," NPR, viewed September 2021, <https://www.npr.org/2020/07/13/890122729/statues-of-conquistador-juan-de-o-ate-come-down-as-new-mexico-wrestles-with-hist>

Weddle, R. S. 2019, "Ortiz Parrilla, Diego," Handbook of Texas, viewed September 2021, <https://www.tshaonline.org/handbook/entries/ortiz-parrilla-diego>

Weiser-Alexander, K. 2021, "Santa Fe, New Mexico – The City Different," Legends of America, viewed September 2021, <https://www.legendsofamerica.com/nm-santafe/>

The Taos Pueblo website, viewed September 2021, <https://taospueblo.com/>

James, G. 2019, "The Battle of the Twin Villages took place right outside Nocona," News Channel 6, viewed September 2021,

<https://www.newschannel6now.com/2019/05/02/battle-twin-villages-took-place-right-outside-nocona/>

Chad Williams, "Twin Villages, Battle of the," THE ENCYCLOPEDIA OF OKLAHOMA HISTORY AND CULTURE, https://www.okhistory.org/publications/enc/entry.php?entry=TW005.

Anne Million, "French," THE ENCYCLOPEDIA OF OKLAHOMA HISTORY AND CULTURE, https://www.okhistory.org/publications/enc/entry.php?entry=FR020.

The Library of Congress website for maps and historical documents: https://www.loc.gov/

"George Vancouver Charts the Pacific Coast of North America from California to Alaska." Science and Its Times: Understanding the Social Significance of Scientific Discovery. Retrieved September 08, 2021 from Encyclopedia.com: https://www.encyclopedia.com/science/encycloped ias-almanacs-transcripts-and-maps/george-vancouver-charts-pacific-coast-north-america-california-alaska

National Park Services 2019, "The Dominguez and Escalante Expedition," Dinosaur Natural Monument CO, UT, viewed September 2021, <https://www.nps.gov/dino/learn/historyculture/the-dominguez-and-escalante-expedition.htm>

History.com Editors 2021, "Lewis and Clark Expedition," A&E Television Networks, viewed September 2021, <https://www.history.com/topics/westward-expansion/lewis-and-clark>

Huban, C. J. 2017, "The Story of Chief Cuerno Verde (Green Horn)," Southern Colorado Territorial Daughters, viewed September 2021, <https://southerncoloradoterritorialdaughters.org/genealogy-history/welcome-to-our-blog-but-what-is-it>

Bagley, W. 2014, "The Astorians Discover South Pass," WyoHistory.org, viewed September 2021, <https://www.wyohistory.org/encyclopedia/astorians-south-pass-discovery>

Weiser, K. 2018, "Stephen Long's Expedition of the Great Plains," Legends of America, viewed September 2021, <https://www.legendsofamerica.com/longs-expedition/>

Jedediah Smith Society and University of the Pacific, "Biography of Jed Smith for Students," Jedediah Smith Society, viewed September 2021, <http://jedediahsmithsociety.org/home/research-information/biography-of-jed-smith-for-students/>

Govaerts, L. 2016, "Real stories behind The Revenant, Part II: Ashley's Hundred," Rogers Archaeology Lab, viewed September 2021, <https://nmnh.typepad.com/rogers_archaeology_lab/2016/03/real-stories-behind-the-revenant-part-ii-ashleys-hundred.html>

Weiser, K. 2021, "William Ashley and the Rocky Mountain Fur Company," Legends of America, viewed September 2021, <https://www.legendsofamerica.com/william-ashley/>

Andrews, E. 2018, "6 Legendary Mountain Men of the American Frontier," A&E Television Networks, viewed September 2021, <https://www.history.com/news/6-legendary-mountain-men-of-the-american-frontier>

Hill, M. 2015, "Mountain Men: History & Facts," Study.com, viewed September 2021, <https://study.com/academy/lesson/mountain-men-history-facts.html>

Ladd, K. 2011, "Three Families of the Old Three Hundred," Stephen F. Austin State University, viewed September 2021, <https://www.sfasu.edu/heritagecenter/3507.asp>

Long, C. 2019, "Old Three Hundred," Handbook of Texas, viewed September 2021, <https://www.tshaonline.org/handbook/entries/old-three-hundred>

Daniels, A. 2018, "Moses Austin's Old 300: Who, What, Why," Midland Reporter Telegram, viewed September 2021, <https://www.mrt.com/news/education/article/Moses-Austin-s-Old-300-Who-What-Why-12765420.php>

Minster, C. 2020, "Biography of Stephen F. Austin, Founding Father of Texan Independence," ThoughtCo, viewed September 2021, <https://www.thoughtco.com/biography-of-stephen-f-austin-2136243>

History.com Editors 2021, "Trail of Tears," A&E Television Networks, viewed September 2021, <https://www.history.com/topics/native-american-history/trail-of-tears>

National Park Service 2020, "What Happened on the Trail of Tears?" National Park Service, viewed September 2021, <https://www.nps.gov/trte/learn/historyculture/what-happened-on-the-trail-of-tears.htm>

Klein, C. 2019, "How Native Americans Struggled to Survive on the Trail of Tears," A&E Television Networks, viewed September 2021, <https://www.nps.gov/trte/learn/historyculture/what-happened-on-the-trail-of-tears.htm>

Anderson, W. L. and Wetmore, R. Y 2006, "Cherokee," NC Pedia, viewed September 2021, <https://www.ncpedia.org/cherokee/origins>

Handbook of Texas 2020, "Cherokee War," Handbook of Texas, viewed September 2021, <https://www.tshaonline.org/handbook/entries/cherokee-war>

History.com Editors 2019, "Manifest Destiny," A&E Television Networks, viewed September 2021, <https://www.history.com/topics/westward-expansion/manifest-destiny>

Bunbury, T. 2018, "What the Irish did for – and to – the Choctaw tribe," Irish Times, viewed September 2021, <https://www.irishtimes.com/culture/heritage/what-the-irish-did-for-and-to-the-choctaw-tribe-1.3423873>

Riggs, E. E. 1916, "The Texas Revolution," Legends of America, viewed September 2021, <https://www.legendsofamerica.com/tx-revolution/>

Weiser-Alexander, K. 2020, "David 'Davy' Crockett – Frontier Hero," Legends of America, viewed September 2021, <https://www.legendsofamerica.com/david-crockett/>

Barker, E. C. and Pohl, J. W. 2021, "Texas Revolution," Handbook of Texas, viewed September 2021, <https://www.tshaonline.org/handbook/entries/texas-revolution>

History.com Editors 2021, "Battle of the Alamo," A&E Television Networks, viewed September 2021, <https://www.history.com/topics/mexico/alamo>

Henson, M. S. 2020, "Anahuac Disturbances," Handbook of Texas, viewed September 2021, <https://www.tshaonline.org/handbook/entries/anahuac-disturbances>

Cox, M. 2018, "A Brief History of the Texas Rangers," Texas Ranger Hall of Fame and Museum, viewed September 2021, <https://www.texasranger.org/texas-ranger-museum/history/brief-history/>

History.com Editors 2019, "Mexican-American War," A&E Television Networks, viewed September 2021, <https://www.history.com/topics/mexican-american-war/mexican-american-war>

Minster, C. 2019, "The Life and Legend of David 'Davy' Crockett," ThoughtCo, viewed September 2021, <https://www.thoughtco.com/biography-of-davy-crockett-2136664>

History.com Editors 2019, "Samuel Colt," A&E Television Networks, viewed September 2021, <https://www.history.com/topics/inventions/samuel-colt>

History.com Editors 2021, "The California Gold Rush," A&E Television Networks, viewed September 2021, <https://www.history.com/topics/westward-expansion/gold-rush-of-1849>

Bell, B. B. 2014, "The Gang Slayer," True West Magazine, viewed September 2021, <https://truewestmagazine.com/the-gang-slayer-1/>

Hernandez, A. 2020, "The Reynolds Gang: Colorado Confederates and Their Buried Treasure," Denver Public Library, viewed September 2021, <https://history.denverlibrary.org/news/reynolds-gang-colorado-confederates-and-their-buried-treasure>

Eberie, J. 2015, "The Reynolds Gang," Colorado Encyclopedia, viewed September 2021, <https://coloradoencyclopedia.org/article/reynolds-gang>

History.com Editors 2021, "Gunfighter Clay Allison Killed," A&E Television Networks, viewed September 2021, <https://coloradoencyclopedia.org/article/reynolds-gang>

Weiser-Alexander, K. 2021, "New Mexico Bad Boy: Clay Allison," Legends of America, viewed September 2021, <https://www.legendsofamerica.com/we-clayallison/>

Metesh, T. L. 2021, "How Western Legend Wild Bill Hickok Died in Deadwood," Free Range American, viewed September 2021, <https://freerangeamerican.us/how-wild-bill-hickok-died/>

Biography.com Editors 2020, "Wild Bill Hickok Biography," A&E Television Networks, viewed September 2021, <https://www.biography.com/personality/wild-bill-hickok>

Kennedy, L. 2020, "5 Legendary Wild West Outlaws," A&E Television Networks, viewed September 2021, <https://www.history.com/news/famous-wild-west-outlaws-billy-the-kid-jesse-james-butch-cassidy>

Weiser-Alexander, K. 2020, "The James-Younger Gang – Terror in the Heartland," Legends of America, viewed September 2021, <https://www.legendsofamerica.com/we-jamesyoungergang/>

Biography.com Editors 2021, "Jesse James Biography," A&E Television Networks, viewed September 2021, <https://www.biography.com/crime-figure/jesse-james>

Nix, E. 2018, "7 Things You May Not Know About Jesse James," A&E Television Networks, viewed September 2021,

<https://www.history.com/news/7-things-you-might-not-know-about-jesse-james>

Stanley, M. E. "Anderson, William 'Bloody Bill,'" Civil War on the Western Border, viewed September 2021, <https://civilwaronthewesternborder.org/encyclopedia/anderson-william-%E2%80%9Cbloody-bill%E2%80%9D>

Andrews, E. 2020, "9 Things You May Not Know About Billy the Kid," A&E Television Networks, viewed September 2021, <https://www.history.com/news/9-things-you-may-not-know-about-billy-the-kid>

History.com Editors 2020, "First Train Robbery in U. S. History," A&E Television Networks, viewed September 2021, <https://www.history.com/this-day-in-history/first-u-s-train-robbery>

Israel, D. K. 2010, "10 Great Train Robberies," Mental Floss, viewed September 2021, <https://www.mentalfloss.com/article/25825/10-great-train-robberies>

Weiser, K. 2019, "Belle Starr – The Bandit Queen," Legends of America, viewed September 2021, <https://www.legendsofamerica.com/we-bellestarr/>

Cogburn, B. 2011, "The Bandit Queen's Treasures," True West Magazine, viewed September 2021, <https://truewestmagazine.com/the-bandit-queens-treasures-2/>

Boissneault, L. 2017, "Murder, Marriage and the Pony Express: Ten Things You Didn't Know About Buffalo Bill," Smithsonian Magazine, viewed September 2021, <https://www.smithsonianmag.com/history/murder-marriage-and-pony-express-10-things-you-didnt-know-about-buffalo-bill-180961736/>

King, G. 2017, "Where the Buffalo No Longer Roamed," Smithsonian Magazine, viewed September 2021, <https://www.smithsonianmag.com/history/where-the-buffalo-no-longer-roamed-3067904/>

History.com Editors 2021, "Murder Ignites Lincoln County War," A&E Television Networks, viewed September 2021, <https://www.history.com/this-day-in-history/murder-ignites-lincoln-county-war>

History.com Editors 2020, "Shootout at the O.K. Corral", A&E Television Networks, viewed September 2021, <https://www.history.com/this-day-in-history/shootout-at-the-ok-corral>

Stuart, M. 2019, "7 Strange Facts About Wyatt Earp and the Gunfight at O.K. Corral," Explore the Archive, viewed September 2021, <https://explorethearchive.com/things-you-didnt-know-about-wyatt-earp-and-the-gunfight-at-the-ok-corral>

Biography.com Editors 2021, "Doc Holliday Biography," A&E Television Networks, viewed September 2021, <https://www.biography.com/personality/doc-holliday>

Nix, E. 2018, "6 Things You Should Know About Wyatt Earp," A&E Television Networks, viewed September 2021, <https://www.history.com/news/6-things-you-should-know-about-wyatt-earp>

Weiser, K. 2019, "Seth Bullock – Finest Type of Frontiersman," Legends of America, viewed September 2021, <https://www.legendsofamerica.com/we-sethbullock/>

Illustration I:
https://commons.wikimedia.org/wiki/File:%22Life_on_the_Plains%22_LCCN2004674924.jpg

Illustration II: by Victor van Werkhooven

https://commons.wikimedia.org/wiki/File:Carte_Lewis_and_Clark_Expedition.png

Illustration III: https://commons.wikimedia.org/wiki/File:Stephens.jpg

Illustration IV:
https://commons.wikimedia.org/wiki/File:Belle_Starr,_Fort_Smith,_Arkansas,_1886.jpg

Illustration V:
https://commons.wikimedia.org/wiki/File:SethBullock.jpg